SPIRITUALITY AND THE STATE

NORTH AMERICAN RELIGIONS

Series Editors: Tracy Fessenden (Religious Studies, Arizona State University), Laura Levitt (Religious Studies, Temple University), and David Harrington Watt (History, Temple University)

In recent years a cadre of industrious, imaginative, and theoretically sophisticated scholars of religion have focused their attention on North America. As a result the field is far more subtle, expansive, and interdisciplinary than it was just two decades ago. The North American Religions series builds on this transformative momentum. Books in the series move among the discourses of ethnography, cultural analysis, and historical study to shed new light on a wide range of religious experiences, practices, and institutions. They explore topics such as lived religion, popular religious movements, religion and social power, religion and cultural reproduction, and the relationship between secular and religious institutions and practices. The series focus primarily, but not exclusively, on religion in the United States in the twentieth and twenty-first centuries.

Books in the series:

Ava Chamberlain, The Notorious Elizabeth Tuttle: Marriage, Murder, and Madness in the Family of Jonathan Edwards

Terry Rey and Alex Stepick, Crossing the Water and Keeping the Faith: Haitian Religion in Miami

Jodi Eichler-Levine, Suffer the Little Children: Uses of the Past in Jewish and African American Children's Literature

Isaac Weiner, Religion Out Loud: Religious Sound, Public Space, and American Pluralism

Hillary Kaell, Walking Where Jesus Walked: American Christians and Holy Land Pilgrimage

Brett Hendrickson, Border Medicine: A Transcultural History of Mexican American Curanderismo

Annie Blazer, Playing for God: Evangelical Women and the Unintended Consequences of Sports Ministry

Elizabeth Pérez, Religion in the Kitchen: Cooking, Talking, and the Making of Black Atlantic Traditions

Kerry Mitchell, Spirituality and the State: Managing Nature and Experience in America's National Parks

Spirituality and the State

Managing Nature and Experience in America's National Parks

Kerry Mitchell

NEW YORK UNIVERSITY PRESS
New York

NEW YORK UNIVERSITY PRESS
New York
www.nyupress.org

References to Internet websites (URLs) were accurate at the time of writing. Neither the author nor New York University Press is responsible for URLs that may have expired or changed since the manuscript was prepared.

Library of Congress Cataloging-in-Publication Data
Names: Mitchell, Kerry (Kerry Archer), author.
Title: Spirituality and the state : managing nature and experience in America's national parks / Kerry Mitchell.
Description: New York : NYU Press, 2016. | Series: North American religions | Includes bibliographical references.
Identifiers: LCCN 2015047789 | ISBN 9781479886418 (cl : alk. paper) | ISBN 9781479873012 (pb : alk. paper)
Subjects: LCSH: Nature—Religious aspects. | National parks and reserves—United States. | Sacred space—United States. | Pilgrims and pilgrimages—United States. | Religion and state—United States.
Classification: LCC BL65.N35 M58 2016 | DDC 201/.763680973—dc23
LC record available at http://lccn.loc.gov/2015047789

New York University Press books are printed on acid-free paper, and their binding materials are chosen for strength and durability. We strive to use environmentally responsible suppliers and materials to the greatest extent possible in publishing our books.

Manufactured in the United States of America

10 9 8 7 6 5 4 3 2 1

Also available as an ebook

Dedicated to my parents, Breon and Lynda Mitchell

CONTENTS

ACKNOWLEDGMENTS

This work has been one of the greatest joys of my life. I thank all whose encouragement, support, open-mindedness, creativity, and critical thought has made it possible. I thank my mentor and advisor, Catherine L. Albanese, whose high standards, careful reading, and openness to projects not her own taught me so much about teaching. Once she saw what I was seeking, she would not let me forget or fall short. My teachers, Tom Carlson, Roger Friedland, and Wade Clark Roof, gave perspectives radically diverse in content and unified in insistence on quality. My friends and fellow scholars in Santa Barbara were my constant companions in this project. They heard my arguments, read my drafts, asked great questions, shared their homes, and celebrated our crossings throughout the years: John and Libby Modern, Wendy Wiseman, Finbarr Curtis, Elijah and Ma Wei Siegler, Mark and Florie Elmore, Drew Bourn, Ellen Posman and Mike Garner, Marie Pagliarini, Anna Bigelow, John Baumann, Suzanne Garner, Joel Geffen, Beth Currans, Revell Carr, Jenna Reinbold, Julie Cordero, Tomas Matza and Nikki Heller, Suzanne Crawford, Sarah Kviat, Evan Berry, Caleb Elfenbein, Kathryn McClymond, and others.

The transition from project to manuscript involved some of the closest reading, and I thank the editors, staff, and reviewers associated with New York University Press, especially Jennifer Hammer, for pushing me back to the central concerns of my work. They activated the years of solitary work and episodic dialogue with a stream of respectful, thoughtful, and critical insights and suggestions. I also thank the editors, readers, reviewers, and conference participants who heard and/or published work that has come out of this project: those associated with the International Society for the Study of Religion, Nature, and Culture (especially Bron Taylor), the Social Science Research Council, the George Wright Society, and the American Academy of Religion.

Institutional support has been crucial throughout this project. The University of California, Santa Barbara, laid the groundwork through generous funding of my studies (with special thanks to Sally Lombrozo). The College of Charleston and Long Island University, Global, have given me a professional home and the daily access to library, office, and tools for scholarship without which my work would be impossible. One institution in particular, the National Park Service, took it as a professional duty to facilitate my research. The rangers and staff of the national parks were incredibly generous with their time, open to critical discussion, and supportive in making arrangements for my work.

To my parents, Breon and Lynda Mitchell, I owe infinite gratitude for more than I can express. From material support to familial care to critical review, their love and generosity stands as the bedrock of this project (and of much more). To my brother, Kieron, my sister-in-law, Courtney, and my nieces, Maddie and Molly, sharing my progress and experiences made the journey so much richer. To my sister, Catherine, my brother-in-law, Steve, and my nieces, Becca and Bella, the distance of continents has kept our meetings less frequent, but I have taken inspiration from the creativity they have expressed in the midst of such full lives. My extended family provided wonderful oases as I journeyed across the country: my cousins Kristina and Sarah and their families, my aunt Nancy, my cousin Jack and his family. I extend special gratitude to those who have passed: my uncle Tim, whose work on landscape painting inspired me, my grandfather Leroy, whose roots continue to ground me, my grandmother Ruby, whose unconditional goodness helps me to let go, my grandparents, "Papa" and Maxine, who while gone before this project started still stand as models of creativity, criticism, and support. Coming lately but most closely, my partner, Georgiya Djibirova, has reconnected me to the passion and discovery that generated the project, and helped me to set the capstone on years of work and life.

In the years since I started the project, a multitude of friends, colleagues, and students have engaged in conversation that has shaped the final work. Too numerous to name them all, my friends and colleagues in Charleston, South Carolina, and my students and colleagues at LIU Global in Brooklyn, especially my traveling companions and coworkers Megan Trulove White, Heidi Hillman, and Debi Goldman, have engaged and encouraged me in my work.

Finally, my analysis and criticism of the public sphere has depended upon the cooperation of so many of its members. A multitude of park visitors, volunteers, and staff took the time to engage me thoughtfully and honestly about intimate features of their lives. While I criticize the systems of experiential management in the parks, I do so in recognition of the great service, joy, and care that have informed the experiences of millions who come to these places of power, beauty, and value. My work may express ambivalence about the parks, but it is a passionate ambivalence, one no less intense for the tensions in which it lives.

Introduction

Seeing me alone one evening in Joshua Tree National Park, some neighboring campers invited me to join them around their campfire. When they asked me what I did, I told them that I studied religion. My neighbor's eyes lit up. He made a broad, sweeping gesture toward the surrounding desert and said, "This is my church."

As our conversation continued, I realized that I did not fully understand what he meant. Surrounding him and the tumbleweed, cactus, red rock, and sand, he had told me, there was religion: something that bound it all together, integrated him as a person, and influenced the way he lived with others. And although I knew that this something was there, I could not see it. To be sure, I could see the desert. But to point to the particular objects out there and ask, "Is this, this here, your church?" or to ask how many miles wide was this church—these would be absurd questions. There was some hidden value to the desert, this man had suggested, that grounded him in a way that a church might. With no visible texts, rituals, doctrines, or structures, how was one to approach this church? How could one understand this kind of religion?

Consider another experience I had not far from the campground. A Crown Victoria Interceptor, a police cruiser emblazoned with the National Park Service insignia, sat in a parking area by the side of the road. I stood outside my vehicle a few spots away, refreshing myself with a bottle of water while pretending to contemplate the view of the surrounding desert. Actually, I was focused on the policeman's conversation. I could hear only his side: "Yeah, someone strung up a line—some kind of tightrope—between two boulders. Looks like he's going to try to walk it. . . . I don't know—some dirtbag . . . [laughter]. Yeah, cleaning out the gene pool." The policeman expressed concern about the mess (legal, bureaucratic, physical) that would be created by an accident. Eventually, it was decided that intervention would be in order.

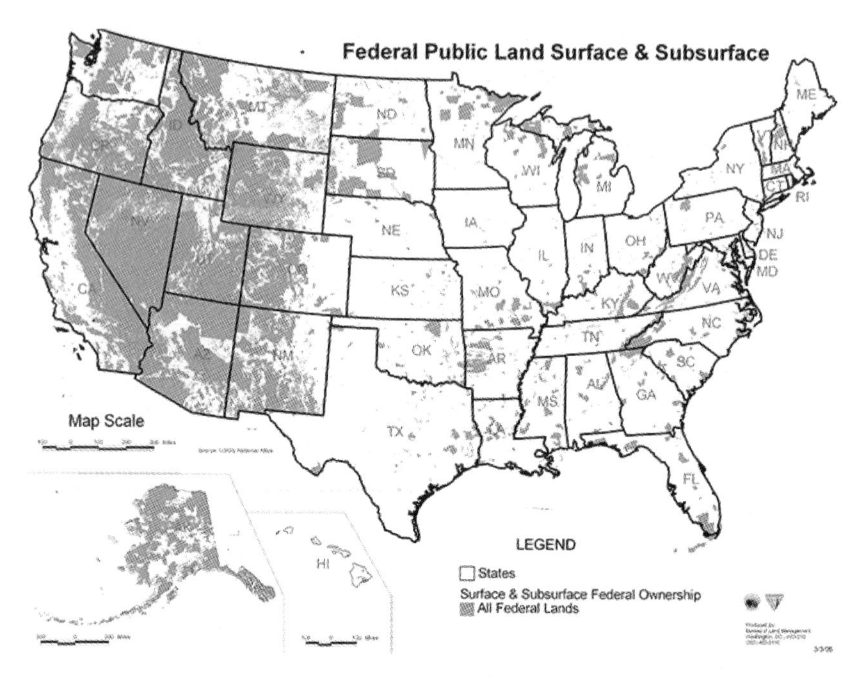

Map of the U.S. showing federal public lands. Source: https://westerncaucus-lummis.house.gov/public-lands, July 8, 2015

These two experiences highlight a particularity about this "church." It was not simply nature. It was public space. It had managers (the state), owners (the nation), and visitors (the public). It was subject to particular laws and regulations. There were doctrines that governed the activity that took place within it—texts on which authority over the space was based. It had a cadre of professionals devoted to its care, including armed men and women making decisions about what could and could not be done. In a certain sense, this church *was* built.

To be clear, I did not read my neighbor as saying "Joshua Tree National Park is my church," nor as "National parks are my church." I interpreted his "church" to refer, at least in a vague way, to nature. But this nature cohabits with a state institution. One third of land in the United States is public. As the map of U.S. public lands illustrates (figure I.1), that proportion is even higher in the western half of the country. Much of that land is "undeveloped." So if one understands the man's church as nature, in the western United States at least, that nature is, largely speaking, state-run.

This book investigates the place of spirituality within the American experiment with public management of land, particularly with respect to national parks. I focus on national parks because they have received the most attention and development on the part of the state and the visiting public. National parks serve as symbolic representations of the nation, including both its natural and cultural heritage. They are tremendously popular destinations, attracting over 350 million visits yearly. They hold political significance out of proportion to their size, visitation, and economic impact. How does their status as the pinnacle of nature in America relate to the spiritual sensibilities that so many visitors express? How does the parks' character as public space influence those sensibilities? How do those sensibilities relate to the state management of the space? In short, how do nature, spirituality, and the state shape each other through their confluence in these park spaces?

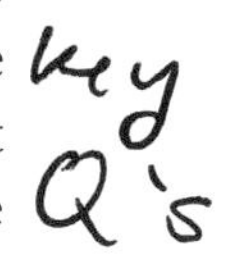

The Critical Stakes

In short form, this book concerns "spirituality in national parks" with a focus on the role of state institutions and the management of space. The larger implications of this volume concern a much broader phenomenon: the form of religion under conditions of secularity. Scholars have shown how "secular" does not mean the absence of religion, but rather the reshaping of it.[1] Indeed, more and more Americans describe themselves as "spiritual" but not "religious," declining to affiliate themselves with any particular religious group.[2] This growing form of religiosity is not well understood as a social phenomenon, being defined largely in terms of individual choice and feeling. By focusing on spirituality in the context of the state management of space, one can better see how the secular works in practice to shape religious life.

Studies of the modern liberal secular state have often downplayed its relation to religion. When taking this relation seriously, such studies have often focused on values and consensus, principles of freedom of conscience, the presence and influence of religious institutions, and governing legal frameworks.[3] This book treats the relation between religion and the modern liberal state at an entirely different level. It explores how the state nurtures spirituality through the management of land, bodies, and sense perception. This volume analyzes the material and embodied relations among the state, religion, and individuals, thereby providing tools for the study of the secular "on the ground."

Secular state power in national parks does not consist primarily of direct command or threat of force. Rather, power proceeds in the service of visions of the public good, particularly a liberal one, and works through the shaping of experience. The sophisticated and intentional use of this power does not negate its value as public service. But critical awareness of this shaping of subjectivity can address some of the limitations, even dangers, of a secular ethos. This book argues that this park-nurtured, secular spirituality is experienced as individual and grounded in nature rather than collective and grounded in society or tradition. The hidden or camouflaged role of the state in the construction of experience in the parks already says much about what the state has to gain from managing subjectivities in this way. Visitors are disciplined to experience a certain structure of authority (the state) as a reflection of nature and their individual freedom and self-realization. Such construction of individual freedom raises a fundamental challenge to the notion of limits for the exercise of power. Liberal political theory centers on the balance between protecting individual freedom on the one hand and restricting freedom in the interest of social order on the other. But when the state defines individual freedom, sets the conditions for it, and does so in a way that resists critical inquiry, then the idea of balance is radically challenged. In a more colloquial metaphor, the state has put its thumb on the scale.

Historian Karl Jacoby's alternative history of the American conservation movement focuses on moments of origin in such naturalization of power. The establishment of parks, wildernesses, and other protected areas turned hunting, cutting trees, and foraging into "poaching," "timber theft," and "trespassing," respectively.[4] The success of conservation efforts outlawed practices that had been part of the ordinary, everyday, "natural" flow of experience for many of those who lived on or near the newly "preserved" land (practices, one should mention, upon which such people had habitually depended for their livelihood, even their survival). What native peoples had earlier experienced with the introduction of private property recurred with settlers and their descendants (and native peoples, again) with the introduction of public property. In contrast to the earlier dispossession of native peoples, however, the establishment of the conservation regime was not justified as an exercise of manifest destiny and a taming of savagery. Rather, conservation justified itself as preservation of the natural order and a collective, public good. Appreciating the history that Jacoby relates, focusing on class and conservation, and the work of several others with respect to native peoples and national parks, one can see the operation of power in efforts to preserve nature—power that has historically privileged certain urban, elite, white understandings and uses of land.[5]

Contemporary national parks bear this history in their structuring of experience. Parks are designed largely for spectating, touring, edification, and transience. The experience of nature in national parks is an urban nature, indeed, a park: a space of leisure, serenity, and class. One may protest that the current regulatory structure of the parks is necessary, that it would be absurd to allow the public to live in national parks on a permanent basis, or that allowing the public to cultivate and harvest in park lands would destroy them. There are certainly sound arguments for such positions, ones with which I would likely agree. But the understanding of national parks as pure nature devoid of politics and interest short-circuits the machinery of critical discourse for making collective decisions that reflect a diversity of perspectives. In other words, the experience of nature as a space of individual freedom and self-fulfillment can, if taken uncritically, erase the sense of social responsibility for the decisions that have determined the particular conditions of the land as it is managed.

Taken as individual and natural, spirituality deepens the investment in state authority. The state gives nature to all, but also to each. In fostering spirituality in the parks, the state sets conditions in which individuals connect with themselves and feel uplifted, recognizing their experiences as personal and private ones even as they involve a sense of connection to higher, universal realities. Through its perceived grounding in nature, the individual, self-realizing, spiritual subjectivity cultivated by the parks (often expressed as a sense of "peace") is to a certain extent pacified. Why would one resist the regulations that preserve the environment in its natural state?[6] This pacification, however, holds an implicit connection to the application of force. Behavior that does not conform to the rules becomes an assault on nature and not just an infringement on a tacit, collective agreement. Such threats become, to a certain extent, existential ones whose neutralization takes on the cast of necessity. Those who will not agree to change their behavior, even after explanations of the natural character of the rules, become not just stubborn, but irrational. If someone cannot be persuaded by reason, what alternative is there to the use of force?

Scholars such as Talal Asad and others have criticized secularity on precisely these grounds. Secular subjectivity, taking as natural certain modes of individuality, discourse, and behavior, implies a relation to the non-secular: collective, social, religious subjectivity and its concomitant claims to authority. When such claims are regarded as alien to natural, authentic being, conflicts with secular orderings of society can take on an absolute and inflexible character. But when both these subjectivities are regarded as contingent and socially constructed, room for more open, flexible negotiation opens up. Such conflicts constitute critical issues not just in the American context but around the world.[7]

Definitions, Principles, and Premises

"Spirituality" needs closer definition. Some use it as a catchall term to indicate religiosity in general. Others use it to indicate an individualized religiosity that is not grounded in institutions. And often the term is used in a way that avoids precise definition.[8] This book uses the term "spirituality" in a way that addresses these common understandings while retaining a distinctive analytical position. I use "spirituality" to indicate a distinctive and individualistic form of religiosity that is socially constructed and that operates in large part through avoidance of definition.

This restricted use of the term does not refer, therefore, to religiosity in general. It does not refer to the set of religious traditions that find expression in the parks. This volume does, however, use the term to refer to openness to various religious traditions. Spirituality, in this sense, is not treated as an identifiable object like a tradition. Rather, this book treats spirituality as an orientation to religiosity that is characterized by individuality, fluidity, and incommunicability.

To say that spirituality is highly individualistic does not deny its social construction. Individualism is a social ethos. This book investigates how that individualism is constructed through the management of bodies, perception, and speech so as to facilitate "spiritual" experience of nature in national parks.

I take the incommunicability of spirituality, its avoidance of self-definition, as socially productive. By that I mean that the vagueness of spirituality allows different forms of social solidarity than those afforded by collective and conscious affirmations of group identity. In national parks, individuals who describe themselves as spiritual while resisting further definition can recognize their experience as a shared one, even a universal one, without talking to or knowing their fellow visitors. Through bodily, aesthetic experience, combined with avoidance of articulation of meaning, visitors can experience the park as public and private at once. Rather than a failure of intellectual sophistication, the incommunicability of spirituality serves as social strategy.

What about nature? It is difficult to answer the question of what nature is beyond human constructions of it. In addition to conceptions of it, one must consider the physical management of spaces called "natural." Romanticized ideals of nature lead many, for example, to identify an intensively managed park as more natural than the broken concrete and weeds of the neglected corners of urban landscapes. The point is not that all nature is social construction, but that the distinction between nature and society is exactly what is at stake in the efforts to take nature as a church. To be clear, innumerable entities and processes operate according to logics that are not under the control of humans. But humans work with nature through their representations of it, and the parks treated in this volume are just such a representation.

This representation often takes paradoxical form. Nature is seen as something deeply connected to the self, yet also as something far beyond it. It can be portrayed as a spirit that unites the community of all life, while at the same time remaining distinct from the communities in which most people live. It can be regarded as something necessarily wild and outside the control of humans, and yet as something that requires human care and management for its integrity. In this book, such paradoxical representations of nature occupy a prominent place, particularly when informing spirituality as defined above.

The state, like all social bodies, is imagined rather than simply, physically existent.[9] It describes a set of relationships that legitimize the exercise of power in the public sphere. So when this volume investigates the role of the state in constructing nature and shaping spirituality, it is concerned less with the specific intentions of individuals with a title and a uniform than it is with the way that specific orderings of space, speech, and behavior acquire legitimacy. In this way, the curvature of a road, the opening up of a vista, and the sense of escaping the city and entering into nature are products of the state. This is true not simply because state employees designed the road, designated the vista point, and cut down trees that blocked the view. More importantly, this is true because the sense of a natural and pleasant arrangement of experience legitimizes cutting down trees, prohibiting building construction visible from the vista point, and collecting fees for entry into the space. In this way, a "spiritual" experience of "connection to nature" becomes an investment in the state insofar as that experience legitimates the specific arrangement of space, speech, and behavior that gave rise to it.

Much work on the state has focused on the power that comes through control of symbolic systems (such as narratives, information, classifications, media). In their work on English state formation, Phillip Corrigan and Derek Sayer wrote, "States . . . *state*; the arcane rituals of a court of law, the formulae of royal assent to an Act of Parliament, visits of school inspectors, are all statements. They define, in great detail, acceptable forms and images of social activity and individual and collective identity. . . . Indeed, in this sense 'the State' never stops talking."[10] In their view, the state represents. The state legitimates its exercise of power through symbolic action. This book takes a complementary but distinct focus. In addition to looking at how power is legitimated through symbols, it looks at the way the state operates through the elision of symbols: through natural vistas, interpretive silences, and the arrangement of bodies. This combination of presentation and representation yields a distinct view of the legitimation of power. In this sense, "the State" is the state: the way that things are and the way that things happen.

The Argument

In national parks, the state is naturalized, nature becomes a state organ, and spirituality becomes a public religion. Through the blurring of the boundaries among nature, state, and individual, spiritual experience invests visitors in the state that has shaped their experience of nature.

While some parts of this process may be intentional, by and large this process occurs unconsciously. The unconscious aspect of this process is a testament to the power of the secular to mask its governing conventions.

This book treats invisibility and paradox as features of social processes rather than analytical barriers. It is not so much that the state masks the "real" operation of power by clothing its officers in green and brown and Sequoia-cone embossed hat bands. Rather, the inability to see the difference between state power and the requirements of the natural environment allows visitors to see their acquiescence to law and policy as harmony with nature.

The paradoxes of state action and natural process, public space and private experience, secular identity and spiritual sensibility operate according to a certain logic. Following the German social theorist Niklas Luhmann, "consider the rhetorical understanding of paradox as more fundamental than the logical one. It is simply a matter of communication that wants to use simultaneously what is incompatible. . . . For the communication of paradoxes, the operative effect is decisive: it causes communication to oscillate, because each position makes it necessary to assert the opposite, for which the same holds in turn."[11] Considered in this way, paradoxes allow for two-pronged communications. The Park Service can present a certain state of the environment as "natural"—that is, as what the environment would look like without human interference. The presentation of such a natural state justifies the intensive operations involving human planning, communication, and labor to achieve or maintain this state. Likewise the presentation of space as public and secular justifies operations yielding experiences that individual visitors share with no one else, often "spiritual" ones. The cumulative effect of such operations constitutes (much of) the power of the state in national parks. That power is itself paradoxical. It is the assertion of a network of interests, hierarchies, values, and choices. It is also the way that things are and the way that things happen. This is the natural state.

Procedure and Methods

Investigating the construction of spiritual value within national parks has been a large and complex task. To provide intellectual focus for this inquiry, I first turned to John Muir, a founding figure for national parks and one who presented the spiritual value of these lands as one of the preeminent reasons for setting them aside. Rather than concentrate on Muir's literary legacy, however, I chose to look at the way that Muir's spiritual vision of nature is memorialized in place, in the management of experience within the national parks that claim him as a namesake. Among these, I selected three sites that cover a range of geographical and social features. The first is the wilderness section of the John Muir Trail, running over two hundred miles from Yosemite National Park through to Sequoia and King's Canyon National Park. The second covers the more heavily touristed areas of Yosemite National Park that are adjacent to the trail, most notably Yosemite Valley and Tuolumne Meadows. The third is Muir Woods National Monument, consisting of an old-growth redwood stand located less than hour's drive from San Francisco. In cultivating Muir's legacy in these sites, the Park Service deals with a wide range of visitors, from long-distance hikers to family vacationers to day trippers. Likewise the geographical features of these sites necessitate a variety of management strategies, ones adapted to wide stretches of wilderness, the large but more developed areas of Yosemite, and the more restricted confines of Muir Woods. While this study involves only a handful of the several hundred units that make up the National Park System, the selected sites represent a range of visitor densities and geographic scales, which, in turn, are broadly characteristic of most national parks.[12]

With regard to method, this work draws on historical, sociological, and philosophical tools. The historical background concentrates largely on texts. Analyzing official policy statements, legislation, and administrative guidelines, Chapter 1 traces the development of the national park ideal from its origin in the nineteenth century and shows how spiritual value has influenced management paradigms for the national parks from their inception.

Drawing on sociological methods, Chapters 2 through 4 serve as case studies of the national park ideal in practice, analyzing how spirituality informs both the production and perception of the environments of the John Muir Trail, Yosemite National Park, and Muir Woods National Monument. Here an important caveat should be noted. While these chapters are based on interviews and surveys of over four hundred park visitors, interviews with rangers, and participant observation in park programs, these chapters do not constitute an ethnography in any classic sense of the term. Two factors precluded an ethnographic study of the parks.

First, as ethnography connotes the study of a community, the park visitors were excluded from ethnographic study. They do not constitute a community. Traveling from far away places for a limited amount of time, visitors step outside of their communities. They spend their visit to the park in solitude or with a limited number of friends and family. Contact with outsiders is often fleeting; perhaps an evening conversation with a neighboring camper or an hour spent listening to a ranger program. Simply put, park visitors do not constitute a "group" with the sets of characteristics that tend to arise from shared living experience in a particular locale over an extended period of time.

Second, park rangers also fell outside the bounds of ethnographic study. Here this preclusion was a matter of permission. Park rangers do indeed form a community: they live and work together, interacting regularly with each other concerning their collective endeavors. But I was not permitted to study them as a community. I was told that soliciting and publishing the private opinions of such a body of government officials would violate the public mandate under which they worked: "subverting the will of Congress" was the phrase one official used.[13] Park rangers represent the public. The Park Service would oppose me in any endeavor to portray them as a group of private citizens with its own particular concerns and attitudes. Of course, there are ways that one can work around this impediment. But in a project aiming to uncover, at least in part, the "public" value of nature and the parks, such a proposed boundary to my research seemed consonant with my goals. I wanted to know how spiritual valuation of the parks might find support from rangers *in their public function*. In order to gain the permission and cooperation of the Park Service, I therefore proposed that my interviews and conversations with rangers would be consultations; as experts, they could illuminate the character of visitor spirituality and who could explain how that spirituality fit into the public value of the parks.

In sum, my analysis of surveys, interviews, conversations with, and observations of visitors and rangers serve as sources "on background" for an exploration of the interplay between public and private spheres.

The "public sphere" is indeed a nebulous category, including what "everybody knows" and what "goes without saying." This analysis of the spirituality of "the public" at the level of lived experience in particular places and times therefore concerns the halo of background intuitions and assumptions, as well as the structural preconditions, that surround the spiritual experiences that find expression in the data. Many of my interpretations go beyond what rangers or visitors may have intended or consciously "thought of" as they spoke and wrote. Indeed, a major theme of this book engages the vagueness and refusal to clarify spiritual meaning, both on the part of rangers and visitors.[14]

I discuss the theoretical implications of this work in Chapter 5, considering the way that visitor spirituality resonates with the structure of the parks as social environments. Here I argue that spirituality acts as a public religion of a particularly liberal stripe. After surveying the theoretical background of public religion, I show how the religious logic that informs park management and visitor spirituality tends toward a liberal model of citizenship. A series of follow-up interviews explores how visitors themselves linked their experience to an understanding of collective identity.

↳ Does this include politicization or pacification?

1

Establishing National Parks

From Ideal to Institution

John Muir, writing of his 1869 experience in the California wilderness of the Sierra Nevada mountain range, described the effects of nature:

> We are now in the mountains and they are in us, kindling enthusiasm, making every nerve quiver, filling every pore and cell of us. Our flesh-and-bone tabernacle seems transparent as glass to the beauty about us, as if truly an inseparable part of it, thrilling with the air and trees, streams and rocks, in the waves of the sun,—a part of all nature, neither old nor young, sick nor well, but immortal. . . . How glorious a conversion, so complete and wholesome it is, scarce memory enough of old bondage days left as a standpoint to view it from![1]

One may wonder what friends and family from Muir's "bondage days" would have made of the "conversion" that invigorated his bodily "tabernacle." Muir had grown up on a Wisconsin farm in the 1850s under the Calvinist rule of his father, a Scottish immigrant who demanded hard labor and strict obedience on the part of his children. While Muir showed little rebellion as a child, his assumption of a nomadic lifestyle after college began a departure from the religious vision that dominated his youth. As an amateur naturalist, Muir began to develop his own spirituality, one that saw a fusion of body and spirit in nature. While initially his writing dealt largely with scientific questions, his appreciation for the sanctity of nature eventually led him to address broader issues of political life. Conveying his spiritual sentiments in some of the most influential periodicals of his time, Muir helped to gain support for the public preservation of wilderness, an effort that bore fruit with the establishment of the first national parks in the late nineteenth century.

What kind of preservation did Muir envision? His writings suggest that in promoting wilderness, he wished to preserve not simply space, but the opportunity to experience nature in a particular way. Muir's way was typically Romantic: the lone wanderer coming face to face with grand scenes of natural beauty, enjoying tranquil repose, joining in ecstatic union with the divinity of nature. His experience depended much upon solitude, risk, adventure, and prolonged, profound reflection. Such an experience, and the spiritual wisdom and love that Muir felt nature could provide to all people, could not abide crowds. Civilization and commercial development were inimical to the revelations he sought. For Muir, the divinity of nature came through personal, intimate encounter. To be sure, this encounter was fed by a broad social and cultural world and was fed to a wide public through his writings. But at its core, such communication of divinity required privacy, and this was what wilderness provided.

Of course, Muir recognized that preserving the opportunity for such personal, intimate experience required more than individual effort. But one notes with irony that to preserve wilderness as a private experience, Muir turned to a definitively public organ: the state. As founder and president of the Sierra Club, he personally lobbied President Theodore Roosevelt and other political and economic elites and thus came to embrace what might otherwise have been viewed as a paradox: retaining the possibilities for intimate, personal connection with wilderness required public control and restriction. Wilderness needed to become public to remain private.

Linking private experience with public interest lies at the core of the National Park Service mission to the present day. Obviously, the complex historical process of the creation of national parks brought with it a whole range of circumstances that Muir could not have anticipated. Historian Alfred Runte has noted how the establishment of Yosemite as a national park gained crucial support from corporate interests that saw Yosemite's snow pack as a reservoir for their agricultural concerns in California's central valley.[2] Later, the language of resource management would encompass the aesthetic and even spiritual aspects of the park. As this chapter shows, park officials would come to view nature in the parks as a good that could be appropriated in a unique way by each visitor, thereby creating a sense of personal investment in the public space of the park. Spiritual experience was seen as one of the strongest expressions of this kind of investment.

In this way Park Service efforts to provide the public with a personal encounter with nature has followed an agenda similar to Muir's, but with a different emphasis. For the Park Service, Muir's vision of a personal, private encounter fits within the structures of public authority and national identity. Visitors are to feel the freedom and enrichment of a personal encounter with nature as their public, national heritage. Furthermore, both echoing and distorting Muir, prominent park officials have seen the spiritual connection between the individual and nature as an investment in the state. To the degree that individuals "find themselves" spiritually in the parks, so the logic goes, they find themselves in the state that sets the conditions for their experience.

Over a period extending roughly from the mid-nineteenth century to the beginning of the twenty-first, the national park ideal found expression in management paradigms that gave rise to the concrete shape of the parks in terms of the number and placement of roads, buildings, and trails, the set of rules governing various activities, and the education that visitors were to receive in the parks. My analysis of three paradigms—recreation, heritage, and systems—shows how Park Service officials sought to integrate private, individual encounters with nature into public, collective enterprises of national identity and state allegiance. Officials occasionally drew on religious language and logic to express this relationship, especially within the heritage paradigm. In their increasing sophistication throughout the history of the parks, these paradigms provide the framework for managing spiritual experience as part of the parks' public mission.

Recreation

Runte has noted how the establishment of national parks was motivated in part by what he called "scenic nationalism," an effort to claim the parks as natural and national cathedrals that would rival and surpass the architectural wonders of Europe.[3] But the management of national parks, and the question of what parks were supposed to "do" for visitors, was also influenced by more mundane social factors. Particularly important among these was the recreation movement, a broad set of social initiatives arising in the second half of the nineteenth century that included, in addition to the promotion of national, state, and municipal parks, the playground movement, the adult education-oriented lyceum movement, and the establishment of a number of voluntary organizations providing, among other services, recreational opportunities to youth and the poor.[4] The recreation movement addressed itself to the increasing industrialization of American society characterized by mass production, repetitive labor, specialization of tasks, and all the resulting stresses and divisions. Out of this context, the recreation movement grew as a way to provide the population with opportunities for rejuvenating and relaxing experiences as well as stimulating and educational ones.

This concern for recreation as a matter of public welfare decisively informed the national park ideal. In the early history of the parks, one figure, Frederick Law Olmsted, Sr., stands out and provides a useful illustration of recreation as a management paradigm.[5] A prominent landscape architect, he advised state officials on park policy as early  as 1865 with regard to the creation of Yosemite as a public park, and was one of the first to theorize the relation of private experience and collective identity in national parks. Specifically, Olmsted's 1865 report to the governor of California, a document that is treated in detail in this section, drew a connection between the individual health benefits provided by natural recreation and the health of the collective "body of the people." Through this metaphor of the body, Olmsted argued that publicly accessible natural areas would build the strength of America as a democratic nation.

Writing as chair of the commission established to develop guidelines for the administration of Yosemite, Olmsted noted the health benefits resulting from the "contemplation of natural scenes."[6] Such recreation yielded increased vigor, productivity, and longevity, while its absence could entail "mental or nervous excitability, moroseness, melancholy or irascibility, incapacitating the subject for the proper exercise of the intellectual or moral forces," and in more extreme cases may have included "mental disability . . . softening of the brain, paralysis, palsy, monomania or insanity."[7] Olmsted's understanding of health centered on harmony, as applying both to psycho-physiological faculties and the temporal rhythm of work and rest. The ill effects of a lack of natural recreation resulted from the constant and unrelieved repetition of everyday activities in both business and household. The weight of habit and repetition brought both the body and the mind out of balance, over-exercising certain faculties while letting others atrophy.

Olmsted drew out the implications of natural recreation for national identity through a comparison with Britain. The invigorating effect of the enjoyment of nature was already well recognized, Olmsted wrote, by the governing elite of the British Empire, who had made it customary to spend time each year in an Alpine sojourn. Such a practice was not simply a perquisite of the ministerial office, but rather, Olmsted asserted, a vital factor in increasing the effectiveness of such officials in their service to the state. Furthermore, Olmsted connected the participation in natural recreation to the much longer "active business life" of the British elite who took up the custom of regular sojourns in nature.

What the British Empire lacked, however, and what Yosemite was to provide America as a nation, was natural recreation for the public at large. Given the opportunity to encounter natural beauty, park visitors would become not only happier people, but more civilized, cultured, and productive citizens: "It is the folly of laws which have permitted and favored the monopoly by privileged classes of many of the means supplied in nature for the gratification, exercise and education of the esthetic faculties that has caused the dullness and weakness and disease of these faculties in the mass of the subjects of kings. And it is against the limitation of the means of such education to the rich that the wise legislation of free governments must be directed."[8] Olmsted alleged that citizens under a monarchy lack aesthetic refinement because, under such a form of government, the natural means of producing such refinement remained the privilege of an elite few. Olmsted argued that this was not simply an injustice. For just as an individual body benefited from the even development of its faculties, so too did a society function as a more whole, harmonious, and balanced body when its components (individual citizens) had been developed to a relatively equal degree. Thus the even distribution of the benefits of nature concerned not just a "free" government but a "wise" and, by implication, "natural" one as well.

Olmsted cited the words of Andrew Jackson Downing, one of the founding figures of landscape architecture in the nineteenth century, in support of this perspective: "The dread of the ignorant exclusive, who has no faith in the refinement of a republic, will stand abashed in the next century, before a whole people whose system of voluntary education embraces (combined with perfect individual freedom) not only schools of rudimentary knowledge, but common enjoyments for all classes in the higher realms of art, letters, science, social recreations and enjoyments."[9] From this perspective, a republic provided a healthier, more vigorous civilization than more hierarchized systems of government, an advance that would impress not simply through its greater justice but also through its cultural richness. The republican education that would stimulate such an advance, Downing suggested, consisted of two essential parts: private agency ("individual freedom") and public equality (common access to high culture). Olmsted mirrored this twofold emphasis on the individual and the collective, the private and the public, in his commentary on Downing's words: "It was in accordance with these views of the destiny of the New World and the duty of the republican government that Congress enacted that the Yosemite should be held, guarded and managed for the free use of the whole body of the people forever."[10] "Free use" referred to private or individual agency while "whole body of the people" referred to the public or collective aspect of republican enjoyment of nature. By integrating this duality of public and private into a metaphor of the body, Olmsted suggested a synthesis of the two with health as a normative principle. The development of the physical and mental faculties of the bodies of individual citizens was to coincide with the increased health of the "body of the people" as a democratic whole.

Interestingly, what stood in the way of a democratic, republican, and individual enjoyment of nature was not any dictatorial or monarchical state. Rather, private property itself provided the threat. Referring to views of Yosemite, Olmsted wrote of "the danger that such scenes might become private property and through the false taste, the caprice, or the requirements of some industrial speculation of their holders, their value to posterity be injured."[11] Private enjoyment of natural scenes needed to be protected from private ownership of the means of access to those scenes. The public sphere was called to enter into the tensions among private interests in order to preserve a certain kind of personal, individual experience of nature. This addresses the curious phrasing of "free use" of lands "held, guarded, and managed" by the state. Individual freedom, according to this perspective, required management and restriction on the part of the government. Here public interest did not simply negate private interest, but rather codified a certain mode of the private: an individual, health-oriented, aesthetic, and recreational approach to nature.

In his vision of public space nurturing the body of the American people, Olmsted provided some of the earliest considerations of the significance of public nature for communal health and identity. And while other politicians and park managers may not have voiced the metaphysical concern for the "body of the people" that Olmsted did, they did share his emphasis on recreation as the main purpose of these public nature parks. This can be seen in the Yellowstone Park Act of 1872, which established the first national park proper as "a public park or pleasuring ground for the benefit and enjoyment of the people."[12] The act assumed the public utility of recreation, of "enjoyment" of nature as a "pleasuring ground." And in terms of policy, successive designation of national parks occurred without any change to this recreational emphasis. For more than fifty years from the time of Olmsted's report, the public function of national parks was dominated, at least in terms of the principles of park management, by the provision of recreational opportunities to the public.

While the recreational paradigm proved vital for park management, this philosophy was not accompanied by a large increase in the number of national parks. At the time of Olmsted's writing, Yosemite was not yet a *national* park: the federal government had ceded Yosemite Valley and the Mariposa Grove of sequoias to the state of California with instructions to maintain these areas as a public park. With the Yellowstone Park Act of 1872, the idea of national parks had touched ground, it is true, but the growth of national parks as a political phenomenon proceeded quite slowly. In the latter half of the nineteenth century, national parks were, for the federal government but also for the populace more broadly, an item of restricted national significance requiring little sacrifice and providing little substantial benefit. The western half of the United States, where the bulk of national parks would come into existence, saw the height of the Indian wars during the late nineteenth century. In this regard, too, nature took on the character of a public, national space, but here one of conquest, eradication, and/or eviction of Native Americans.

The ongoing wars, distance from major population centers, and difficulties of travel restricted visitation to national parks during this period. In view of these considerations, it is not surprising that only four large national parks were created in the nineteenth century.[13]

Steady growth of the national park movement occurred in the early twentieth century, coinciding with the end of the Indian wars and population increase in the West. Fourteen parks and national monuments were established by 1916, the year Congress created the National Park Service to manage such lands. The development of recreational tourism dominated the management agenda for these national public spaces, but not completely. The National Monuments held little in the way of touristic attraction, at least at the time, and were reserved as sites of scientific and archaeological interest. But it was not until the National Park Service Organic Act of 1916 that the preservation of nature in and of itself came to expression as a particularly national interest. Historians of national parks have noted how even with this codification of nature preservation, recreational interests and a utilitarian worldview dominated both congressional intentions and park management during this early phase.[14] But for national heritage, which would later become a centerpiece of expressions of the public significance of national parks, this emphasis on the inherent worth of nature was an important step.

Heritage

Recreation has continued as a fundamental concern of park management to the present day. Equally important in today's parks is the preservation of national heritage, whose history as a management principle this section will treat. Under the notion of heritage, the Park Service preserves certain sites or environments as symbolic representations of the nation. A house that functioned as part of the Underground Railroad, for instance, is used by the Park Service to symbolize American history in terms of race, oppression, and freedom.[15] A particular wetlands environment is preserved as a symbol of physical America—that is, as an example of an ecosystem typical to the American land mass both historically and in the present.[16] Visitors may have "fun" in such areas, and they may benefit from all the aesthetic and athletic stimulation that Olmsted cited, but under the heritage paradigm such sites are to provide visitors with something more: namely, an encounter with a larger whole of which they are a part (nature, America). In contrast to Olmsted's concern for recreation, heritage makes national parks a locus of individual and national self-consciousness. Individuals come to a greater cognizance of their place within American history and the history of the planet. In short, visitors are to achieve a greater awareness of their own nature through their encounter with national parks.[17]

There is no definitive historical origin for this concern with heritage, and heritage never supplanted recreation as a management principle.[18] Rather the two overlapped. The National Park Service Organic Act of 1916 provides a useful illustration of this coexistence. Written in large part by Frederick Law Olmsted, Jr. (son of Olmsted, Sr.), the act stated that the parks were to "conserve the scenery and the natural and historic objects and the wildlife therein and to provide for the enjoyment of the same in such manner . . . that will leave them unimpaired for the enjoyment of future generations."[19] Recreation took priority here. The first object of conservation was "scenery" that was to be maintained for "enjoyment." The use of the word "scenery" implied that the land was not conserved for its inherent value, but for the way it struck the eye, for the pleasing image it provided. "Enjoyment" can take on several different meanings, but when applied to scenery, it is difficult to argue for any other purpose than one of recreation. Despite this evocation of leisure, however, the Organic Act added an important nuance to the national park ideal.

"Unimpaired for future generations" served as the key phrase. Historian Richard Sellars has remarked that Olmsted, Jr., added these words "almost offhandedly" in the process of drafting the bill.[20] Regardless of the level of importance that Olmsted, Jr., may have placed on them, these words would later become the quintessential expression of the Park Service's mission and a ubiquitous citation within Park Service literature. How does this phrase modify the understanding of nature preservation? By way of contrast, a return to the Yellowstone Park Act of 1872 proves useful. That act mandated "the preservation, from injury or spoilation, of all timber, mineral deposits, natural curiosities, or wonders . . . and their retention in their natural condition."[21] This can be seen as a foundational formula for preservation, but it did not encompass the notion of heritage. The phrase "retention in their natural condition" did state that the site would be maintained in a certain stasis over time. But preservation of a "natural condition" did not, in itself, address the historical continuity *of society* that lay at the heart of heritage.

In contrast, the Organic Act of 1916 highlighted collective identity by linking preservation to a notion of kinship: the parks were to preserve nature for "future generations." Preservation needed to provide for the public not just in the present, but also in the future. The act thus linked the continuity of nature with the continuity of society. And the act also suggested that the present be maintained not only into the future, but also out of the past, for the preservation of "natural and historic objects" pointed backward in time as well. Taken together, the preservation of objects for future generations created a symbolic link between the past and the future. From the notion of a "pleasuring ground" the national park ideal had now taken on a dual extension in time: a site that while providing enjoyment would also serve as a link from the past to the present and into the future. Parks became a public inheritance, a gift that citizens were to receive from their forebears and pass on to their children.

In the exposition of the heritage paradigm, Park Service officials continued to assert recreational enjoyment of nature as a public good. But those who asserted nature as national heritage tended to view recreational enjoyment of nature as a *competing* public good. That is, they saw recreational values and heritage values as, to some degree, limiting each other. Such a view was in evidence only six years after the foundational act of 1916, when the Park Service produced a resolution on the dangers of development in the parks. "The Superintendents' Resolution on Overdevelopment," arising from the National Park Service Conference in 1922, did affirm recreational development, stating that roads, trails, and services were needed "so that the parks may better fulfill their mission of healthful recreation and education to a larger number of people."[22] This stood in complete accord with the sentiments expressed by the elder Olmsted some fifty years earlier. Recreation was here recognized not merely as pleasure, but as a vehicle for public health. The superintendents affirmed the provision of recreational opportunities, for which development was necessary, as a sine qua non of park management.

But while the act of 1916 expressed the preservation of nature and the provision of recreation as noncontradictory principles, the superintendent's resolution of 1922 expressed its concern for natural heritage as a *limitation* on recreational interests. In an explanatory letter accompanying the resolution, Roger Toll, superintendent of Rocky Mountain National Park, evoked a mythical vision of American history to adjudicate the conflict between nature as heritage and nature as a site for development. That is, he alluded to a myth of progress in asserting the necessity of development while also evoking a myth of the Fall in asserting the destructive character of industry.[23] After a nod to the recreational purpose of national parks, Toll elaborated this mythical vision:

> Another object for which the parks were created, is to set aside for future generations, certain areas that are typical of our finest scenery. They are to be held free from commercial exploitation. . . . In order that our nation may grow and prosper, forests must be cut, streams must be turned onto dry lands, cataracts must give up their power, meadows must be shorn to feed the flocks. These things are necessary. Scenery must often be destroyed by commerce, beauty must often be sacrificed to industry. But in order that we shall not squander all of our birthright, a few jewels of scenery are set aside for ourselves and for posterity to enjoy.[24]

Here development did not simply refer to a means to improve recreational opportunities, but was rather woven into a story of American history. Consonant with a myth of progress, Toll's vision presented development as a vital factor in the growth of the nation. But rather than regarding development as an unmitigated triumph of manifest destiny, Toll saw this as a necessary evil. Scenery was "destroyed" by development, and beauty was "sacrificed." In terms of the relationship to nature, development was a fall from a state of wholeness. Nature was given to America as a "birthright" and was sacrificed for the sake of growth. But the total sacrifice of that birthright would "squander" nature as a national heritage.

Compared with the recreational emphasis of the Olmsteds, this assertion of the symbolic value of national parks shifted the standards used to shape policy. The recreational value of nature as expressed by Olmsted, Sr., involved a practical immersion in an experience of the present. According to his theory, industry involved repetitious tasks oriented towards future goals and deferred satisfaction, while recreation yielded its healthful effects through practical enjoyment of the present. In contrast, the heritage value of nature involved a symbolic immersion in the past and a sense of continuity running into the future. That is, nature did not simply provide healthy respite from work, but rather participation in the birth of the nation that was to be preserved for all time. From this perspective the development that facilitated recreational enjoyment involved a symbolic impact that was potentially detrimental. Development symbolized progress and the triumph of manifest destiny as well as a fall from a state of natural wholeness with which America was originally graced.

The religious overtones of this perspective become even more apparent in the paragraph immediately following the passage cited above.

> Not all of nature's treasures are to be seen from the seat of an automobile; one does not receive at twenty miles an hour, the inspiration that results from a pilgrimage on foot; and an automobile horn is less effective than the silence of solitude, to awaken thoughts deep and abiding. Someone had said, "Great views make great thoughts, great thoughts make great men." The national parks should be a real factor in the building of a better, stronger race.[25]

Such an experience of nature manifested in a sense of elevation, one endowed with religious overtones. Given the context of policy advocacy within a state institution, the reference to race-building illuminates the national character of the parks. Combining the previously established benefits of recreation with the assertion of the symbolic return to the birth of the nation, this building up of the "race" wove individual experience, bodily health, a religious sense of elevation, and national identity into a natural whole.

In terms of implications for practice, one should note that for Toll, appreciating the symbolic value of nature was not simply or even primarily a mental operation. Rather, the symbolic return to the birth of the nation involved particular bodily orientations and attitudes. It required the physical effort of hiking on foot, a social withdrawal through isolation, and a sensory environment absent of human sound and language. Individuals may have experienced nature in crowds, enjoyed all the comforts of civilization, utilized all the technological tools for recreation, and still have made good use the park. But, Toll suggested, to enjoy the full benefits and particularly to participate in the national character of the park, visitors needed to venture reverentially and with physical effort into solitude.

As this idea of preserving nature as a memorial to national origins started to take a more central role in policy statements, the expression of the value of nature took on a more absolutist cast. In 1925, Hubert Work, secretary of the interior and the immediate superior of the director of the National Park Service, wrote a memorandum to "restate" park policy:

> This policy is based on three broad, accepted principles: First, that the national parks and national monuments must be maintained untouched by the inroad of modern civilization in order that unspoiled bits of native America may be preserved by future generations as well as our own; Second, that they are set apart for the use, education, health, and pleasure of all the people; Third, that the national interest must take precedence in all decisions affecting public or private enterprise in the parks and monuments.[26]

This put a new element into first place among principles of park management. Whereas the report of Olmsted, Sr., and the Yellowstone Park Act of 1872 made recreation the primary purpose of the parks, Work made "use, education, health, and pleasure" a secondary principle and inscribed the symbolic return to national origins as primary.[27] Furthermore, Work recapitulated the myth of the Fall implied in Toll's letter, and in fact went farther. Nature has not been "sacrificed" but largely "spoiled" through the course of American history. The growth of civilization has entailed not merely consumption, but desecration of nature. A picture of nature "untouched" by civilization reinforced this language of purity. These remnants of nature "must" be preserved, he wrote, and not simply in the interest of the highest benefit or efficiency. Rather Work made it clear that preserving nature meant preserving America itself.

This nuance of purity and absolutism filtered down to official documents farther down the chain of command. Horace Albright, writing as director of the National Park Service in 1931, prepared a policy statement regarding predatory animals, seeking to protect those that might be hunted or systematically removed from park environments. Albright's statement stands in strict continuance of Work's perspective:

> Every policy developed is an attempt to meet the purposes for which the parks were formed; First, the national parks must be maintained in absolutely unimpaired form for the use of future generations as well as those of our own time; second, they are set apart for the use, observation, health, pleasure, and inspiration of the people; and third, the national interest must dictate all decisions affecting public or private enterprise in the parks.[28]

The three-tiered structure of priorities mirrored Work's memorandum in each of its parts, with the second and third principles reiterating Work's almost verbatim.[29] True, the statement of the first principle did not use the language of "unspoiled bits of native America." Rather Albright inscribed a concern for purity into a restatement of the mission statement contained in the act of 1916. That act stated that the Park Service should leave the parks "unimpaired for the enjoyment of future generations." Albright added the word "absolutely" in front of "unimpaired" in his rephrasing of the fundamental principle. The language of purity came out even more forcefully in the specific policy statement regarding predatory animals: "all animal life should be kept inviolate within the parks."[30] "Inviolate" echoed the concern voiced by Work that nature should remain "untouched" and "unspoiled," a choice of phrasing that brings to mind the connotations of sexual purity contained in the phrase "virgin territory." Together with the insistence that nature be preserved "absolutely unimpaired," these purist policy directives raised the symbolic value of national parks to the level of the sacred.

Such explicit religious language appeared in Albright's directive regarding park planning, also dated 1931. Office Order No. 228 commanded park superintendents to develop a plan for construction within their parks. Each park superintendent was to map out the areas of the park and describe the development plan for each area. The following is excerpted from Albright's general outline that he provided as a guide for the superintendents:

> 2. Wilderness (Sacred Areas) Areas. (Outlined on Park Topographic Map or Park General Plan.)
>
> A. Wilderness Areas—large areas to be generally protected as undeveloped wilderness areas.

B. Sacred Areas—small areas to be protected against all development for the protection of a special natural feature—i.e., 1/8 mile radius around Old Faithful Geyser. Similar areas around important waterfalls—a special group of trees or geological feature, etc.[31]

Beyond this brief outline, Albright did not elaborate on his understanding of "sacred." However, his use of the term resonated with the allusions to religious significance made in other Park Service documents. First, only "natural" areas fell under the designation of sacred. Second, the sacred was to be protected by a prohibition against "development," which, given the context, implied durable artificial structures such as roads, parking lots, trails, public utilities, and buildings.[32] Third, the sacred was to be marked. That is, the directive commanded that clear geographical lines be drawn to mark off the sacred from the non-sacred. All of these aspects appeared in the earlier documents discussed. Albright's Office Order No. 228 was innovative in its degree of clarity in defining the sacred: the directive called for clear lines on a map and strict prohibitions based on those boundaries.

In sum, the heritage paradigm added a new thread to the national park ideal, one that was woven in and around the recreational paradigm that preceded it. Toll, Work, and Albright pulled away from the recreational paradigm by viewing recreation in terms of heritage and decrying the symbolic impact of the development necessary for recreational activities. At the same time, Toll emphasized certain recreational modes, such as solo hiking, as being conducive to an experience of heritage. One could consider such a view as a compromise. In another way, however, the heritage paradigm came to express a higher synthesis. The core dynamic of the national park ideal—that is, the mediation of private experience and public identity—was no longer simply a matter of physical and social health. Under the heritage paradigm, the integration of the individual and the collective became a matter of the sacred as well.

Systems

With the stock market crash of 1929 and the Great Depression that followed, the management of national parks underwent significant changes. The agenda for nature preservation, at least as a state free of human development, lost some of its momentum. Instead, the public works projects of the 1930s resulted in a major infusion of money and labor devoted to the touristic infrastructure of the parks: visitor facilities, roads, and trails. Many conservationists found the pace of such development alarming, and both within and without the Park Service calls came to preserve the proper "atmosphere" in the parks.[33] Further, the entry of the United States into World War II made certain park resources, notably timber, targets for extraction. Faced with calls for greater development and extraction, park officials sought new arguments to defend their management of parks. Toward this end, they expanded the national park ideal to include a conception of systemic integrity that would be threatened by swift and radical changes. Both integrating and going beyond the recreational and heritage paradigms that preceded it, the systems management paradigm viewed the parks as a complex of interlocking networks that needed to be harmonized with one another in order to preserve them and fulfill their mission. While this paradigm initially applied to the "natural" systems of the park, it soon grew to embrace the social networks in which the parks participated as well. A complex, multipurpose approach to management, the systems paradigm has remained the dominant mode of organization within the parks today. With regard to the public mission of the parks, the systems paradigm was presented as a refinement of democratic and pluralistic ideals, one whose strength resided in the harmonious management of difference rather than the pursuit of singular management goals.

One can find origins of the systems paradigm in ecological concerns. National Park Service Director Newton B. Drury's "The National Parks in Wartime," published in *American Forests* in 1943, provided one of the earliest official expressions of the ecological value of the parks. Further, his defense illustrates how recreational and heritage values were incorporated into the new paradigm.

With the wartime economy's need for lighter and stronger materials came calls for the logging of certain types of trees located in national parks. In an effort to prevent this, Drury argued that the war made a higher call for natural preservation. One element of this argument arose out of the recreational paradigm. Preserved in their natural state, Drury argued, parks provided the maximum of refreshing and healthful effects:

"Affording an environment that gives relief from the tension of a warring world, the parks are, even now, being looked upon as a factor in the physical and mental rehabilitation that will be increasingly desirable as the war progresses."[34] Drury then noted the expanding use of national parks by military personnel on furlough and implied that the relief afforded by contemplation of nature would improve morale.

But the value of nature was not restricted to improvement of physical and mental health, Drury continued. Rather, natural preservation went to the heart of the motivation for the war, a motivation that centered on national heritage:

> In defining the purpose of this war, President Roosevelt has said that we are protecting a great past. Evidences of this past, both as human history and natural history, are contained in areas of which the National Park Service is custodian. . . . Pride in America swells in the hearts of all who look upon the mile-deep chasm of the Grand Canyon, the geysers and hot springs of Yellowstone, the thundering waterfalls of Yosemite, the towering Sequoias, and the sweep of mighty forests on the Olympic Peninsula. Consciously or unconsciously there is built up within all who have had such experiences an increased faith in our country. Can these experiences fail to strengthen the conviction that this is a nation worth fighting for?[35]

This passage illustrates both the distinction between history and heritage and the tendency to conflate the two. Note that Drury's reference to America's natural history is accompanied by a description of nature that has nothing to do with history. Drury's language speaks exclusively to the spatial characteristics and sensory impact of nature. How visions of a "mile-deep chasm," a "thundering waterfall," or the "towering Sequoias" may be related to the nation's history, and how such visions might arouse pride in the nation are not explained here. In terms of heritage, however, and as opposed to history, such rhetoric made more sense. Earlier in the article Drury wrote that "Americans take pride and courage in the fact that the national parks and monuments are being protected and will be available for future enjoyment."[36] As an experience of greatness that would be preserved for one's descendants, for the nation's descendants, nature became a means for linking present and future generations over time. In terms of this temporal dimension, natural heritage took on a character related to but distinct from natural history.

Nor did Drury ignore the past. In concluding the article, he wrote that the parks were preserved "so that this and future generations will see the untamed America that was, and understand the compelling influences that built and strengthened this nation."[37] Evoking both a mythology of national origins and a sense of inheritance passed on to the nation's future, Drury presented the parks as symbols of collective identity. That symbolic function, Drury suggested, took on even greater importance in wartime.

But Drury's article introduced another theme that went beyond heritage. In addition to playing a symbolic role, he claimed, parks displayed an ecological harmony that, if disturbed, could resulted in their ruin. Drury evoked both heritage and ecological values to contrast with extractive, commercial interests: "The magnificent park forests at the lower elevations . . . though having potentially high commercial value, are worthy of permanent preservation as outdoor museums for the benefit of this and future generations. If we should cut these forests, which include outstanding specimens hundreds of years of age, we not only would lose these forest giants forever, but also lose something far more fragile—the delicate ecological balance which exists among all the elements of the forest."[38] This invocation of "ecological balance" modifies and expands the call for preservation of the forest. If parks were to be "outdoor museum[s]," one could argue that parks need contain only a limited number of examples of organisms or species to serve their purpose. The call for maintaining a "delicate ecological balance," however, demands a broader preservation of the forest. The value of national parks, Drury suggested, went beyond a vision of original America and included a network of natural processes and relationships.[39]

The concluding paragraphs of the article synthesized heritage and ecological values. In the penultimate paragraph, Drury singled out John C. Merriam's work on conservation, *The Garment of God*, to bolster the case for preservation.[40] Drury paraphrased the message of that work as an assertion "that man cannot live in an isolated present separated from past and future. The nation which forgets its past will have no future worth remembering."[41] While the exact meaning of Merriam's title was not explicated, the context in which Drury cited the work implied a connection between preservation of nature and the continuity of the nation within a theological framework. In the final paragraph, and in reference to the parks, Drury wrote, "As long as the basic law that created them endures, we are assured of at least those few places in the world where forests continue to evolve normally, where animal life remains in harmonious relationship to its environment, and where the ways of nature and its works may still be studied in the original design."[42] Given the earlier reference to *The Garment of God*, the phrase "original design" invokes a divine creator. Furthermore, the language of this passage allows for a conflation of divine and national origins in nature. The "basic law" that protected nature in national parks, the Organic Act of 1916, coincided with the law of God expressed in the "original design." As long as the first endured, so would the second.

This assertion of the harmony of natural law and the law of the state nuanced the nationalist aspect of the heritage paradigm. The heritage paradigm mandated the preservation of particular visions of landscape that could be attributed to the pioneers as national ancestors. Such visions were intended to create bonds among the people, a sense of collective identity along ethnic lines (particularly European American), which was to result in a sense of national unity. The preservation of nature as a network of processes and relationships, however, went beyond the maintenance of a certain visual field. Rather than focusing on vision, the "ecological" perspective focused on law—that is, on the structures that regulated relationships within the ecosystem. In terms of society, the heritage paradigm focused on the nation as an ethnic entity bound together by sensations of collective unity. In contrast, the systems paradigm, seen here in a concern for ecology, focused on the state as an ethical entity bound by law and collective behavior.[43] In other words, rather than invoking a natural nation, the systems paradigm invoked a natural state.[44]

For Drury these paradigms did not stand in contradiction. Both justified the preservation of nature as a connection to common origins. From the perspective of the heritage paradigm, these origins were historical. Maintaining a vision of pristine nature evoked a sense of sympathy with the pioneers a hundred years earlier. From the perspective of the systems paradigm, origins were ontological. Maintaining certain patterns of natural relationship kept humans in touch with the fundamental processes that govern the world. In Drury's article, reference to a divine creator served as a foundation of both paradigms at the same time.

In "The National Parks in Wartime," Drury drew on a number of justifications that had previously served in defense of national parks. His invocation of ecology, however brief, was quite original for a director of the Park Service at that time. Later official expressions of the national park ideal, especially in the immediate postwar environment, dropped the ecological language. The logic of systemic integrity that he invoked, however, found application well beyond the arena of nature. An appreciation for systems informed the social management of the parks and grew to include the state as the regulative system of the parks. Two developments accompanied this shift: (1) the use of economic language to describe state management; and (2) the incorporation of spirit as a value amenable to such management.

The concern for social management was influenced by historical developments following World War II. With the postwar economic, boom national parks experienced a significant increase in visitation. In 1941 twenty-one million people visited the parks. By 1955, that number had increased to fifty million, and the Park Service predicted eighty million visitors by 1966.[45] By the mid-1950s, the facilities created during the Depression era had exceeded their capacity and the environment of the parks were being sorely strained: sewage facilities were overworked, roads and campgrounds became more clogged, understaffing resulted in long lines and delayed maintenance, and increased traffic kicked up dust and trampled vegetation. In 1953 the prominent historian Bernard DeVoto wrote an article for *Harper's Magazine* in which he suggested closing the national parks to let them recover.[46] Instead, the Park Service developed a comprehensive plan for renovation. Known as "Mission 66," it consisted of a ten-year multimillion dollar plan for improving the infrastructure in the parks, including more accommodations, road improvements, increased staff, better housing for staff, increased trail maintenance, and a variety of other projects oriented toward visitor services.

Meanwhile, increased tourism had raised the financial value of national parks to a new level. Commercial revenues created by the tourist industry had always been factored into park management, but up until the 1950s the commercial value of the parks was extremely limited with respect to the broader economic environment. With the increase in tourism, however, parks began to a play a much larger role in state and national economies. Park Service officials took advantage of this new significance to argue for increased funding. Furthermore, they integrated an economic perspective into their expressions of the national park ideal. The significance of this integration lay not only in the addition of financial value to those previously expressed, but also in the notion of economy itself. Parks, officials argued, played a role in systems of relationship that went well beyond their borders. Those systems included not only financial dimensions but also symbolic and cultural ones. Preserving the full value of national parks, these officials implied, required wise management of those systems in which they participated.[47]

This systemic perspective can be found in Park Service Director Conrad Wirth's justification for Mission 66, dated 1956. In an address to President Dwight D. Eisenhower and his cabinet, Director Wirth invoked financial, recreational, educational, and heritage values of the parks. These values did not stand separately from one another, however. Rather, Wirth argued, they were united under a central economic metaphor:

> The intangible benefits of refreshment, understanding, and inspiration are not the only dividends. . . . With working hours going down and leisure time going up, vacation travel and vacation spending are, in fact, among the . . . biggest industries. . . . The more the parks are used for their inherent, cultural, and recreational values, the more they contribute to the economy of the Nation. Here is one resource that earns its greatest human and economic profit the less it is used up.[48]

While presenting all the values of the parks in economic terms, Wirth asserted that the differences among them lay in their tangibility: recreational, educational, and heritage values could not be strictly calculated. However, Wirth presented all the values of the park as contributions to a single "economy of the Nation."

As these different values contributed to a single economy, they called for a single management strategy: conservation. Expressing ecological concerns through an economic metaphor, Wirth described conservation as wise management of an investment. Parks produced their greatest "dividends" and "profit" if their physical content, the principle of the investment, remained intact and was not "used up." Furthermore, this investment applied not only to recreational and heritage values per se, but also to the specifically "spiritual" value of national parks:

> To put the National Parks in shape is an investment in the physical, mental, and spiritual well-being of Americans as individuals. It is a gainful investment contributing substantially to the national economy. . . . It is an investment in good citizenship.
>
> Where else do so many Americans under the most pleasant circumstances come face to face with their Government? Where else but on historic ground can they better renew the idealism that prompted the patriots to their deeds of valor? Where else but in the great out-of-doors as God made it can we better recapture the spirit and something of the qualities of the pioneers? Pride in their Government, love of the land, and faith in the American tradition—these are the real products of our national parks.[49]

Wirth's invocation of the "spiritual" was illustrated by reference to the "spirit . . . of the pioneers" as found in nature "as God made it." Such phrasing fell in line with earlier expositions of the heritage paradigm that linked nation, nature, and God. Wirth offered an innovation with respect to earlier expressions by presenting the "spiritual well-being" of the citizenry as one element of a national economic system and an "investment" that required wise management.

This conception of "investment" put the value of national parks in a new light. Earlier documents referred to the parks as "treasures," a metaphor that connoted wealth. By describing the parks in terms of "investment," however, Wirth implied that parks contained wealth that produced more wealth. The added wealth referred not only, and not primarily, to financial wealth. Rather, the "real products" of national parks, of the "investment," consisted of the people's "pride in their government, love of the land, and faith in the American tradition." The wealth produced by national parks consisted of a set of symbolic associations informed by emotion and a sense of allegiance. Further, these "real products" may have been intended to produce further wealth themselves. Earlier in the presentation, Wirth compared the park system to a factory, "a plant operating at 200% capacity."[50] From this perspective, the "products" of the "plant" would yield a "profit." In other words, Wirth suggested that "pride in their government, love of the land, and faith in the American tradition" could be conceived as a *source* of wealth for the government and the nation. In terms of value, the "treasures" of national parks thus served as capital: wealth that could produce more wealth. This capital had financial, symbolic, and spiritual dimensions.

This distinction between capital and wealth highlighted the emphasis on system. Parks stood as one element within a system of national extent. Wirth suggested that if the parks fell into disrepair, the national economy, as a whole and broadly conceived, would suffer. While he did not reiterate Drury's concern for the "delicate ecological balance among all the elements of the forest" or of nature, the same logic of balance, interconnection, and systemic relation informed Wirth's presentation. Wirth's economic metaphor thus mirrored a logic of ecology and applied it to a national system of financial, symbolic, and spiritual production.

This emphasis on parks as part of a total and unified system was accompanied by a specific distinction between the nation and the state. Regarding the nation, the second paragraph of the quotation above stressed the heritage value of the parks: preservation of historical sites aimed to "renew the idealism that prompted the patriots to their deeds of valor"; preservation of nature intended to "recapture the spirit . . . of the pioneers." Such language evoked the continuity of the collective, and particularly the nation, over time. But in addition to his mention of heritage values, Wirth added a new element that had not appeared in earlier expressions of the national park ideal. In national parks, visitors "come face to face with their Government." Apart from sensations of national unity, to what could this encounter with "Government" have referred?

One could argue that with the great increase in visitation, park management could no longer remain hidden. As parks became a denser social space, perhaps the order of that social space came into visitor consciousness in a more powerful way. DeVoto suggested this in his proposal, published three years before Wirth's presentation, to close the national parks. He wrote:

> The chief official of a national park is called the Superintendent. He is a dedicated man. He is also a patient, frustrated, and sorely harassed man.

> Sit in his office for an hour some morning and listen to what is said to him by the traveling public and by his administrative assistant, the Chief Ranger.
>
> Some of his visitors are polite; some aren't; all have grievances. A middle-aged couple with a Cadillac make a formal protest: it is annoying that they must wait three-quarters of an hour to get a table at Lookout Point Lodge, but when it comes to queuing up in order to use the toilets at the Point—well, really! A woman in travel-stained denim is angry because Indian Creek Camp Ground is intolerably dusty. Clouds of dust hang over it, dust sifts into the sleeping bags at night, dust settles on the food and the children and the foliage, she has breathed dust throughout her two-week stay. Another woman reports that the toilet at Inspiration Cliff Camp Ground has been clogged since early last evening and that one of the tables there went to pieces at breakfast time. A man pounds the desk and shouts that he hit a chuck-hole on Rimrock Drive and broke a spring; the Drive, he says, is a car-killer and will soon be a man-killer. Another enraged tourist reports that a guardrail collapsed when his little girl leaned against it and that she nearly fell into the gorge.[51]

The list of grievances extended another half page. DeVoto's broadside concerned the ordering of the social space in national parks, and he made it clear that in terms of visitor impressions not only did the parks offer a view of "America" as a transhistorical collective space, but they also represented "the United States Government."[52] The display of nature and of America now stood side by side with the display of the state.

Such a perspective appeared in a more positive vein in Wirth's Mission 66 presentation three years later. While he mentioned heritage and other values as a foundation of park management, Wirth's discussion of the contents of the plan focused on the smooth workings of the social order. Mission 66, he asserted, would provide adequate accommodations, improve safety, and decrease crowding. He stressed the need to "improve the flow of traffic," "double total capacity," and manage the increasing "recreational use load."[53] A "one-package" program was necessary, Wirth suggested, "so that when we build a road, the lodges, campgrounds, public use buildings, utility systems and the other things the road leads to will be ready for use at the same time."[54] Wirth's language stressed the efficiency of social workings and served as the context to his concluding (optimistic and anticipatory) rhetoric. Efficient management, Wirth suggested, held symbolic value in and of itself: "Where else do so many Americans under the most pleasant circumstances come face to face with their Government?" Wise management of the parks, Wirth suggested, would create a consciousness of and allegiance to the broader system of management carried out by the state.

While Wirth designed his presentation to convince a small number of individuals at the highest levels of government, the logic of capital can also be seen in a text focusing on the day-to-day work of park rangers. Freeman Tilden's *Interpreting Our Heritage*, originally published in 1957, served as a foundational work for the Park Service in its educational function of interpreting the features of the parks for the visiting public.[55] In providing guidance to rangers, Tilden drew on economic metaphors to describe the value of the parks, calling them "treasures" that promoted "the enrichment of the human mind and spirit."[56] Indeed, an economic logic informed his conception of conservation, and he employed the notion of investment much as Wirth did. Tilden wrote: "We can *use* these precious resources, so long as we do not *use them up*. Put it this way: We should not dissipate our capital, but we should zealously dispense the interest."[57] For Tilden, interpretation did not simply communicate information, but employed the symbolic wealth of the parks so as to enrich the public.

Tilden meant this enrichment to effect an investment in national identity. In stressing the need to make interpretation personally engaging, he used the words of Ralph Waldo Emerson: "As we read, we must become Greeks, Romans, Turks, priest, king, martyr and executioner; must fasten these images to some reality in our secret experiences."[58] The nationalist import of such an imaginative enterprise becomes clear in Tilden's citation of C. E. Merriam, a University of Chicago professor and leading member of the behavioral movement in political science: "The underlying design is of course to set up a group of the living, the dead, and those who are yet unborn, a group of which the individual finds himself a part. . . . He is lifted beyond and above himself into higher worlds where he walks with all his great ancestors, one of an illustrious group whose blood is in his veins and whose domain and reputation he proudly bears."[59] Through these citations Tilden promoted interpretation as an enterprise that would result in the collective bonding of visitors through their imaginative investment in a common heritage. The stories told in national parks would become the nation's stories, the stories in which citizens would live and for which they would fight.

Tilden recognized, however, that such bonding occurred most effectively through those "secret experiences" within each individual visitor rather than a self-conscious affirmation of group identity. For this reason he outlined a strategy of implication, of strategic silences whose context would facilitate investment in a common heritage. He wrote that "the interpreter acts only as a scout and a guide. He leads his group to the most alluring scenes he has discovered, and is silent." This combination of guidance and restraint would render plausible the sense of private possession of public space. Absent explicit statements on the part of rangers, the park would become for the visitor "a precious personal possession. It is the individual's shock, *his* apprehension, *his* discovery: and what he discovers is more than what he sees or hears. He has discovered something of himself, hitherto unrealized."[60] The collective bonding in these natural scenes would therefore inhere in individuality itself, in a sense that these public spaces were sites of personal self-realization.

The language of such collective and individual self-realization, for Tilden as for others noted in this chapter, centered on spirit. In that space opened by interpretive silence, the ranger would evoke "reverence for what, in our natural world of fitness and beauty, is not factual but of the spirit; for that which is beyond diction; for the very soul of that which the interpreter makes a living and potent reality in a cloudy experience."[61] Through an institutional mandate to appeal to the individuality of visitors, Tilden portrayed the parks as vehicles of mass communication, indeed of mass investment of visitors in public space. His centralization of spirit within this enterprise made this work a promotion of spirituality as public religion.

Tilden's perspective falls largely within the heritage paradigm and resonates with nationalism. Following Tilden, rangers could promote among visitors an identification with pioneers and settlers in the face of a pure, natural landscape, a collective return to national origins. However, the techniques that he outlined, and in particular his privileging of individuality, harmonized with the systems paradigm that was rising to prominence at the time of his writing. That is, he gave guidelines for communicating the value of a complex environment to a complex visiting public. Those interpretive silences could be filled with different meanings for each visitor, drawing on a variety of aspects of the environment according to the visitor's individual proclivities. The resultant investment in public space would therefore constitute an investment in the state that shaped and maintained the environment as a vehicle for individual self-realization. In these ways, then, Tilden's work spoke both to the collective heritage of the nation and to the management of difference performed by the state.

* * *

These three paradigms of recreation, heritage, and systems provide the framework for managing spirituality as public religion. While Olmsted's formulation of the recreational value of the parks lacked religious language, the link he forged between individual and collective health was metaphysical: an imagination of the social as a body in which democratic ideals fostered good circulation and harmonious development. Both building on and departing from a focus on recreation, the expositors of the heritage paradigm introduced explicitly religious language. Heritage became a sacred possession: natural scenes bespoke a collective history and an inheritance for future generations, a linkage among past, present, and future that had to be protected and approached reverentially. Under the systems paradigm as expressed by Drury, the spiritual dimensions of recreation and heritage were channeled toward law. Nature as a system displayed the law of God, a law that found reflection in the state when it preserved nature in its "original design." Thus the evocation of "spiritual well-being" invested visitors in the state as the system of organization of the parks. In sum, park officials have drawn on religious language and logic in sophisticated ways in order to link the nature of national parks to the public good. This has provided a framework for a public religion, one in which spiritual appreciation of nature was to yield a sense of collective identity and an investment in structures of authority.

As parks developed and became more complex environments, the scientific, recreational, symbolic, ecological, political, and other values of the parks were treated as a set of interconnected elements that could not be managed independently from one another. In other words, park officials working under the systems paradigm rarely advocated the pursuit of one goal to the exclusion of all others. Rather, official park documents showed a tendency to integrate various goals with one another. In this way the systems paradigm did not act as an overarching perspective to which all others must conform. Rather, the systems paradigm was multi-perspectival.

This multi-perspectival tendency did not mean that the paradigm was neutral. With an increasing diversity of tensions and accommodations among various goals, the focus of park management became structural stability more than conformity to singular ideals. In other words, faced with the goals of scientific knowledge of the parks, provision of recreational opportunities, preservation of the symbolic value of scenery, maintenance of the ecosystems of the parks, adjustment to changing political circumstances, and others concerns, park management tended to abandon any focus on one particular goal and instead expressed concern for the creation of balance within the structure of the parks. Of course, in practice this balance may have resulted in a privileging of one set of interests over another. However, the balance struck in one management decision would not necessarily have been replicated in other decisions for other areas. The complexity of the park environment therefore could have shielded management from accusations of partiality: managers could point to some area of the park, or of the park system in general, where an interest neglected by one decision took a more prominent position.

This refusal to privilege one perspective above all others may explain the general lack of religious and/or spiritual language in later expressions of the national park ideal. From the 1960s on, one finds an increasing tendency toward management for management's sake: thus the emphasis on structural stability. Recreational, heritage, ecological, and economic values, all of which were accompanied with religious expression, no longer drew on a transcendent justification. Their continued maintenance within the overall system of the parks arose out of the structural inertia of the park, with adjustment and change occurring on a case-by-case basis. Religious expression did not disappear from expressions of the ideal value of the parks. Rather, the religious dimensions of the national park ideal, previously given explicit expression, became implicit within the organizational structures of the parks. The basis for those structures lies in the growing sophistication and institutionalization of the systems management paradigm. The historical process of tension and accommodation within this paradigm shows a growing trend toward synthesis, one based in the blurring of the nature/culture distinction under the structures of the state.

Toward Synthesis

Mission 66 moved away from concerns for nature preservation and ecology expressed earlier in the century. But with the increasing prominence of the environmental movement in the 1960s, ecology took a more central place in expressions of the national park ideal. This focus on ecology did not privilege the economic language used in management of the parks as social space. However, ecological perspectives maintained the emphasis on management of systems contained in earlier postwar documents. Furthermore, this recognition of parks as systems involved a blurring of nature and culture. Ecologists suggested that both human and nonhuman activity participated in the ordered flows, patterns, and systems of relationship that made up the environment. Wise management of national parks thus required a paradigm that would apply to both social and "natural" space.

This perspective focusing on natural and social systems involved, first of all, the establishment of systems of knowledge. In a presentation addressed to the National Park Service in 1959, biologist Stanley Cain stressed the importance of nature as an "ecological laboratory."[62] Interestingly, Cain did not propose that research in such a place would likely result in major scientific breakthroughs. Rather, Cain asserted that the encounter with nature as an object of knowledge and understanding stood at the root of public appreciation of nature. The public, he suggested, invested itself in nature largely through intellectual reflection. From this perspective, and in contrast to previous tendencies in national park research, the study of nature in the parks needed to go beyond specific management concerns. Park research needed to "run the complete systematic gamut," Cain suggested, plumbing the "breadth and depth" of the ecological system.[63] Without such knowledge, Cain implied, the Park Service failed to serve the visitor whose appreciation was enriched by systematic knowledge.

This knowledge of systems focused on the social. Cain advocated studying nature in "the communities which are formed." Park naturalists were to work toward an understanding of "the composition and structure of all communities" with a focus on patterns of relationship: "the important actions, reactions, and coactions in each community."[64] From this perspective, Cain proposed knowledge of nature as knowledge of social organization, including territorial integrity ("territories, ranges, and home ranges"), economic exchange ("producer and consumer relations"), and the dimensions of social units ("population size and density").[65] Such a perspective admitted no distinction between nature and culture. Human action could disrupt the equilibrium of certain ecosystems, but this did not constitute an ontological contamination of nature with the human. Rather, such action implied disruption of another society, one upon which the human species may have been more or less dependent.

Although Cain downplayed management concerns in this proposal, his focus on nature as a structure of organization laid the groundwork for management of nature and society in the parks under a single management paradigm. Such a perspective can be seen in "A Back Country Management Plan for Sequoia and Kings Canyon National Parks," written in 1960 and released service-wide in 1963 to serve as a model for wilderness management. This document offered a definition of conservation that viewed society and nature as a single whole. Specifically, it proposed a synthesis of economic and ecological values under the rubric of conservation: "The ultimate aim of conservation is to leave our earth as rich and productive as we found it. William Dean Howells said, 'A nation is great not because it mines coal, cuts timbers or builds railways, but because it has learned how to produce, build and grow without destroying the bases of its future existence.'"[66] In terms of value systems discussed earlier in this chapter, this statement drew on the heritage paradigm with the phrase "as we found it." Such wording implied that parts of the earth were "discovered" by a certain collectivity and thus invoked the European colonization of the Americas. As in earlier expressions of the heritage paradigm, this one stressed the need for connecting a natural past (nature "as we found it") to a national future (to "leave our earth" in a way that preserved the nation's "future existence"). But the national emphasis of the heritage paradigm was, through the synthesis of economy and ecology evoked here, linked to the state. The nation's greatness, Howells asserted, depends on its wise and efficient management of the systems of production and exchange that fed it. In other words, a nation was great because of its system of organization. From this perspective, nature provided society not only with resources to be consumed, but more importantly with models of efficient and sustainable organization: "As our society continues to increase in complexity and in population, such an understanding of natural, balanced environments will become increasingly essential for developing ways of living harmoniously, rather than destructively, on our Nation's lands."[67] In addition to providing a source of national wealth, nature taught humans how to govern and manage themselves and thus functioned as an informational resource for the state.

In the application of such a perspective to park management, the authors of the "Back Country Management Plan" invoked the concept of natural law: "National Parks, preserved as natural ecological entities, can supply man with a more complete understanding of the natural laws that may govern his future—and possibly his ultimate survival—in lands and environments everywhere."[68] The phrasing of "laws" that "govern" anticipated a coincidence of natural and social management, for the authors of the document went on to present their management principles as being in conformity with natural law. The smooth continuity between management of natural resources and social management can be seen in the notion of "carrying capacity":

> This concept has long been applied with precision to the management of domestic livestock. Likewise, since the thirties, it has been standard procedure to base wildlife management programs on careful studies of the wildlife ranges to determine, and operate within, their carrying capacities. As human use of wilderness ranges begins to approach a saturation point, management has the responsibility of identifying basic factors that limit the carrying capacities of each area, and of tailoring the respective management programs to conform to these natural limitations.[69]

Domestic livestock, wildlife, and humans thus fell under the same management principle. Park officials managed them all through reference to "natural limitations," and thus implicitly through natural law.

Such a perspective involved cultural management as well. In justifying wilderness regulations in terms of natural law, the authors wrote,

"When the present Committee determined from observation the minimum distance required for wilderness-type privacy between high country campsites, it was, in effect, determining the camper-carrying capacities of these areas."[70] The earlier description of carrying capacity saw it as conforming to natural limitations. The state of nature evoked in the regulation of campsites therefore involved a conception of "privacy" that could not be considered as a solely aesthetic or cultural phenomenon. Instead, "privacy" was regulated under the concept of natural limitation or law considered in terms of a temporary "home range" of the organisms (campers) managed under the paradigm. Park management here integrated a certain wilderness aesthetic into the conception of the natural order, thus giving park regulations the force of both natural law and scientific management.[71]

Park officials knew that invocations of ecology would be recognized as a tool for management of humans. "A Back Country Management Plan" addressed potential resistance to such a social agenda in its last section, entitled "Wilderness Protection vs. Personal Freedom":

> When human populations expand they become subject to the biological limitations that govern other dense populations: The greater the number of individuals the greater the loss of individual freedom of action. An illustration of this in the daily lives of all of us is afforded by the congestion, delays, and complicated regulations on today's crowded highways.
>
> Wilderness users may with justice complain that they seek wilderness to escape the regimentation of daily life. But the time is past, for example, when a Boy Scout can use his axe to cut fresh pine branches for his bed in the old tradition. Today we have no choice but to agree with Snyder (1961) when he suggests that, ". . . when we speak loosely of an 'untouched' wilderness we must actually be reconciled and receptive to an area managed in a degree relative to the number of people who enter it."
>
> The Committee recognizes a major responsibility to preserve all possible freedom in the wilderness, but feel the answer to complaints over present day restrictions is not "bureaucracy" but "Born too late."[72]

As in earlier sections of the document, this citation set the regulation of human population in the context of natural law: human populations were as subject to "biological limitations" as any other species. From this perspective, the authors asserted that the infringement on "individual freedom" resulted from the laws of nature. In their illustration of natural law, the authors implied a coincidence of the state of nature and the state as government. Traffic regulation on the highways was presented as a manifestation of "biological limitations."

Such a perspective blurred any essential distinction between nature and civilization. Referring to such a distinction, and to the public's investment in it in their attitudes towards recreation, the authors were remarkably frank: the distinction was dead; wilderness as a space free from civilization no longer existed. From the standpoint of ecology, the expanding population fell under the governance of natural law, and the preservation of wilderness required management in accordance with this law. Maintaining wilderness in a recognizable form, the authors asserted, required a kind of management and regulation that simply could not be said to leave wild spaces "untouched." Such regulation, furthermore, was not presented as the manifestation of any particular political will. "We have no choice," the authors wrote: natural law and the passage of time demanded the regulation of wilderness.

In denying any absolute separation of nature and culture, the systems paradigm departed from earlier constructions of the heritage paradigm. The prewar documents discussed above asserted the otherness of nature, the virginity of territory. On this view, the social import of nature depended on difference: landscapes stood as the common "other" that citizens shared with their ancestors. From a systems perspective, however, there was no essential difference between nature and the human. Humans manifested a set of patterns and systems that interacted with other sets of patterns and systems. According to the "Back Country Management Plan," systems in which humans were relatively uninvolved tended to exhibit greater stability, and this rendered their value to humans as models for natural/social regulation.

The rise of the systems paradigm did not supplant heritage. Rather, park officials sought a consonance, a synthesis of the different paradigms that shaped the parks. For the emergent systems paradigm, one document expressed such a synthesis above all others. Commonly called "the Leopold report," after one of the members of the advisory board on wildlife management, this set of policies went far beyond its original mandate of wildlife management and offered a reformulation of the national park ideal.[73] In this report, the authors described the return to an original state of nature as an act of theater, an illusion with great symbolic and social value. While earlier authors recognized the illusory quality of this symbolic return, they tended to conceive of this illusion largely in visual terms. In contrast, the authors of the Leopold report focused not on visions of landscape, but on the recreation of the "biotic associations" (that is, predator-prey relations, seasonal migration patterns, and others) that existed at the birth of the nation.[74] Such an endeavor, they proposed, would add depth and authenticity to the spectacle of natural/national origins, depth that a purely visual approach lacked. From this viewpoint, ecological management provided a more faithful rendition of national heritage than preservation of scenery ever could.

This language of "illusion," specified below, reflected a consensus among park officials that, whether as a visual scene or a set of biological relationships, the state of nature at the birth of the nation could not be completely restored. The Leopold report discredited any notion of "untouched" nature by recounting the history of logging, grazing, predator control, fire suppression, extinction of native species, and introduction of exotic species, all of which have shaped the national parks. The authors wrote: "The resultant biotic associations in many of our parks are artifacts, pure and simple. They represent a complex ecologic history but they do not necessarily represent primitive America." The authors claimed that nature as a state absent of human influence has, through the action of history, ceased to exist. Further, this report viewed the full restoration of natural origins not only as an ontological impossibility, but as a political impossibility as well: "The wolf and the grizzly bear cannot readily be reintroduced into ranching communities, and the factor of human use of the parks is subject only to regulation, not elimination." From this perspective, the statement that "exotic plants, animals, and diseases are here to stay" reflected both recognition of a physical state and resignation to a political reality.[75]

Restoration of national/natural origins thus stood as an unachievable ideal, but one that nevertheless served as a focal point: "If the goal cannot be fully achieved it can be approached. A reasonable illusion of primitive America could be recreated, using the utmost in skill, judgment, and ecologic sensitivity. This in our opinion should be the objective of every national park and monument."[76] Given the wider context of the document, "skill, judgment, and ecologic sensitivity" referred to management of systems of interrelationship, both natural and social. Park officials, this report suggested, needed to understand not only how ecological systems were organized internally, but also how those systems were involved in broader economic and political systems.

Ecological systems could take many forms, and in principle management did not need to privilege any one particular form. The heritage function of national parks, however, gave management of ecological systems a specific historical focus that it would otherwise lack. Consonant with earlier expressions of the heritage paradigm, the Leopold report advocated recreating the ecological system at the time of national origins. And like earlier notions of national origins in official literature, this ecological conception of national origins was based on race. "As a primary goal, we would recommend that the biotic associations within each park be maintained, or where necessary recreated, as nearly as possible in the condition that prevailed when the area was first visited by the white man."[77] This historical focus for ecology sought to symbolize a collective (white, Euro-American) identity not simply in an image of pristine landscape, but in the structures of the park environment itself.

By the end of the 1960s, official expressions of the national park ideal consisted of a synthesis of recreation and heritage under the systems paradigm. The rising prominence of an ecological perspective within such expressions did not result in a prioritization of nature preservation per se, but rather in a broad institutional recognition of national parks as systems. State officials recognized that such systems involved physical, symbolic, and political dimensions, and officials adapted their management strategies accordingly. For instance, in terms of concern for physical systems, the National Environmental Policy Act of 1969 mandated, as part of a broad overhaul of federal policy, environmental impact reports (EIR) for a host of government projects.[78] For the National Park Service, this meant that proposals for new roads, buildings, facilities, and other projects had to be accompanied by a written analysis of the impact such projects might have on the larger environmental system of the parks. Combined with a mandate for public comment sessions, the

EIR requirement ingrained a systematic perspective into the procedures of park planning.

Systematic thinking was not restricted itself to the local environment of the parks, but became integrated at a larger, more symbolic level as well. The General Authorities Act of 1970 stated that park lands,

> though distinct in character, are united through their inter-related purposes and resources into one national park system as cumulative expressions of a single national heritage; that, individually and collectively, these areas derive increased national dignity and recognition of their superb environmental quality through their inclusion jointly with each other in one national park system preserved and managed for the benefit and inspiration of all people of the United States.[79]

In keeping with the perspective of many earlier documents, this act expressed the primary value of national parks in terms of national heritage. Furthermore, and reflecting the trend toward an ecological perspective, such heritage value depended largely on the "superb environmental quality" of these lands. But the notion of "system," which according to the act was central to the value of national parks, did not express a set of biological relations within or around the parks. Rather, the "inter-related purposes and resources" referred to the gamut of all functions fulfilled by national parks, including provision of recreational opportunities, preservation of historic sites, management of wilderness areas, and every other purpose mentioned in previous legislation. These various functions, the act asserted, constituted a single system expressing a "single national heritage." The act thus introduced a dynamic that would come to dominate park management philosophy to the present day: public heritage consisted of a multiplicity of discrete elements that formed a whole only through their relation to each other. Such a dynamic suggested that no one park encapsulated the American heritage as a whole. Rather, heritage was viewed as plural in its contents and singular in its organization. The unity of heritage was therefore expressed not in terms of any core essence, but rather in terms of relations within a system. In this way, the act could assert that administration under a single system actually increased the public value of these parks. Furthermore, the act suggested that such increased value occurred through "inclusion" in the system itself. The act thus asserted that the decision to designate land as a national park actually conferred value and did not simply reflect or preserve it.

This idea, that, in itself, the designation "national park" actually increased the value of any particular piece of land, coincided with an accelerating growth of the system. The period from 1960 to 1980 saw nearly 150 additions to the National Park System, compared with less than fifty for the two preceding decades. Proposals for new parks became so numerous that opponents referred to them as "park barrel" legislation. Regardless of the motivation for their inclusion in the system, the variety of these new units presented a challenge to the park officials charged with managing them under a common authority. New units that fell under Park Service management ranged from National Historic Sites such as the Saugus Iron Works and the Carl Sandburg Home to large wilderness areas such as the Big Cypress National Preserve and the Gates of the Arctic National Monument. The assertion that these sites all expressed a "single national heritage" did not clarify what these various types of land held in common nor how, precisely, they should be managed. In response to this challenge, state officials elaborated their conceptions of system to encompass this variety and, in the case of the Vail Agenda of 1992, drew on the economic metaphor of investment management to do so.

Officially titled "National Parks for the 21st Century: The Vail Agenda," this report was commissioned as part of a service-wide conference held in Vail, Colorado, in 1992 and recapitulated many of the concerns contained in the "State of the Parks" report of 1980 and the General Accounting Office report on the parks in 1987. In addition to remarking on the chronic problem of understaffing (greatly exacerbated by the addition of new units), the Vail Agenda also highlighted the increasingly diverse character of the system. "The resources of the Park System now encompass a markedly diffuse range of public values. Citizen support for and interest in individual units varies greatly, as do the contributions each unit makes to the national heritage. Requisite personnel skills, organizational structures, and management demands also vary greatly."[80] Put bluntly, in the political climate of the time, any piece of property deemed nationally significant, even in the most general way, could become a candidate for inclusion in the park system.

The Park Service bureaucracy found itself performing all the roles of a property manager without a clear conception of what value its properties held in common. In terms of management strategy, the report's response to this situation bordered on despair: "Effective management of such a diffuse system requires the abandonment of any hope for a single, simple management philosophy."[81] Whether environmental education, historical preservation, or provision of recreation, the various purposes the parks served could no longer, according to this report, fall under a unidimensional strategy.

In line with the language of the Mission 66 proposal almost fifty years earlier, the authors of the Vail Agenda drew upon the economic metaphor of investment to address the public value of the parks. But whereas that earlier presentation used the investment metaphor to stress the preservation of principle, the Vail Agenda called upon the same metaphor to address the diversity of assets: "The National Park Service manages a portfolio of assets; it must learn and implement the strategies of a portfolio manager. This means recognizing that all the units and programs of the agency contribute to public value, but that the ways that these contributions are made and the forms that they take are varied."[82] Much like Conrad Wirth's Mission 66 presentation, this statement constructed "public value," or heritage, through the notion of capital. Through their preservation, these sites produced public value just as an investment produced interest. Thus these sites not only contained public value as "national treasures," but as a kind of public capital also produced ("contribute to") public value. Going beyond the framework of the Mission 66 presentation, however, the portfolio management metaphor implied that the value of a site could not be encompassed or explained by the individual particularity of that site. Rather, just as the worth of an investment depended on the portfolio in which it participated, so too could the value of a park be fully comprehended only through reference to the system of parks as a whole. If park managers wanted to understand the value of their particular park, they needed to refer to the system of parks as a whole and find their particular place within it.

In sum, parks took their public value through reference to other parks. This system of public value has become, at least in part, self-referential. This can be seen in guidelines for park designation found on the official Park Service website. In reference to natural areas, the website states that candidates for inclusion within the park system should fall under one of several categories, including, for example, landscapes or ecosystems that are currently typical and widespread, were formerly typical and widespread but are now rare, have always been rare in general, were rare within their particular context, or were exceptionally diverse.[83]

In terms of their contents, these categories focus on biological and/or physical formations: "biotic areas," "land forms," "ecological components," and so forth. These elements can refer to systems. For instance, a wetlands "biotic area" can be treated as an ecosystem, and a "land form" of canyons can be conceived in terms of geological and hydrological systems. However, the relationship among the different elements within the categories is neither biological nor physical. In other words, and to state the obvious, the national park system is not a physical system. Rather, at least in terms of these categories, the parks form a typological or symbolic system. In terms of the system, the individual sites function as symbols, and their worthiness for inclusion in the system depends upon their symbolic character.

Such a symbolic function is not, in itself, new. Earlier documents discussed national parks as symbols of "primitive America" and of nature in its "original design." However, in those earlier documents, the symbolic value of such parks was never conceived in terms of a system, in terms of a set of distinct, interconnected elements that together form an integrated conceptual whole. By contrast, these guidelines for park designation sought just such a systematic unity to the set of national parks.

Such an arrangement represented America through the organization of complexity. That is, in terms of these categories, a national park does not by itself represent America, but only one element of a network that makes up America. America is conceived as complexity, as a variety of different elements or "forms" (some widespread, some rare, some both over time). The unity of that complexity is an effect of organization.

This systematic approach creates public value by organizing complexity. Parks are valuable for the individual part they play in a complex, differentiated system. This systematic organization of complexity is to be mirrored at all levels of park management. Returning briefly to the Vail Agenda, note that the authors stressed variety within the parks as a central theme, applying to visitor interest and involvement, to the qualities of the parks themselves, and to the value those qualities represented.

Furthermore, the document stated that this variety was necessarily reflected in the Park Service as an institution: "Requisite personnel skills, organizational structures, and management demands also vary greatly." According to the Vail Agenda, the Park Service needed to mirror the complexity of its environment within its own internal organization.

While the Vail Agenda offered a multitude of statements regarding the reality, worth, and necessity of complexity, one passage will suffice to illustrate how this emphasis on complexity plays into management concerns at the level of visitor experience:

> The diversity of visitors makes it unlikely that there can be *the* park experience: can a fourteen-year-old girl from Idaho experience Pearl Harbor like a seventy-year-old veteran of the attack? And why should she be expected to? It is one thing for managers to provide a planned spectrum of recreation opportunities (say, from concession lodging to wilderness campsites); it is another to attempt to socially engineer the emotional reactions of the citizenry to the resources of their parks.[84]

This passage suggests that recognition of complexity should be factored into management practices without seeking to dissolve that complexity. The diversity of visitor backgrounds and interests needs to be addressed by a diversity of visitor services (exemplified by the provision of a "spectrum of recreation opportunities"), which, in turn, allow for a diversity of visitor reactions. The reference to social "engineering" does not seek to discourage systematic management of visitor experience, but rather to encourage the integration of complexity into the management system.

In these more recent developments in the national park ideal and its expression in particular management paradigms, complexity, or "diversity" as it is otherwise termed, became the defining concept for the national character of the park system.[85] The Vail Agenda stated:

> If each unit is a unique contribution to the system, then the system becomes a unique collection of national heritage, a benchmark of who we are as a people. And since cultural diversity is our national experience (*E Pluribus Unum*: out of many, one), the national park system must be a collection of culturally diverse resources. The criterion for inclusion must

> be national significance, but of a special kind: the significance should relate to the building of the nation out of so many different peoples and environments.[86]

The authors did not present such a perspective simply as a reflection of reality. Rather, they realized that the recognition and management of complexity actually participated in the life of the nation. Park use "is partly an act of nation building."[87] In offering a complex public body with a complex representation of its environment (both temporal and spatial), the National Park System built collective unity out of that complexity itself.

This relationship between diversity and unity, complexity and organization, spoke directly to the public/private distinction that lay at the center of the Park Service mission. The National Park System addressed this distinction by incorporating it within its own organization. The diversity of individual citizens was mirrored by a diversity of management strategies structured in accordance with that diversity. At a broader level, parks represented a plurality of individual, unique contributions to public value, and that public value was to be safeguarded and enhanced through the systematic construction and management of that plurality.

* * *

Throughout the historical development of the national park ideal, a dynamic of public and private has informed the management paradigms that govern park planning. What role did religious modes play in this relation between public and private? While absent in the recreational paradigm, references to "God," "sacred," and the "spiritual" served to connect public and private under the heritage paradigm. Through the absence of the signs of other humans, public natural spaces were to allow a sense of individual connection with national origins, divine creation, and ancestral spirit all at the same time. In contrast to this earlier perspective, government literature from the 1970s through the present contains little reference to God or spirit in discussing the national park ideal. What does one make of the decline in the prominence of religious language?

In national parks the relationship between public and private, state and citizen, occurs through a nature that appears as "given." With this given status, nature becomes a symbol that can reflect back on the nation and the state with added value, as detailed in this chapter. To the degree that the workings of symbolic capital become exposed, however, the efficacy of this operation comes under threat. The continued pronouncement of a connection between nature and nation could lead to the destruction of the relationship. Nature could come to be recognized as a product of state labor intended to serve the interest of a particular regime. With this in mind, one can see the efficacy of silence on such spiritual connections between the public and private domains. That silence allows the connections to appear natural, to go without saying.

Such silence underscores the secular character of the parks. By letting the landscape "do the talking," state authorities let the authority of the state shine through a veil of nature. The separation of church and state, whether considered legally or as a matter of custom, becomes a blur of landscape and law. This is not to say that the state surreptitiously implants a particular religiosity within visitors. Rather, park managers prepare the landscape in such a way to make it hospitable for particular kinds of aesthetic, individualized, and private experiences that are often called "spiritual."

2

The John Muir Trail

The Properties of Wilderness

Running 212 miles from Yosemite Valley to Mt. Whitney, the John Muir Trail, or the "JMT" as it is often called, traverses one of the longest stretches of wild country in the lower forty-eight states. For the most part the trail runs along the height of the Sierra Nevada mountain range, and in one hundred-mile section, hikers never come closer than a day's journey from any road. This undeveloped character of the JMT does not result from neglect. The National Park Service and the National Forest manage the trail under a variety of legal mandates, the most prominent of which is the official designation "wilderness." This and every other such administrative specification demands thorough attention on the part of public lands managers. However, while signs at the entry points announce the bureaucratic divisions, there is little to distinguish one administrative regime from another. For the vast majority of the trail, the only recognizable sign of human presence consists of the trail itself.

This muted presence of the government results from a concerted management strategy based in the Wilderness Act of 1964. The act describes wilderness as an area that "generally appears to have been affected primarily by the forces of nature, with the imprint of man's work substantially unnoticeable."[1] At the base of Mt. Whitney (the southern end of the JMT), not far from the entrance to the wilderness just half a mile up the trail, the presence of humans is unmistakable. A parking lot remains full throughout the summer months. Thirty yards up the road an outdoor café serves hikers half-pound burgers in baskets overflowing with french fries, and inside one can purchase maps, souvenirs, candy, and cold beer.

Moving up off the road from the parking lot, the trail climbs several miles and several thousand feet to reach the crest of the Sierra Nevada, and along this stretch one finds no cafés, roads, vehicles, or permanent dwellings. Still, the "imprint of man's work" is hard to escape. Of course, the trail is always there, but the most obvious sign of human presence is the humans themselves. The vast majority of these are not JMT hikers. As the highest peak in the lower forty-eight states, and just a few hours drive from Los Angeles, Mt. Whitney attracts a full complement of short-term visitors every day of the summer months. The ascent (twenty-one miles round trip) can be made over the course of a long weekend, offering visitors an opportunity to claim a distinctive athletic achievement without an extensive sacrifice of free time. The ascent has become so popular that the Forest Service has limited per-day visitation to approximately two hundred visitors, each of whom must apply for permits through a lottery opened months in advance. The result is a steady stream of hikers flowing up and down the mountain.

No government official with whom I spoke claimed that such a condition was ideal. And as an end point of the JMT, the Mt. Whitney Zone (as the short term permits designate it) can provide something of a shock for long-distance hikers coming off the last, long stretch of their journey.[2] The southbound JMT hikers have just spent two to four weeks in which they may have crossed paths with only a handful of people per day. Most show evidence of the "forces of nature" on their bodies. The sun, high altitude, and several weeks of hiking bring out a deep and even tan. The men (the vast majority are men) usually dispense with shaving gear and display stubble of distinctive length and irregularity. The dirt of the trail smooths their tans even further, and while not redolent out of doors and beyond a range of a few feet, enclosed spaces often bring out a strong bodily odor.

Signs of the forces of nature can also be seen in their packs: tightly bound, close fitting, balanced, and relatively small. Over the course of three weeks, gravity and the task of walking encourages (through fatigue and pain) certain adjustments and a streamlined form. Such streamlining extends to bodily movement as well: little side-to-side sway, a regular gait, and a slightly bent but stout forward lean. On a more interior level, the journey changes the hikers' body chemistry: their blood absorbs more oxygen. Their muscles have acquired greater stamina. These factors, along with the acquired habits of regular hydration, affect mood: despite the load they have carried over great distance, JMT hikers speak and smile easily and with little breathlessness.

Such signs contrast sharply with the short-term visitors to Mt. Whitney. Generally clean-shaven and unremarkable in their smell, the majority of Whitney hikers lack the physical conditioning to ascend the peak comfortably. Having driven, most often, from near sea level to eight thousand feet to reach the trailhead, short-term visitors run a greater risk of altitude sickness. Even a night's sleep in the thinner air does not guarantee that the next day's climb will not bring dizziness, headache, and nausea. Inexperience in packing compounds the difficulties. Whitney hikers almost always carry a larger, heavier load than their long-distance comrades, and the overnight packs are distinctive for their greater likelihood to swing, sag, or rest slightly askew on their bearers' shoulders. The forces of nature work differently on these bodies: fatigue causes shoulders to slump against their straps, the pain of seldom-used muscles encourages more lateral swings and shifts of weight (a temporary and ultimately more exhausting relief), and lack of oxygen, rapid loss of fluids, and general physical strain draw faces downward, the ragged breath less welcoming of interruption for greeting or conversation.

For the JMT hikers, reentry into "civilization" begins with these first encounters in the Mt. Whitney Zone. With the higher social density come anonymous, unacknowledged crossing of paths, virtually unheard of in the back country. The base camp for the Whitney ascent is a small village, a cluster of tents tethered like brightly colored balloons to a nearby latrine. The trail leading down to the parking lot yields short-term hikers just beginning their ascent, the weight of their misshapen, ponderous packs not yet breaking their unconcerned smiles. This trail also bears their return as they often stomp through an exhaustion created as much by their lack of conditioning and inadequate planning as by the altitude and slope of the mountain. To recall the phrasing of the Wilderness Act, these faces and forms do not necessarily appear "to have been affected primarily by the forces of nature," and before the JMT hikers reach the bottom of the trail and cross into the parking lot, "the imprint of man's work" has already caught their attention. The JMT hikers carry wilderness in and on their bodies, in the ways that they move, speak, and interact. For them, wilderness and civilization are ways of seeing the world as much as they are the world that is seen, ways of being in the world and not simply the world that is.

The Wilderness/Civilization Difference

Such a portrait of the Whitney Portal illustrates the complicated nature of the difference between wilderness and civilization. On the one hand, the official boundaries separating the two are indisputably real. On one side of the line, roads, parking lots, and businesses are permitted; on the other, they are forbidden. Anyone who ignores the boundary runs the risk of activating law enforcement and legal procedures with predictable, concrete results. On the other hand, the border marks the middle of a grey area. In crossing that line into the wilderness, hikers carry civilization with them, in the packs, boots, tents, maps, and food that they have bought, in the permits that they have acquired, and in the plans that guide their action. At the same time, hikers carry wilderness with them even as they rest within civilization. One is always subject to "forces of nature" such as gravity, weather conditions, genetics, and aging. Further, the anticipation of wilderness guides behavior in civilization. The scheduling of vacation time, the decision to join a local gym, and the purchases of hiking gear are all "civilized" activities that may depend upon wilderness.

Such observations highlight the implausibility of any conception of wilderness as "untouched by the inroad of modern civilization."[3] The JMT was originally built as a stock trail, blasted out with dynamite, engineered with specific requirements for its gradient (slope), and reengineered and rerouted to ease travel along it. The trail receives regular maintenance governed by a complex budgetary and bureaucratic procedure, just as it did when it was being built. In the case of the high Sierras, there is no question about an "inroad of modern civilization." The JMT was built and is maintained like a road.[4]

This fact, however, does not dissolve the difference between wilderness and civilization. Granted, no public land agency operates with a view of nature as a space free of civilized influence. Rather, wilderness is infused with its difference from civilization. That difference does not define civilization or wilderness in terms of preexistent, essential qualities. Rather, a multitude of regulations, management practices, permissions, and prohibitions make distinctions between wilderness and non-wilderness and govern operations accordingly. These distinctions constitute a network of decision-making procedures that act upon the environment and change its shape.

Historically, the "natural" quality of wilderness arises out of such socially constructed distinctions. Prior to public appropriation, the inhabitants of the large swaths of land in the high Sierras that would later become wilderness, park, and national forest land did not use a wilderness/civilization distinction: Native Americans had established routes for crossing the Sierras, they utilized the meadows to gather resources for subsistence and for trade, and they resided periodically in the valleys. Around the end of the nineteenth century, Euro-American mining and grazing operations supplanted the patterns of native land management. Native Americans were removed not because they were considered as contaminants in a "natural" setting, but because they were not civilized in the "proper" (capitalistic, white) way. Later, with the designation of Yosemite National Park, for example, large areas of land that were at the time being used for residence and economic exploitation came under a different management regime. In the case of Yosemite, the United States Cavalry removed grazing operations, thereby changing the appearance and substance of the meadows. Closely cropped meadows, alternately muddy and packed down from the weight of sheep hooves, were transformed by the artificial boundaries that guided cavalry operations. With the expulsion of sheep from Yosemite, the meadows inside the boundary became soft and spongy, evenly covered with grasses and flowering plants. Through the legal fiction of designating land as "natural," it gradually came to appear as natural. This change in social categorization was as substantial in its consequences as it was fictitious in its origins.

The decision to remove land from commercial exploitation did not make the land unprofitable, as the tourist industry would later show, and it certainly did not remove human presence and management. The history of wilderness in the Sierras shows a multiplication of management strategies and operations of observation. Wildlife biologists, hydrologists, geologists, fire technicians, and an array of others have mapped out the land, have written procedures for measuring changes in the land, and have come to operate in increasingly precise ways in their management. The change is not in the presence of human management, but in its visibility. Over the course of the last forty years, wilderness management has striven for invisibility.

As mentioned above, the call for such invisibility is codified in the Wilderness Act of 1964. Note that this act does not define wilderness as "untouched by the inroad of modern civilization," but rather as an area that "generally appears to have been affected primarily by the forces of nature, with the imprint of man's work substantially unnoticeable."[5] The logic of the act does not depend on the presence or absence of civilization in any absolute sense. Rather, the act calls for the appearance of nature and the concealment of culture. While in its immediate context one could read "substantially" to mean "largely," the rest of the act highlights the notion of substance itself. Within wilderness, civilization is to remain invisible in its substance. Durable, visible, artificial structures pose the greatest threat to the appearance of wilderness. The less "substantial" signs of civilization do not pose a threat to such an appearance.

But what, precisely, "appears"? It is not "nature" by itself, but rather the distinction between nature and culture that appears. The absences of civilization within wilderness are noticeable, and those absences, just as much as the wind, water, and topography, shape the experience of wilderness. The absence of grocery stores, mechanized transportation, electricity, asphalt, and concrete is "felt" by visitors. It is not just that the elements missing are from their sensory environment. Rather, and more importantly, the systems of organization that depend upon visible, substantial structures begin to disappear. Sets of priorities, patterns of behavior, and structures of expectation that govern life in civilization cease to operate in wilderness. Anticipations of an imminent change of scenery, for instance, depend upon mechanized transportation and the distinct environments of home, work, and shopping areas. In wilderness, however, the pace of walking lengthens the different stages of the day and prolongs the views that are available to the eye. It is not so much that these views become more noticeable, but rather that the duration of the views becomes more noticeable. In this way the absence of certain ingrained, almost unconscious modes of civilization (in the preceding example, the pace of perceptual change) renders those modes more tangible, articulable, and noticeable. In other words, through creating wilderness as a space of difference and distinction, a space defined by the invisibility of civilization, certain aspects of civilization are, ironically, rendered even more visible.

The previous chapter showed how national parks were seen as "intangible" resources, the maintenance of which National Park Service Director Conrad Wirth referred to as "an investment in . . . spiritual well-being."[6] What motivates the state to make such an investment? On one level, the specific features of hiker spirituality (such as solitude allowing for self-reflection and new perspectives) depend on the way that wilderness is managed. Hikers find solitude because the state guarantees that solitude through a permitting system and through the general prohibition of services that would provide food, shelter, and other needs. Hikers find greater opportunities for self-reflection because the state-managed trail allows them to engage in the long, repetitive task of walking rather than the more absorbing and varied tasks of finding one's way over unmarked terrain. Through minimizing the sensual presence of civilization, and through the enforced absence of its operative systems, the state provides hikers with opportunities for new perspectives on their lives within civilization. In these ways hikers are implicitly and structurally dependent on the state for the particular quality of their experience. But the state does not give nature only to hikers. Parks are public spaces. To the degree that hikers find their true nature in these spaces, they find themselves in the state, in a space of discipline, management, and regulation that yields value in their lives. That discipline extends into their subjectivity, into the way they perceive multiple aspects of their lives. To the degree that hikers find such a disciplined perspective enriching, and the reported sense of liberated individuality suggests that they do, hikers are implicitly invested in the structures of state authority that constitutes that discipline.

Spirituality in Context

From June 25 to August 3 of 2002 I recorded formal interviews with thirty-two JMT hikers and spoke with a dozen others more informally.[7] While the National Forest and Park Services do not keep any statistical data on JMT hikers other than gross numbers, my contact with hikers provided a demographic profile that yielded some striking results. The hikers I interviewed were 99 percent white, 85 percent male, clustered in the mid-twenties but ranging from eighteen to sixty years of age, and were generally well-educated. Because of the significant number of students and/or recent graduates, a statement on the average income level could be deceptive (I gave two hikers with "under $20,000" incomes a ride to their parents' million-dollar home in Ventura). A handful chose to hike the trail solo, but most traveled in groups of two or three, and the majority were hiking the trail for the first time.

I introduced the project to the hikers by saying that I was working on a project on "religious and/or spiritual approaches to nature in national parks." In response to the central questions of the interview, "Do you consider yourself a religious and/or spiritual person?" and "Was there anything religious and/or spiritual about your experience here?" roughly a quarter of the hikers (n=9) described themselves as neither spiritual nor religious. Approximately half (n=15) described themselves as spiritual and either rejected or did not use the term "religious," and a handful (n=5) were comfortable with either term. Notably, only four mentioned an affiliation with a religious organization or community, and two of those declined to use the term "spiritual" to describe themselves or their experience.[8]

With respect to age, gender, education, and ethnicity, Susan Power Bratton's work on spirituality along the Appalachian Trail identified a similar demographic profile of the long-distance hikers she surveyed.[9] In contrast to the survey of JMT hikers, however, over half of her respondents expressed a substantial engagement with religiosity, whether through attendance of services or participation in conventionally recognized religious practice such as prayer.[10] Regional differences might explain the lack of professed religious affiliation among the JMT hikers surveyed here: whereas, the majority in Bratton's study came from the southeastern United States, the majority of hikers in this survey came from the West or West Coast in the survey presented here.[11] While differences in survey methods make rigorous comparison of these two studies problematic, nevertheless the divergence with respect to religiosity suggests caution in extending the results of either survey to characterize long-distance hikers more generally across the United States. That said, with respect to national averages, both studies indicate a relatively high percentage of the religiously unaffiliated. As this book asks how religion takes shape under conditions of secularity, it will be useful to consider a larger social and historical context for trends in religious disaffiliation and the rise of spirituality as a category distinct from religion.[12]

Given their demographic profile, the tendency of hikers to be "unchurched" is not surprising. The Pew Forum on Religion in Public Life conducted a large-scale quantitative survey in 2012 on the decline in religious affiliation in the United States.[13] In outlining the demographic contours of the religiously unaffiliated, the study noted within the general trend high percentages of young, white males in the western part of the country. The study also noted that disaffiliation did not indicate a total rejection of religiosity. Most of the religiously unaffiliated believed in God and felt a deep connection with nature, with significant numbers describing themselves as spiritual but not religious. These findings dovetail with the results of the present study and indicate that this population stands right in line with a trend that is increasing in the United States more generally.

Sociologists of American religion have noted a long-standing pattern of church attendance and membership that would anticipate such disaffection. As a rule, Americans have been more likely to attend church while under their parents' control, but then drop out or rein in their enthusiasm as they emerge into independence. Upon marriage and especially upon child-rearing, they have tended to return to church.[14] In addition, one may note another long-standing trend in American religion: women have tended to be more active and regular in church participation than men. Given these factors of age and gender, one would expect that a coterie dominated by twenty-something-year-old males would exhibit only loose attachment to particular religious traditions.

Hikers' preference for the term "spiritual" as opposed to "religious," however, requires closer examination. Historian Leigh Schmidt has shown how the contemporary phenomenon of "spirituality," considered as a mode of religiosity that distinguishes itself from attachment to any specific religious tradition, can be traced to nineteenth-century religious liberalism and liberal Protestantism in particular.[15] Focusing on a more restricted historical scale, sociologist Wade Clark Roof connected contemporary spirituality with the general social upheaval of the 1960s. Seeking to explain why the Baby Boom generation did not return to church in their child-bearing years as had previous generations, he noted the affluence, high levels of education, and strong dissatisfaction with institutions that characterized many who lived through the 1960s. The freedom that affluence afforded, the exposure to a diversity of worldviews, and an idealism that could not accept the conservatism of institutions all fed the development of a culture of spiritual seeking, one unbounded by the demands of particular religious traditions.[16]

Within this larger context, hikers' use of the term "spiritual" indicates their particular social and cultural location. Taking a longer historical view, note that religious liberalism and liberal Protestantism have been associated with affluence, relatively high levels of education, and whiteness—all characteristics of this group of hikers. Taking a shorter historical view, note the broad cultural influence of the 1960s and the Baby Boom generation, both characterized by high levels of affluence and education as well as a culture of disaffection with respect to religious institutions. In line with these historical considerations, the Pew study indicated a more progressive or liberal political orientation among the religiously unaffiliated.[17] Here, too, hikers shared the characteristics of those for whom "spiritual" is an important identifying category.

What about the content of spirituality? Schmidt identified a number of themes that characterized what he saw as a liberal mode of religiosity: an appreciation for meditative, solitary, and even mystical encounter with the transcendent; a tendency to locate that transcendence in immanence—that is, within the individual and/or the world—with a consequent universalism that sees all religious paths as expressions of a common human nature; and a dual and tension-filled commitment to social justice and personal creativity.[18] While he did not explicitly identify the period of the 1960s as liberal, Roof described its influence on American religiosity in similar terms: as an embrace of pluralism, an emphasis on free and individual choice, a valorization of open horizons of possibility (and of seeking per se), and a commitment to "post-material values, to pursuing greater equality, peace, environmental protection, and quality-of-life."[19] Roof employed the metaphor of the market to describe the freedom that the 1960s engendered, a rhetorical choice shared by Robert Wuthnow in his broad-based treatment of American spirituality since the 1950s. Contrasting an older mode of religiosity that emphasized "dwelling" with a more recent spirituality of "seeking," Wuthnow characterized the latter in terms of a cutting-edge, post-material, information-based, service economy in which individuals are free to explore, consume, and tailor religious products to meet their particular specifications.[20] Responding to and partially affirming criticisms of contemporary spirituality as self-centered and narcissistic,

Wuthnow proposed "practice" as a model for understanding and constructing spirituality in a way that could escape the pitfalls of both dwelling and seeking.[21]

While emphasizing the private dimensions of spirituality, its rootedness in individual experience and free choice, each of these authors strove to provide spirituality with a public face, whether that of a particular tradition (religious liberalism), a mode of social organization (the market), or a call for an alternative (practice). These strategies responded to the criticism that the individuality and freedom associated with contemporary spirituality was not liberty so much as license, and therefore socially pernicious. While each went to some lengths to provide some public legitimacy to spirituality, none of them theorized it as a form of public religion per se, and this despite the ubiquity and inclusiveness of the term.

Spirituality on the Trail

Of the twenty-two hikers who described themselves as spiritual and/or religious, only two declined to describe their experience along the trail in such terms.[22] Conversely, one hiker who declined the labels "religious" or "spiritual" nevertheless described her experience using language commonly associated with those terms.[23] All told, then, two-thirds (n=21) of the hikers found their experience along the trail as religiously or, to highlight the predominant term, spiritually significant.

In characterizing their experience, the vast majority of hikers (84 percent, n=27) made use of a wilderness/civilization distinction. Hikers used the term "wilderness" itself, but for the purposes of analysis I have also included "back country," "nature," "outdoors," "outside," "what God created," and "removed context" under the rubric of wilderness, especially when these terms were employed as one element of an opposing pair. These opposing terms referring to "civilization" include, in addition to that term itself, "the city," "society," "the world," "man," and "civilian life."[24] Within this basic framework, I identified three prominent themes running through hikers' description of the contrast between wilderness and civilization. The most prominent theme is "perspective," a theme that appeared in over half (56 percent, n=18) of the interviews. This theme refers to the way hikers found the contrast between wilderness and civilization to lead to new ways of viewing themselves, society, or the world more broadly. This first theme included more abstract evaluations than did the second, which was nevertheless closely related: "perception." Under this theme a large majority of the hikers (59 percent, n=19) discussed changes, precipitated by the movement between civilization and wilderness, in their sense of time, their judgment of distance, their experience of pleasure, and the pace and rhythm of their thinking. Finally, slightly less than half of the hikers (44 percent, n=14) commented on the sense of community they experienced with other hikers, and the lack of such community in civilization.

Hikers made use of the wilderness/civilization dichotomy to evoke a whole range of distinctions, including focus/distraction, simplicity/complexity, calm/turmoil, need/desire, spectacular/mundane, newness/familiarity, nature/human, divine origination/human origination. Their experience brought these distinctions into focus, these hikers asserted, and allowed them to manage these distinctions in new ways by showing them what they really needed, what they could do without, and how they could live without all the amenities of civilization. When speaking of the spiritual aspect of their experience, hikers focused on the revelation of these distinctions and the implicit reorientations that resulted from this revelation.

By way of contrast, although hikers regarded their sense of community as a significant and enriching aspect of the hike, they did not characterize this sense of community as spiritual. Hikers who spoke to this theme found other hikers more open, friendly, sympathetic, and helpful than the people they routinely encountered in civilization. But this aspect of their experience did not come to the forefront when I asked them about the spiritual dimension of their experience.

Perspective

Of the twenty-one hikers who identified their experience as religiously or spiritually significant, two-thirds (n=14) described a newfound sense of perspective on themselves, their environment, and the relation between the two. This theme found expression in a variety of ways. For example, some expressed a sense of connection (n=4) in which hiking the trail showed how separated from nature they "normally" were and allowed for a bridging of that divide. One individual who encapsulated his spirituality with the phrase "Nature is my god" explained this sense of connection: "I just craved being outside and getting away from things that were manmade. Just feel like I'm a part of it."[25] While such a feeling could occur before an expansive wilderness vista, as it did for this hiker, for another the sense of spiritual connection involved smaller scales of operation. From such a perspective, wilderness yielded the benefit of "really feeling part of something. You know what water you're drinking. You're scooping it out of the river and putting it in here. And you're fishing and catching the fish right out of that lake."[26] Another hiker attested, "I think everything around me is a god . . . every rock . . . every tree . . . everything. And I don't think every car, every building, every sidewalk—I don't get that same feeling." This hiker saw a sense of connection in terms of a process involving the coordination of waking and sleeping with the cycle of the sun: "You get into the earth's rhythm."[27] Each of these hikers expressed a sense of spiritual connection through a wilderness/civilization distinction. It was through contrast that the connection came to be revealed, a gaining of perspective made possible by the difference of wilderness.

Under this same theme of perspective, others found benefit in prolonged self-reflection (n=8), which, in itself, revealed ingrained tendencies to ignore or avoid particular issues. One hiker who described himself as an atheist and his solo hiking as "a fundamental type of religion" explained the value of his experience: "Just to be able to spend that much time in my own head, it gave me a lot of time to think things through, as opposed to thinking about it and then it gets interrupted. I would think about something for three days. Really mull it over."[28] For this hiker, walking the trail provided an opportunity to meditate on a career change and his impending fatherhood, and also led him to a sense of gratitude for the affluence he currently enjoyed despite a year of unemployment. For a much younger "spiritual" hiker, a teenager, her self-reflection in the wilderness allowed a greater sense of independence and self-confidence: "Before I went on this trip I think I was more reliant on my friends, more centered on what my friends were doing, trying to be more—fit in with the group. And now I've figured out that I'm maturing and that I'm ready to become my own person. I need to figure out who I am before I can do that. I think it helped a lot, being out there."[29] For this hiker, self-awareness linked to a perspective on and critique of society. She stated that "when you're in society there's this bigger influence," an influence whose absence in the wilderness she characterized as both remarkable and liberating.

In several cases, those who reported spiritually significant shifts of perspective placed a critique of civilization in the foreground, specifically with respect to materialism (n=9). One hiker focused on conspicuous consumption: "We live in a very much overindulged society. It's like we're drunk with over-indulgence: food, cars, houses, three cars, a couple of buildings, four to five thousand square-foot homes with two dual packs on the roof. And they can only sleep in one room. Like a little castle. Like the Egyptian kings built pyramids for themselves."[30] The theme of anti-materialism as a whole, however, did not set the bar of criticism as high as did this hiker's allusion to the Pharaohs' splendor. More often the basic amenities of modern life came under fire, particularly for the way such amenities shaped one's ability to engage with the world. In the words of one hiker who described himself as spiritual but not religious, "As the human race we've come to a place where we're not in place if we're not in a house with a toilet with fast food at the touch of our fingers on the telephone. We don't know how to act."[31] Wilderness experience, this hiker asserted, helped him to break out of those habits that had "spoiled" him and led him to find satisfaction without a range of conveniences. As another hiker put it, referring to the lessons of long-distance hiking, "You can live for five months with twenty pounds of stuff on your back. You don't need a house full of things to make you happy. In fact the fewer things you have in essence makes you happier out on the trail."[32] From this hiker's viewpoint, wilderness experience did more than help one to escape the materialism of "consumer society." The experience of hiking, he suggested, reversed that materialism so that the absence of encumbrance made a direct contribution to one's enjoyment.

In terms of the social referent of these critiques, note the breadth of the terms "society," "human race," "consumer society," "our culture," and "civilization." While these hikers likely referred primarily to an American context, the logic of their critique extends to include basic aspects of modernity, particularly the economic system of capitalism that encourages production and consumption well beyond the needs of survival. Such social criticism did not target a particular community among other communities.[33] Rather it painted a picture of the way "everybody" tended to live. The broad scope of these criticisms contrasts with the fairly narrow scope of the proposed remedy: individual experience. These hikers presented the changes in their embodied, individual engagement with their surroundings as the socially edifying aspect of wilderness. Encouragement for local, particular communal actions based on collective agreement was notably absent from the interviews.[34]

One interview illustrates the theme of perspective and each of its subthemes in particular depth. John has been teaching environmental education to middle school students in a small town in northern California. At the time of the interview he was twenty-five years old and single. His job gave him time during the summer months for a hike such as the JMT. Being out in wilderness, he asserted, gave him a sense of spiritual connection, one that arose out of the removal from a civilized environment. He asserted that this connection was often covered over or obstructed by individual inattention and/or the distractions of society. The connection did not restrict itself to an awareness of nature, therefore, but was also and at the same time a reflection on life in civilization. Thus there arose for John a sense of social connection that was distinct by virtue of its infusion with a wilderness perspective.

Before being asked directly, he offered this characterization: "I honestly come to this experience being pretty spiritual . . . , being someone who wants to know more about what's around me and to connect to that."[35] When asked to elaborate, he said his was "an earth-based spirituality, a connection and a wanting for more connection with nature and a real respect for nature, communion with it. That's my spirituality. There's no tenet that I specifically adhere to. I try to be present." From John's perspective, a connection with nature required work, desire, effort, thought: it was not simply given, nor was it ever complete (it was both connection and a "wanting for more" connection). This, of course, presumed a certain division or separation from nature, one that yielded the possibility of reconciliation and the call for "communion," "real respect," and "presence" as tasks that were not self-evident.

In terms of practice, John noted that even hiking itself can leave one disconnected from nature: "You're just going. You're seeing this much of the wilderness that you're walking through. You're seeing the trail. You're not necessarily present with the things around you." For this reason John stressed the importance of taking time to sit and simply observe. As he was hiking the trail solo, the evening provided ample time for such observation. After dinner he would sit down and literally address himself to his surroundings: "just trying to be present with things around, and was actually verbal about that, like 'hello trees,' 'hello mountain,' stuff like that. And then watching, being observant." John felt that this practice opened up a whole world that otherwise remained opaque and created a heightened awareness of his spatial surroundings that resulted in a decreased awareness of time. This was not a metaphysical revelation, John suggested, but rather a result of redistribution of everyday modes of attention. And while the shifts in focus may have been simple, he found the shifts in awareness "amazing."

This awareness, this sense of connection, involved both an analytical and ethical dimension that John expressed in terms of "respect." In answering the question of what role humans played in such an earth-based spirituality, John said:

> "It has a lot to do with trying to be as respectful as possible to the things that are around me. . . . More than anything, acknowledging that humans aren't the only things out here, that we're just part of the huge puzzle. And that we have a place in this. And it's an interesting marriage between religion and science because you can talk about humans as predators and you can look at the food chain idea of where we fit into things. And I tend to move back to that a little bit. I do think that all things are put here for a purpose, for a reason. There is some sort of scheme. There is some sort of a—not plan, but it works for a reason. There's a reason for things that happen, call it fate, whatever. But we move away from that the more we move away from . . . doing things as maybe folks would have done many many millions of years ago, thousands of years ago."

In this response, awareness of one's surroundings moved from a basic recognition and sense of presence ("acknowledging that humans aren't the only things out here") to a sense of relative position ("we're just part of the huge puzzle;" "we have a place in this"), to an understanding of systemic relationship ("the food chain idea of where we fit into things"), to a sense of an all-encompassing, rational design ("all things are put here for a purpose, for a reason. There is some sort of scheme"), to a sense of social-historical location in relation to that universal design ("we move away from that the more we move away from . . . doing things as maybe folks would have done many many millions of years ago"). In this definition of his spirituality, John drew a chain of connections from the simplest of local observations to the most all-encompassing of global understandings. In fleshing out his earlier, shorthand definition of his spirituality as a desire "to know more about what's around me and to connect to that," John emphasized universality. This sense of connection and presence ran from solitary, contemporary experience to the course of world and natural history. John encapsulated this universality with the notion of a "marriage between religion and science" in which factual, empirical relationships took the quality of spiritual connections between individual and world.

While such a vision was universalistic in its scale, it was not all-inclusive. Individual experience and world/natural history here stood as poles, but intermediate terms such as local community were conspicuously absent. John's view of "church" brings this absence into sharp relief. In discussing his upbringing as an Episcopalian, John explained: "So much of why people enjoy going to church seems a lot to do with the people who go to church with them rather than what the rector is saying to them, what the sermon is about. And those are . . . good . . . food for thought. It has a lot more to do with communing, connecting with people. People don't really seem to connect with what I've been thinking about." The connection that John found spiritually enriching put the individual in touch with a broader level of reality—that is, with nature, history, society. John recognized that religious communities foster a sense of connection as well, but a connection to other people and, more specifically, to other people in the community. For John this was not enough. Seen in this light, John's rejection of the Bible was not the decisive factor in his movement away from his religious upbringing. While parts of the biblical narrative outraged John ("I'm not connecting with Old Testament right now, and will never connect with Old Testament. I've read that and it's a fucked up story"), other parts inspired a certain respect ("I do connect with some of it that strikes a chord"). More fundamental for deciphering John's attitude toward his religious upbringing is how he perceived the church community's lack of connection to a broader vision of the world, whether a vision communicated by the biblical narrative, by the rector in a sermon, or by a source external to the tradition.

In place of community, John emphasized society broadly conceived, and in particular a sense of collective error related to processes of modernity and industrialization. He contrasted that modern, industrial collective identity with a more fundamental identity: human nature defined in terms of systemic relation to other elements of the environment:

> "As we spend more time getting involved with technology and what-not we start to move away from our natural place in that order. . . . That order does mean something to me. That's how I see how we fit into things, that food chain order, that idea that we are part of this animal kingdom. . . . Observing nature you realize that animals take what they need. They don't take more than they need. And people take a hell of a lot more than they need. That might be why I began to have some sort of spirituality—has a lot to do with this idea of conservation. I think the two are married, conservation and an earth-based spirituality."

Here John repeated the reference to marriage, specifying the "marriage between religion and science" as the union of "conservation and an earth-based spirituality." This gave normative, ethical import to the connections he outlined earlier. The human place within a broader order implied an imperative to harmonize with that order. While the obstacle to such harmony was greed, the natural, sustainable course of action addressed the satisfaction of needs, not desires.

These ethical imperatives applied to a "we" and "people" that John did not strictly define. His broadside against greed could have applied equally well to individuals in the amalgamation of their private behaviors as it could to modern, industrialized society as structured by law and public policy. While broad and loosely defined, however, the collectivity John indicted was not without a certain determinate character. Specifically, the "we" did not specify a particular community within society, a group among other groups. Rather, the "we" and "people" are unbounded in their scope. John's sense of collective error applied to those who participated in processes of increasing technological dependence and consumption, a "we" that was not presented as one collectivity among others, but rather as "everyone."

I pressed John on this point. Later in the interview John spoke of keeping land in an "original" state, and in explaining what this meant, he made use of the dichotomy of human/nature. From his perspective, the original state was pure nature, devoid of human influence, and humans entered the scene at some point in history and began to move away from that state. When I offered a revision of that sense of "originally" to indicate ethnic and national identity, however, John embraced the analysis. He went on to use "we" to refer to white Americans (in contrast to "they" referring to Native Americans) and said that he would be "totally comfortable" with defining "originally" as a state before "white colonization." However, John's usage of "we" retained its universalistic usage, for he treated Native Americans as a past phenomenon. He spoke of them purely in the past tense, and only minutes later in the interview he used "we" and "people" with no sense of any other coexisting collectivity that might have had any bearing on the fate of the environment. His understanding of the "we" that bore the burden of preserving the environment was therefore both universalistic and particularistic at the same time. It referred to "everyone" in the sense that it applied to all who participated in consumerism and the increasing use of technology, and it referred to white Americans as a group that was historically responsible for the dominance of consumerism and the increasing use of technology.

When John spoke of his spirituality in terms of a sense of perspective, he spoke of an act of self-reflection that revealed not only his individual connection to nature, but also a collective connection to a cosmic order: "how we fit into things." The "we" involved in John's spirituality went beyond a biological universal ("humans") to include the collectivity of individuals/society (exclusive of local communities) under the sway of technology and consumption and located socio-historically within the framework of white ethnicity and colonialist national origins. With these further more precise distinctions, one can identify the spirituality here expressed as particularly modern and liberal in its orientation. John emphasized his own independent access to spiritual truth, one that revealed a vision of universal humanity progressing historically in a linear fashion, and he highlighted individuals (outside of particular communities) reflecting on and experiencing a connection with a universal, rational order of nature and history. Furthermore, he let white ethnicity and a particular national identity function as equivalents of this universality.

Perception

For those who found their hiking experience religiously or spiritually significant, over two-thirds (n=15) described perceptual changes governed by the wilderness/civilization distinction. As a theme of hiker spirituality, "perception" was closely related to "perspective": they both involved new ways of seeing. When hikers spoke in terms of evaluation and described new ways of viewing themselves or the world, I coded their responses as "perspective." When they highlighted the senses and described changes in the way they reacted to stimuli, I coded their responses as "perception." As one might imagine, these two categories often accompanied one another (n=15).

Perspective/Perception Cross-Tabulation

		Theme of Perception		Total
		Yes	No	
Theme of Perspective	Yes	15	3	18
	No	4	10	14
Total		19	13	32

Within the theme of perception, some described the spiritual dimension of hiking the trail as an accumulation of small changes (n=7), the experience yielding, through contrast with civilized life, a greater appreciation for material comforts, increased patience in the face of inconvenience and adversity, and a resulting sense of relaxation and gratitude. Such a viewpoint linked the asceticism of wilderness living to a more enriching, even luxurious experience within civilization: "Because you reduce yourself to a minimum . . . , you come back and everything is at your fingertips. Everything is comfortable."[36] Another hiker illustrated this point: "When we get home we turn the faucet on, we're like, 'Nice! I can get a glass of water. Sweet!'"[37] This change in the way hikers perceived their environment led to more abstract reflections as well. Relating to the theme of perspective, one hiker highlighted the pace of wilderness experience: "The fact that you walk at three miles an hour, it's not the sixty-seven miles an hour down the interstate freeway. You actually get a chance to see stuff and think."[38] Another hiker tied such a shift in the perceptual environment to the theme of self-reflection specifically. Regarding a resolution to volunteer, for instance, he said, "If I was [going] down the street, it's really easy for me to turn that off. 'Whoa, red light.' Stopped the car, and then you've just shifted gears all the sudden. So you conveniently not get stuck dealing with the things that you think are issues for yourself."[39] In terms of spiritual experience, these hikers suggested, the difference between the perceptual environments of wilderness and civilization opened up new possibilities for reflection. For these hikers, such reflection never applied purely to themselves or to their environment, but rather involved the relationship between self and environment, a relationship that involved a whole network of interactions.

In contrast to these comments on mundane experience, hikers highlighted grander perceptual shifts that I have categorized as expressions of the "sublime" (n=11): feelings of awe, smallness, insignificance, and being overwhelmed. One may note that all four hikers who mentioned an affiliation with a religious organization fell into this category.[40] And as one might expect, those who expressed such sentiments tended to link them to a religious and/or spiritual appreciation of their experience (n=8). Evoking a creationist understanding of geological history, one hiker remarked that "there's so much of the Bible that is still visible there. If you've studied it, and then you get out and think about it being flooded. And you start thinking, wow. . . . It's just awesome to think about it when you're at fourteen thousand [feet]. Father God destroyed this. And yet he created this."[41] Invoking the category of spirituality specifically, one member of the Church of Christ echoed such sentiments: "You're beating yourself up against this thing that's so huge, and that thing has to be—that's sort of spiritual, too. There's this big thing out there that you can't get your arms around. And that is evidence to me that I'm just a speck or a small thing in this creation."[42] And, of course, expressions of the vast and overwhelming quality of the environment did not need to refer to a biblical model. Another hiker who considers himself spiritual but not religious described an encounter with a storm: "It was so exhilarating . . . , Mother Nature's awesome power, showing she's still in charge." Interestingly, hikers never evaluated such feelings of powerlessness and insignificance negatively. The hiker above continued, "But at the same time I felt no—I was not scared in the least that any harm would come to me. I don't know how to describe it, but I was not worried." [43] The loss of control could even be found liberating and/or relaxing, as another hiker explained: "I like that feeling when you're just so small. It's just really comforting to feel you're just part of it."[44] Such expressions of awesome power and destructive potential went hand in hand with sentiments of peace, relaxation, and security—a sense of being relieved of responsibility for one's immediate fate. These expressions of the sublime stood against the backdrop of the wilderness/civilization distinction. Largely by way of implication, civilized life was portrayed as one infused with burdens of self-control and worry and lacking in the potential for inspiration and wonder.

One interview illustrates how such shifts in modes of perception can result in a broad reorientation that many hikers called "spiritual." At the time of the interview, Matt was in his mid-twenties, single, and shared custody of a child from a previous relationship.[45] His journey along the JMT had particular significance for him as it was to be his last for quite some time: facing an indictment, he was scheduled to go to trial in early fall. Shortly after completing the JMT, he was incarcerated. Matt hiked the trail with two friends he met through an outdoors club in central California. I spoke with them three days into their hike.

Matt framed his remarks with an invocation of humility. He encapsulated the human condition with the phrase "a flea on an elephant's ass," and in elaborating on the inflated sense of importance humans hold with respect to their own perspective, he offered an analogy:

> "I think that God gave us so much and we get stuck. Do you have any kids? I have a daughter, and sometimes you come home from a trip and you bring home a toy. And you give her the toy and you give her a kiss and she's sitting on the floor playing with the toy forever. And you're like, "No, come here, give me a hug." And they're too busy playing with the toy and they've missed the point. They're too busy playing with what you've given them than playing with you. And I think it's the same thing with the earth.

> This is a beautiful playground we've been given. But we're too busy . . . worshipping the things we've been given instead of who gave it to us."[46]

Here Matt singled out ingratitude as a fundamental, almost innate, aspect of the human condition. Humans have been given an enormous gift, but rather than intensifying their relationship with the giver, they have focused their attention on the gift itself. Matt did not describe this ingratitude, however, in terms of selfishness per se. Rather, he tied the failure to appreciate life as a gift to certain patterns of focus and attention, to natural, almost innocent (attributable to a nine-year-old) habits of perception. This habitual focus on "the things we've been given" has led to shortsightedness, Matt asserted, an inability to see beyond the objects at hand, and a collapse of interpersonal relationship into relationship with "things."

On Matt's view this worship of the "things" of this earth did not need to refer exclusively to the natural world or to the material world as a whole. Immediately after his comments about the gift and the giver, Matt went on to criticize "the Baptists, the Methodists, [and] the Pentecostals" for being "stuck": "People are stuck in one spot. . . . There are people who believe in healings and people who believe in tongues and on and on and on. And that's what it is. They've all stopped short of the promised land." For Matt, even intensely felt, transformative religious beliefs did not, in themselves, constitute a fully realized spiritual vision. In the tendency to focus on those beliefs and practices, the spiritual life of an individual or community could stagnate when not placed within a larger context, as a step in the journey to "the promised land."

In this context Matt disavowed the term "religious" in describing himself, and instead used the term "spiritual." In fleshing out this distinction Matt implied that religion served as a certain mediation of spirituality: "religion is our understanding of spirituality." However, and in line with his comments concerning Baptists, Methodists, and Pentecostals, this mediation was not necessary nor was it predominantly positive: "Religion is the only thing that keeps you away from God, right? I feel that way." In parallel with John's comments regarding religion, Matt's use of the word "spiritual" indicates a more direct relationship between the individual and universal, all-encompassing realities (here, God). But whereas John emphasized religion's tendency to focus on community rather than society, Matt highlighted the focusing itself, the tendency toward shortsightedness that Matt saw as endemic to civilized life in general.

For Matt, the sublime quality of nature served to reverse such tendencies. "It's magnificent to see the power of nature. It's magnificent to see that it's all in working order. In fact, if you know anything about it—hydrological features of the globe—if you understand how it all works it's just really, really amazing. . . . So it's humbling. We're just a small part. And that doesn't include the reference of time. This is just a small amount of time that we're perceiving." Such an appreciation for nature went beyond passive enjoyment of scenery. Rather, Matt suggested, it set human life within a larger perspective. The appreciation of nature's complexity as a working system, set within the immensity of its temporal dimension, evoked a sensation of wonder: "You're in awe." But beyond that, it effected an interior transformation: "It makes you humble." For the purposes of this analysis, note that Matt tied this transformation to the perception of space and time, dimensions that life in civilization tended to reduce in scale.

For Matt, this reduced scale, one tied to certain modes of perception, was exactly what wilderness changed. "Our perception of things after being on the trail, I've noticed this after a couple of weeks, but these PCTers [Pacific Crest Trail hikers] are like, 'Whoa, rode in a car! That was crazy!'[47] That's really wild, but most people couldn't even perceive that, to be living in a two or three mile an hour world, versus airplanes and cars." From Matt's perspective, the failure to appreciate the amenities of civilization was not simply a moral failure, a reflection of a general ingratitude. Rather, it involved a basic incapacitation of one's powers of perception. Those who spent all their time in civilization did not experience changes in velocity, for example, in the way that back country hikers did. For those in the city, the habitual use of mechanized transportation resulted in a dulled perception of speed. In contrast, life in the back country, where one almost never moved faster than a few miles an hour, yielded a heightened spatial awareness inaccessible to those living at faster speeds.

Such changes in perception were not confined to the sensation of wonderment. Describing the task of finding a parking space, Matt said, "You see people complaining about things. Everyone's doing circles trying to find the closest parking spot to the mall. I'm like, 'There's one right out there.' 'Oh, that's so far.' It's thirty more feet! Get off the merry-go-round and go park. It's just amazing to me how people perceive things." On the scale of feet, both persons in this anecdote might have agreed that the distance in question measured thirty feet. However, their judgments may have differed greatly on the scale of close/far. With the changed perspective resulting from time spent in the wilderness, Matt suggested, one perceived distances, not incorrectly, as shorter.

Wilderness immersion had a significant impact on perception of time as well. When I asked Matt how he might carry some of these changed perspectives into civilized life, he said: "It's like waiting in line at a fast food restaurant. It's no big deal. Some people are getting impatient, honking their horn. I don't know how to explain it—little tiny things. We expect too much. We expect everything like that [snaps fingers]." Analogous to the change in perception of distance is a change Matt described in the perception of time on a scale of long/short. In terms of the pace of wilderness experience, Matt viewed the time spent waiting in line at a fast food restaurant as inconsequential.

While individually these changes may have been small, they added up to an experience that Matt called "spiritual." He expressed this in terms of a general sense of the value of life. On several occasions Matt noted the tendency of those immersed in civilization to complain, to be dissatisfied. In contrast, he suggested, the perceptual changes evoked by wilderness yielded greater satisfaction when applied to civilized life. Matt saw the resulting sense of satisfaction (with wait times and travel distances, for example) as a humble appreciation of reality. In contrast, the inability to perceive times, distances, and speeds along a more extended scale yielded arrogance with respect to the amenities of civilization. People immersed in civilization became "spoiled," Matt suggested, and felt entitled to the levels of convenience and service that they had been afforded. Such ingratitude, he stressed, was the paradigmatic failure to appreciate the gifts of God. Conversely, the gratitude facilitated by wilderness experience was a spiritual transformation.

Community

In terms of a social vision, the two preceding sections highlight the individual and society. In contrast, this third section emphasizes a sense of community, specifically, the community of other long-distance hikers.[48]

In their evaluations of these others along the trail, hikers were uniformly positive, highlighting the friendliness, openness, helpfulness, and sympathy that characterized their encounters with fellow hikers. One hiker noted how the intimacy of their interaction did not require communication: "You don't even have to introduce yourself. Everybody knows what everybody's going through. And you talk trail a little bit, what's ahead, what's back. But everybody just kind of knows what's happening, and what kind of a person you are to even be doing this."[49] None felt that the social interactions they experienced in civilization were more enriching or worthwhile than those they had experienced in the wilderness. But while buoyed by their sense of wilderness community, none of the hikers placed such appreciation at the forefront of their discussion of spirituality.

For example, while one hiker was effusive in her characterization of other hikers, she suggested that her appreciation for the hiker community operated at a level distinct from and more restricted than the experience of cosmic connectedness that her companion had earlier affirmed as spiritually significant: "Apart from all the airy fairy stuff, you just meet great people and great things just—it just all comes together."[50] In other words, the clearly spiritual dimensions of their spirituality, described in a self-deprecatory manner as "airy-fairy," remained separate from the social relations that stood in a realm by themselves. Perhaps most important, however, the possible attribution of spiritual significance to a sense of community simply clashed with the emphasis on solitary and individual experience. For one hiker, the recognition of the hiker community arose as a qualification with respect to his "religion" of wilderness. Regarding the latter, he stated, "It's like I need it to keep me balanced, going backpacking, being in the outdoors, getting away from people, society. And then the people you run into out there are usually top-notch people. . . . So even when you meet people out there it's different than when you meet people in normal day-to-day."[51] Other long-distance hikers were not the impediment to spiritual experience that civilized people were, but they were not presented as conducive to such experience either.

With respect to what he valued about wilderness experience, another hiker expressed the neutrality of the hiker community more directly: "People you run into in the back country are usually real friendly. . . . You're immersed in total beauty and friendly people, or no people, which is even better sometimes. Relatively speaking compared to being in the city."[52] Again, while complimentary towards others along the trail, this hiker felt a need to excuse their presence in describing what drew him to wilderness. To illustrate this difference between spiritual experience and communal relationship, I will treat one interview in detail.

Scott and Heather were siblings, and the outdoors had been part of their family life for as long as they could remember. Raised just outside Atlanta, they lived in a house that bordered a rural, forested area that served as their playground. Beyond their daily life, hiking figured prominently in their family vacations: every summer of their childhood they would spend two weeks hiking and camping in or around national parks. In their mid-twenties at the time of the interview, Heather and Scott had made such treks a regular feature of their adult lives. Heather taught wilderness education, and Scott had been planning to hike the JMT for several years.

When I asked what had drawn them to the wilderness, Scott first noted his desire to get away from "society . . . cars, fast food, shopping, dealing with money . . . all the extra baggage."[53] He then noted the effect such an escape had on his relationship with others: "The wilderness . . . really does bring you closer to the people you're with. . . . Because you know those people really well, because you can't get distracted by anything else. There's no chance to get distracted. It's you and the people you're with, every day, all the time. . . . When you're dealing with survival . . . , when you bring it down to that base level of existence, I think it brings you closer." Seen in light of his earlier comment regarding "extra baggage," Scott portrayed civilization in terms of distraction. The things one found in society were in the way, and their absence in the wilderness allowed one to move closer to other people. Interestingly, Scott did not entertain the idea that wilderness could serve as a distraction, not even in the slightest degree ("there's no chance to get distracted"). Indeed, Scott implied quite the opposite: the task of survival was so much more demanding in the wilderness, and this strengthened social bonds.

This heightened sense of bonding applied not only to one's own hiking group, but also to strangers encountered on the trail. Scott elaborated:

> "When you see people coming off the trail, they understand exactly what you're going through or where you're at, because they're pretty much in

> the same position. There's a unique bonding. Whereas if you meet someone in the city, it's almost like—first, you don't have an excuse to talk to them, but also they can be so different-minded than you. Like I could be a carpenter and you could be a music teacher and the amount of overlap that we will have is probably minimal. Whereas when you're out there, there's a lot."

For all the various backgrounds that hikers brought to the wilderness, Scott suggested, the experience of back-country hiking remained remarkably homogeneous. All hikers needed to provide themselves with the basics of survival: finding water and suitable shelter, carrying enough food, keeping warm, and not getting lost. Scott pointed out that these tasks provided a common ground of experience and thus a basis for empathy. Further, Scott noted, these common tasks prompted social exchanges. Hikers traveling in opposite directions needed to know what lay ahead on the trail, information that could be vital to survival.[54] Such exchange of information could also lead to material exchange, or more properly, to material gifts. Extra food and equipment could be a major burden, and the opportunity to lighten one's pack and help a fellow hiker was rarely missed. Such gifts did not need to stem from clear self-interest. Scott and Heather were offered hiking poles and a water filter by someone exiting the trail, and while that person may not have felt any urgent need for these items, their value approached one hundred dollars—not a small sum to give a stranger.

Scott drew a strong contrast between the hiking community and life in "the city." In the city, Scott suggested, separate occupations led to an experience of others as "different-minded." He implied that without sharing the same tasks and the same daily experience, city dwellers came to live in different mental worlds. Further, this difference remained unmediated because one had "no excuse" to begin an exchange. Wilderness encouraged social exchange at every opportunity, partly to meet the demands of survival, but also and simply, Heather noted, because "it's exciting. You see [only] five people a day." In contrast, civilized life did not encourage such exchanges. Scott, after all, implied that the task of survival in the city was handled through "cars, fast food, shopping, dealing with money," and not through more open-ended social exchange.

Although Scott and Heather recognized the sense of community with others as a major benefit of their trip, neither of them saw this aspect of their experience as "spiritual." When the category did come up, both Scott and Heather related it to solitary experiences and not to the sense of social bonding they found otherwise so enriching. For instance, Heather considered her spirituality as more "internal" and "personal" in contrast to religion as more "organized." When I asked her to relate her spirituality to specific behavior, she first highlighted writing, noting that on this trip she lacked the opportunity since they "were never really still" and she could not "take the time to soak it all in." Reflecting further, she identified as spiritual "those moments where you're soaking it in and when you're hiking—it was nice hiking on my own sometimes, to soak it all in." In describing her spirituality, Heather linked a sense of reflection and immersion ("soaking it all in") with expressly solitary exercises (writing and solo hiking). This stands in stark contrast with her hunger and appreciation, after twenty-three days on the trail, for civilization and social contact. While she found both the solitary and the communal aspects of the hike enriching, she located her spirituality squarely in the solitary aspect.

Scott echoed his sister's sentiments in his own comments. While near the beginning of the interview Scott declined to identify himself as either spiritual or religious, he later identified one of his experiences as at least potentially "spiritual." Just as his sister did, he highlighted solitude.

> "One night in particular we were in an especially beautiful place. We were in a bowl of mountains all around us, which was pretty unique. And the sun was starting to set, we'd eaten dinner, brushed our teeth, everything was ready for us to go to bed, but for some reason I just stayed up, in the cool air. And you couldn't see the sun go down but you could tell the sun was going down by the way it was reflecting off all the shadows of the peaks. And as the sun went down what mountains were lit and what mountains turned into shadow changed. I must have been out there for ninety minutes or so. I don't know how long it was. But it was great. I just watched the changes and just sat there. It was really, really peaceful. I was really glad I did that. Because we had no layover days we didn't have—a lot of times we hiked, we were so hungry, we ate, brushed our teeth, we were so tired we went to bed. 'I can't wait to put my head on the pillow.'

> But for that night I didn't and I'm so glad I didn't. I just enjoyed it. I suppose you could call that spiritual."

This experience stands out as exceptional in Scott's and Heather's hike, as well as in their emphasis on sharing common tasks. Here Scott stepped out of the rhythm of those common activities (eating, brushing teeth, and so forth), and spent time in solitary reflection, an immersion in observation and passive absorption in contrast to the goal- and task-oriented perspective that guided the rest of the hike. Of all the experiences that Scott related to me, he associated the word "spiritual" with only this one: a moment of solitude standing outside of the pattern of the hike as a whole.

For Scott and Heather, hiking the John Muir Trail was a largely "non-spiritual" experience. Although they both allowed certain room for the category of the spiritual, saying certain moments either were or could be called "spiritual," they characterized these moments as exceptional to the general trend of the hike, both in terms of the mode of activity (solitary reflection versus communal accomplishment of tasks) and in terms of the overall benefits and significance of wilderness experience. For Scott and Heather, hiking the JMT brought them closer to each other and to others on the trail, and also gave them a sense of self-confidence through a more precise awareness of dangers and personal limitations. But while they echoed what many others said about the significance of hiking the JMT, they did not make "spirituality" a central category for understanding their experience.

Conclusion

How do the experiences of those hiking the JMT fit into broader contexts? Both the present study and Bratton's study of the Appalachian Trail find that hikers did not tend to relate the communal dimensions of their experience to a sense of spirituality.[55] This accords with general understandings of spirituality as focusing on the individual at the expense of traditionally recognized religious organizations or traditions. Beyond that, both studies show a strong tendency to find spiritual significance in the hiking experience expressed in terms of personal well-being.[56] Differences of methodology hinder point-to-point comparisons, as does a general tendency in Bratton's study to focus on traditional categories of religious identity and practice. Nevertheless, the findings of both studies suggest strong religious and/or spiritual significance within an activity often regarded as "secular."

In terms of the broader context of American spirituality, one may note the consonance between the experiences of these hikers and the characterizations advanced in the scholarly literature. With respect to Leigh Schmidt's work, the hiker interviews displayed an appreciation for meditative, solitary, and mystical encounter with an immanent transcendent.[57] Hikers described prolonged periods of engagement in a repetitive task that allowed for uninterrupted reflection on themselves, their tendencies, and their environment. They located the spiritual aspect of such meditative experience in themselves as individuals and not in any community, no matter how positively they valued the latter. And mystical overtones infused their descriptions of being awestruck and overwhelmed by an environment governed by scales of time and space far beyond what they could comprehend or control. Further, the transcendence described by hikers held a deeply immanent quality. Encounters with the sublime referred just as easily to nature scientifically understood as they did to creation under the biblical model. And in thinking of transcendence not as a being but as a logical form, note that hikers saw wilderness as a space of transcendence with respect to "society," "the world," and "normal reality." The deeply individual and embodied occupation of this space constituted the spiritual movement that hikers described in terms of perspectival and perceptual shifts. In these ways the experiences of JMT hikers share major features of nineteenth century religious liberalism that Schmidt identified as the forerunner to contemporary American spirituality.

These themes of perspective and perception resonate with Wade Clark Roof's emphasis on the open horizons of possibility within contemporary spirituality. Hikers came to recognize the contingency of their habitual evaluation of themselves and their world, a contingency that informed even their sensory encounters with their environment. They recognized that their sense of the importance of various tasks and goals, their frustration with inconvenience and delay, and their appreciation for amenities and services were not simply encounters with a fixed reality. The experience of wilderness, these hikers attested, infused life in civilization with the liberating possibility of radical and enriching change, a change they recognized as spiritual.

Recalling Robert Wuthnow's polemic, one may rightly view long-distance hiking as a spiritual practice. The embodied, disciplined nature of this endeavor grounded hiker spirituality in individual experience. At the same time this practice displayed a strong communal dimension, even if hikers put this dimension at arm's length from what they understand to be the spiritual import of wilderness. With this grounding in practice, the individuality and open-ended character of hiker spirituality can be readily differentiated from the caricature of spiritual seekers who picked and chose the elements of their spirituality based on fancy or whim. Conversely, the destabilizing self-reflection encouraged by the practice distanced it from any automatic conformism to tradition that Wuthnow associated with a spirituality of dwelling.

While hiker spirituality resonates with many of the characterizations in the scholarly literature, there are marked differences. With respect to religious liberalism, this study found scant grounds to argue that hikers participated in a tradition. There was no "community of memory," no reports of common expressions of ideas that these various hikers accessed in the form of media.[58] If this spirituality was a "tradition," it was vastly different from tradition understood as a sharing of stories, a sense of a distinctive history, the use of a common vocabulary, and a commitment to collective understanding. Rather, this study shows that spirituality could arise as an effect of social management but without reliance on a particular community for its transmission. Hikers claimed that their spirituality arose out of the difference between wilderness and civilization. That difference, as described in the historical treatment of the JMT, was a product of state management. The difference arose as an artifact of law and public policy, levels of social organization that transcend both local communities and traditions conventionally understood.

Regarding the metaphor of a "spiritual marketplace," Roof portrayed the social formation of spirituality in terms of individual interests and agency on the one hand and the provision of religious products on the other. Such an observation was a macroeconomic one. Roof did not offer a microeconomic analysis of the process by which a particular "spiritual" enterprise distributes its products to a variety of consumers. Applying such a microeconomic perspective to wilderness spirituality, one can see the decision to hike the JMT as a selection of one "product" from among a range of others. These hikers, with their particular spiritual interests and tendencies, chose the trail rather than a church, retreat, or workshop. But one should also note the exclusivity and anti-market consequences of that decision. Rather than embracing ease and a proliferation of choices in shaping one's spirituality, these hikers put themselves in an environment that limited their options. If they wished to tailor their spirituality while on the trail, they would have had to do so without any access to the market besides what they carried in their heads. They could have chosen to "return" the product by leaving the trail, but this choice may itself have required an arduous and uncertain journey, perhaps even a spiritual one. But more than this, hikers described spiritual shifts in perspective that ran counter to the ethos of market consumerism. For one, hikers valorized an escape from the central vehicle of market consumerism: media. Hikers lauded the absence in the wilderness of television, radio, billboards—all the sensory bombardment that drove consumerism. It is difficult to see how this hiker spirituality could square with a more media-intensive spirituality that has thrived on reading books, watching audio-visual materials, attending seminars and workshops, and otherwise exposing oneself to a wide range of stimuli. Hikers found spiritual value in the minimization of stimuli, and they felt that the perceptual shifts that they experienced rendered them less acquisitive, less in need of sensory novelty, less in need of making choices constantly. Certainly I found no evidence that hikers had dropped out of the spiritual marketplace. But hikers did report conditions that would slow the pace of their participation in that marketplace.

Wuthnow's polemic suggests spiritual practice as a remedy to the instability of seeking and the stagnation of dwelling. By way of contrast, one may note that the spiritual process that hikers described was something of a spiritual nomadism. One should take this in the anthropological sense of nomadism—that is, not as an aimless wandering but as a serial pattern of dwelling. Hikers found spiritual value in wilderness, but primarily as a temporary experience, one whose value was infused with the anticipation of returning to civilization. Wilderness, from this perspective, was a place to spend a season and gather the spiritual refreshment particular to that environment. One then went back "home" to civilization with the bounty one had acquired. Conversely, however, one may recognize the spiritual seeking that informed this nomadism. Hikers claimed that their return to civilization would be infused with alternative ways of seeing and acting, making their wilderness experiences a resource for change in their lives. In this way, hikers asserted, the habitual patterns that governed civilized life could be borne as temporary choices, ones that looked out onto other ways of being to which the hikers would have now had (easier) access. From the perspective of hiker spirituality, therefore, seeking and dwelling were neither antithetical nor discrete. For hikers, seeking and dwelling were moments of their spiritual lives, moments that interpenetrated one another in the course of the movement from civilization to wilderness and back again.

With respect to public religion, recall the absences and invisibilities that characterized wilderness. The absence of the signs of civilization, and of the management that has governed wilderness, constituted the public character of the space. In considering the public value of wilderness, particularly in its capacity as a spiritual resource, one may relate these absences to the constitution of liberty. Hikers could affirm a sense of escape from daily burdens, of new possibilities for perceiving and evaluating their environment, because of a contrast created by state management. This absence that created liberty constructed individuality at the same time. Through the disappearance of social others, hikers were left with only themselves and nature (to which hikers understood themselves to belong) to explain the character of their experience. In other words, with the absence of society, hikers were left with self-reflection. To call this public religion is not to say that hikers related their spirituality to their government. Rather, the indistinguishability of natural law and land management, of individual freedom and social construction, rendered a natural quality to the state. The spirituality that invested visitors in the law and freedom of nature also invested them, at the same time and in the same movement, in the structures of state management.

3

Yosemite National Park

The Spirit of Complexity

Visitors to Yosemite Valley, the northern starting point for the John Muir Trail, encounter a variety of impressive scenes along the drive. Panoramic vistas of the valley, immortalized in classic nineteenth-century landscape paintings by Albert Bierstadt, Thomas Moran, and others, stand like open gates along the southern and northern approaches. From the north, motorists follow a mountain road that opens up to a wide granite gorge with Bridal Veil Falls at its head. From the south, visitors exit a tunnel and find the peaks of El Capitan, Half Dome, and the Three Brothers forming a monumental frame for the green valley below. After the two roads merge on the flat valley floor, visitors follow a winding road through the forest, an Arcadian enclosure that opens onto a meadow and the stark profile of the three-thousand-foot cliff face of El Capitan, the largest rock monolith in the United States. As the road continues, views of the other major features of Yosemite arise within living frames, the forest opening up to photo opportunities and their requisite parking lots. The beauty and ease that visitors encounter along this promenade, however, do not answer the questions of where to eat and sleep and how to organize one's time. And as if waking from a dream, summertime visitors are eventually led to a large dirt parking lot flanked by restrooms, shuttle bus stops, milling crowds, and strings of visitors looking for the walkway or their car.

Because of heavy visitor volume, automobile traffic in the valley is restricted. To get to the visitor center, one must park at the periphery of Yosemite Village and take a bus. In the summertime the buses are crowded, and when they let off at the visitor center, one emerges from the press and heat of bodies to a view of a meadow through the trees. No visitor center in sight. "Turn around," the driver instructs. "Cross the street. The visitor center is straight ahead." The bus pulls off, the lanes of

Yosemite Valley as seen from Tunnel View. Photo by the author.

traffic clear, and one crosses the street onto a small, amorphous plaza, its borders made somewhat indistinct by a wide footpath that runs in front of the wood and stone structure that stands just up ahead.

This is the visitor center, although its designation is easy to miss. Modest signs with white lettering identifying the building stand off to the right against the facade, slightly obscured by bushes. Such obscurity is intentional. In response to occasional complaints, park rangers offer the explanation that they do not want signage to interfere with the scenery. Indeed, above and to the left, through a wide gap in the canopy, Yosemite Falls kicks out from the granite headlands three thousand feet above the valley floor, arcs of white spray easing down into a gentle and even-flowing mist.

Inside the visitor center, a squad of rangers and volunteers stands behind a wood-paneled counter answering questions. The space is open. The cashier's counter sits on the left side of the room, and the center holds benches as well as a relief model of the park. Through an opening on the left side of the room, one enters a small bookstore. Postcards, videos, and books dominate the inventory of this modest shop, with only a smattering of the small, gifty souvenirs found elsewhere in Yosemite Village. This is a more serious store, its shelves containing denser, more scholarly works in addition to lighter fare, all revolving around the themes of Yosemite, nature, and conservation.

Exposed wood and stone work characterize the interior of the visitor center, and earth tones predominate. The rangers blend into their surroundings; grey shirts and green pants soften their silhouettes. Small touches are noteworthy: their leather belts are graced with sequoia cones in relief, as are the leather straps that ring their hats. Authority is added by badges, patches, and a design that stems from turn-of-the-century cavalry uniforms. Change the color scheme to blue, and the ranger would be hard to distinguish from a state trooper.

A single wall and open threshold separates the right side of the bookstore from a larger exhibit area treating the history of Yosemite. Geology, flora, fauna, human history, and extensive emphasis on ecological threats and local heroes of the park dominate this winding tour, including a prominent display of Muir's image and words. The last panel presents one of Muir's most often quoted passages, "When we try to pick out anything by itself, we find it hitched to everything else in the universe," and stresses the global and spiritual aspect of conservation of the park: "Yosemite is connected to the rest of the world ecologically and spiritually. We may see the park boundaries on a map, but plants and animals do not recognize this imaginary line, and it doesn't provide a barrier to outside problems like air pollution. To protect all the ecosystems and species connected to Yosemite, the entire planet must be protected."

One cannot dwell too long on the exhibits, however, before the public-address system announces the next showing of the main presentation: a twenty-three-and-a-half-minute orientation film entitled *Spirit of Yosemite*, shown every half hour. Exiting out the back of the visitor center, crossing an interior courtyard, one enters an auditorium. This room is entirely different from the others. The high walls are a restrained light blue, and the grey, high-backed, cushioned chairs stand in elegant ascending rows. It is a small, seventy-person amphitheater that one might find in a first-class conference center. The projection screen is immense and is flanked by tall black speakers set into the walls. The sound environment is also distinct. As one enters the room, the chaotic babble of visitors flattens and dies away, deflected by the acoustics of the room's design.

Visitors drift in and seat themselves, lowering their voices in instinctual respect for the space. Each chair is something of a cocoon, its soft, broad shoulders and padded armrests enclosing the visitor and focusing attention toward the screen. The rows are placed at a steep angle: the heads of other visitors are visible just above one's knees and are largely obscured by the chair backs. One has the sensation of being alone before the screen.

The room gently darkens and the film begins. The whisperings of visitor conversation relax into the background as from all sides the sound of a rolling cymbal, chimes, and a single note from a choir flows into the room. Images of evergreens arise under the slow motion surf of a thick mist. The camera pans back to reveal a forest under pools and streams of morning fog, white wisps curling up against an adjacent cliff wall. Cymbals and strings gradually rise to a crescendo to reveal three jagged peaks jutting out from the clouds. With the close of the opening movement, the mists and music give way to the spray of a waterfall. The music dies, and a roar grows out from the walls. A white flood pummels granite ledges, channeling into foamy streams that flow down in curtains behind the arcing spray of a cataract. The sound environment has now been totally monopolized, and as a succession of violent eruptions wash over burnished brown granite, the roar descends into a deeper fullness. The second movement closes with a waterfall in full flood, its spray jumping out from its granite frame like a thunderhead.

As the roar recedes into the background, the scene shifts to forest and quiet pools reflecting a waterfall in the distance. The birdsong of the forest heralds the reappearance of the musical score. A rhythmic oscillation of strings, two notes from a clarinet, and low intonations from a piano build in volume as the forest opens to a meadow with Yosemite Falls in the distance. As the camera moves to grand, sweeping vistas of Yosemite Valley, the narration begins. After two and a half minutes of instrumental music and natural scenes and sounds, a slow tenor voiceover, its pauses pregnant with music and panorama, intones: "It has been called nature's grand cathedral. Yosemite Valley is one tiny spot on the planet where the dynamic forces of nature are focused like sunlight passing through a lens, a land of powerful change where the elements of sun and stone, fire and ice, collide and harmonize in astonishing ways, a place where most who visit sense the presence of a spirit." The final words do not mark the end of the movement. With a substantial narrative pause, the music builds to another crescendo as the camera flies over a raging mountain stream, a rainbow arcing out along the spray. As the scene moves from the snowy meadows of the high country to a small rivulet running along a mossy boulder and then to a green shoot breaking out of a delicate lattice of melting ice, the narrator concludes his introductory oration: "And beyond the sheer cliffs of Yosemite Valley there exist other realms, other domains, each one unique, each one supporting a distinct community of living things, each one moved and shaped by the same spirit, the spirit of Yosemite."

What is the significance of calling Yosemite Valley a cathedral, of calling it "nature's" cathedral? What does it mean to say that "most who visit sense the presence of a spirit?" And what does it mean to speak of communities united under spirit? Note the distinctiveness of such a loose definition. The film does not simply state that there is a spirit, nor does it define this spirit in such a way that the viewer could agree, disagree, or reformulate the term. If one is hoping to find consistent and specific definitions of the film's central concept and motif, one will be disappointed. After its opening movements, the film continues much as it began. Music and striking visual scenes predominate. The narration is spare, almost incantatory in its tone, and broad in its semantic sweep. While the film offers a history of Yosemite Valley and its surroundings, conveying information is clearly not its primary task.

So what is its task? What are the tasks of Yosemite Valley, of the roads, the views, the structures and services? Yosemite Valley presents an ambiguous relationship between nature and culture. Panoramic visions of nature are set inside particular cultural frames: vistas depend on the placement of roads and parking turnoffs, the speed of traffic influences the opportunities of visitors to view scenery, and orientation services manage the context in which visitors encounter their environment. These are not simply services that make visitor experience more enjoyable. Rather, these and other features of Yosemite constitute a coordinated construction of nature, one that capitalizes on the landscape in order to suggest a value that visitors can appropriate individually. Value takes shape through spirit in a variety of (public) ways. "The spirit of Yosemite" indicates not only nature, but the organization of experiential possibility in the park, an economy of relations managed by the state.

Of course, in the developed areas of Yosemite this process of experiential management differs from the one that governs the wilderness along the John Muir Trail. There, wilderness heightens the distinction between nature and culture, and reflection on this distinction constitutes the spiritual experience of many who have hiked the JMT. The more heavily "civilized" areas of Yosemite, however, efface the distinction between nature and culture. They hide or camouflage it or, put more precisely, seek to harmonize nature and culture in an inconspicuous way. So while wilderness seeks to render culture invisible, Yosemite Valley renders culture indistinct.

The "spirit of Yosemite" evokes one world of harmonious enclosure. While enjoying the amenities of cultural infrastructure, visitors speak of a "spiritual connection" to nature devoid of the danger, insecurity, and discomfort that wilderness experience can entail. Their sense of peaceful envelopment within a majestic environment ignores the structured access to that natural environment that culture provides. Managers design structures and services to provide safe, controlled, and inconspicuous access to the environment.

Such an intensively managed experience of nature yields an irony. In harmonizing nature and culture, park managers create a culture not found outside of the park and a nature not found in wilderness. The effacement of the nature/culture difference, therefore, makes the park distinctive. Put another way, the value of Yosemite lies in this effacement. Visitors come to the more developed areas of Yosemite to "escape" the conspicuous presence of culture (crowds, structures, traffic, noise) and to avoid the more conspicuous presence of nature (discomfort, fatigue, uncertainty, danger). The smoothing out of the contrast between nature and culture is the product of social organization, a product that visitors consume largely through spiritual experience.[1]

This singular world of harmonious enclosure manifests a further irony: a highly differentiated structure of experiential possibilities. Visitors can spend anywhere from five dollars to five hundred dollars per night for accommodations, spread over five different types of lodging. They can stay just for an afternoon or for months depending on their budget. These variations in type of lodging and length of stay mean that a visit to Yosemite can take vastly different forms. More important, the meaning of park experience can take different forms. The Park Service does not transmit a singular vision of park experience. Rather its communication fosters individualized constructions of meaning. When visitors articulate the meaning of their experiences and thereby mark them with their individuality, an operation they tend to call "spiritual," they invest themselves in the park. In so doing, they implicitly invest themselves in the social organization that has provided the conditions for their self-realization. That social organization is the state, represented most conspicuously by the rangers in paramilitary uniform, and more inconspicuously in the harmonious organization of nature and visitor in the park. This double representation of the state, in both its manifest and its hidden dimensions, taps into multiple authorities: the authority of nature whose protection and preservation demands adherence to certain regulations and codes of behavior, the authority of individuals who require social management to keep them from running over each other and to create their impressions of spiritual solitude, and the authority of the nation whose flags, insignias, and other symbols claim nature for America. In blurring the boundaries between nature and culture, the state taps all of these authorities and becomes a manifestation of each, whether in the guise of protector of nature, guarantor of individual freedom, or steward of national heritage.

Historical Genesis

This spiritual harmonization of nature and culture stems partly from shifts, beginning roughly in the eighteenth century, in conceptions of beauty and the sublime in their application to landscape. These shifts retain their force in the present day and precondition visitors to view landscapes such as Yosemite as spectacular and not horrible or awful.[2] On a more concrete level, however, this harmonization stems from the physical shaping of the environment that stands as a precondition to seeing the valley at all. Of course the roads and trails bringing visitors to Yosemite count as one of these physical preconditions. But a more fundamental precondition involves the elimination of trees that would otherwise block one's view of the valley. This elimination of trees began with the Ahwahneechee, the tribe that shaped the landscape of the valley prior to its "discovery" in 1851 by those of European descent. By regularly setting fires, the Ahwahneechee burned up the unwanted saplings that would otherwise replace the fire-tolerant, acorn-producing oaks and the game-attracting meadows on which the tribe depended for survival. This practice opened up the landscape in such a way that the soaring cliff walls were almost always visible to anyone on the flat valley floor.

The views created by this practice led to interest in the valley for those of European descent. In the late nineteenth century, increasingly affluent urbanites began to seek and spend money on the recreational opportunities afforded in "natural" settings. As Frederick Law Olmsted, Sr., mentioned in his 1865 report on Yosemite (discussed in Chapter 1), traveling to scenic environments was an established recreational practice of the European elite. Journeys to scenic wonders such as Yosemite thus allowed Americans to participate in the leisure pursuits of their high-class European counterparts. Such an opportunity took on added significance given that America did not have the elaborate palaces, cathedrals, and monuments of the European landscape. Suffering in comparison, nineteenth-century Americans began to claim in natural landscape features an architectural grandeur that not only rivaled Europe, but surpassed it.[3]

In this regard, Yosemite Valley became an ideal destination. On the one hand, the peaceful, gentle qualities of the valley floor created an environment that one might find in the gardens of a city. The valley's meandering river, wide, sunlit meadows, and flat terrain offered short, easy walks in the sun and by the water, with plenty of flat, grassy areas for a picnic. On the other hand, the soaring cliff walls that enclosed the valley provided the visitor with the visual sweep of monumental architecture expansive in its historical scale. Such impressions were reflected in the names of the valley's features, such as "Cathedral Rocks" and "Royal Arches." But this was not to reduce Yosemite to human dimensions, for these architectural and scenic wonders exceeded the size of Europe's monuments. In this respect, promoters of Yosemite promised the visitor a spectacle superior to the grandeur of European civilization, a testament not to the glory of the world's architects, but to the architecture of the world.

Through such claims Yosemite was presented as a unity of nature and culture, a unity that depended upon seeing nature as architectural and organic at once. In an essay for *Century* magazine in 1890, John Muir highlighted this unity in advocating the designation of Yosemite as a national park, describing the Sierra valleys as "mountain streets full of life and light, graded and sculptured by the ancient glaciers."[4] Referring here to the natural action of glaciers in terms of civil engineering ("streets" that are "graded") and art ("sculptured"), Muir went on to convey the unity of nature and culture through a variety of architectural images. But in the case of Yosemite Valley, one metaphor took center stage. "Comprehensively seen," Muir wrote, Yosemite "looks like some immense hall or temple lighted from above." The religious metaphor served as a particularly unifying reference. The characteristics of Yosemite, Muir suggested, not only provided beauty and recreation, but also allowed a spiritual union. In this temple, Muir wrote, "Nature [has] gathered her choicest treasures . . . to draw her lovers into close and confiding communion with her."[5] For Muir, this "communion" encompassed human and animal, animate and inanimate, nature and culture. The description of a timeless and unbounded creative force that could express personal, loving intimacy recalled certain theological traditions, and in his writings Muir often used the terms "Nature" and "God" interchangeably. The description of Yosemite through the metaphor of the temple reinforced this unity of nature and the divine, the impersonal and the personal.

Muir's eloquent praise of Yosemite and other areas, along with the subsequent passage of legislation making Yosemite a national park, contributed to his de facto canonization as the "Father of National Parks." But a closer look at the legislative history of Yosemite reveals the limits of Muir's influence. Historian Alfred Runte has convincingly argued that economic interests were ultimately decisive in the designation of Yosemite as a national park. Further, Runte asserts, the history of management in the valley showed a consistent tendency to favor economic development of a tourist industry rather than a strict concern for natural preservation. Given these observations, what is the status of the spiritual values that Muir attested to in his essay?

While Muir's rhetoric may not have had a direct, decisive effect in the original establishment of Yosemite as a national park, it is instructive to note that the theme of unity between nature and culture was not, in fact, irrelevant to the historical course of events. Indeed, Yosemite was founded on an assumption of harmony between nature and human concerns. The natural qualities of Yosemite, proponents of the park argued, could be preserved without undue sacrifice to the engine of civilization. In fact, as Runte's scholarship shows, Yosemite became a park because the preservation of "untouched" landscape was viewed as (1) happily coincident with the economic interests of agriculture in California's central valley and (2) directly linked to the economic interests of the railroad whose passenger traffic would increase with the rise in nature tourism.[6]

Such an observation does not equate Muir's vision with that of Southern Pacific Railroad. Nevertheless, it does stress that highlighting the differences between nature and culture (a central operation of wilderness, as seen in the previous chapter), was not a guiding concern in the establishment of Yosemite as a national park. Both as a spiritual paradise and as an economic engine of tourism and agriculture, Yosemite was envisioned by early proponents as a place where nature and culture agreed. Shaping this agreement became the task of management as the park came into being.

In the early history of the park, such agreement of nature and culture was viewed almost exclusively in terms of aesthetic harmony. That is to say, management treated the park as scenery. As long as touristic development did not interfere with the view, it was generally permitted. The check on development did not arise out of a commitment to nature as a set of systemic relationships. Rather, a sense of visual propriety informed park management.[7] The tendency to identify nature as scenery has been long recognized as a dominant trend in park management, particularly in more critical histories offered by Runte, Richard Sellars, and others.[8] The necessary correlate of such a trend, however, has gone underappreciated. For just as nature was treated in terms of scenery, so was culture.[9] In the process both nature and culture took shape in a way that can be attributed neither to a model of strict natural preservation, nor to bald economic exploitation, nor to a contest between the two.

For the sake of brevity, I illustrate this point with two examples rather than survey the history of Yosemite comprehensively. First, when in 1928 the Curry Company, a concessionaire in Yosemite Valley, requested permission to expand its parking lot to accommodate more visitors, a Park

Service advisory board issued a negative report with the following reasoning. According to the chair of the board, Frederick Law Olmsted, Jr., not only would the parking lot cause "a very serious loss to the attractiveness" of the camp, but it would replace "a distinguished and so pleasantly memorable view" of Royal Arches and the Tenaya Canyon with "a necessarily ugly, bare, parking yard" and would make the experience of the camp more "overcrowded and overgrown and citified." Finally, Olmsted concluded, "a great parking yard, as seen from Glacier Point, for example, would seem like a desecration."[10] According to Olmsted, the sacred and natural quality of Yosemite Valley resided first and foremost in a panoramic view of its total expanse. Further, the visual intrusion of an expanded parking lot would have destroyed the natural/cultural harmony of the camp by making it more "citified." Such a perspective made potential desecration of natural/cultural harmony a matter of visual impact.

But aesthetic considerations were not entirely visual. Management of Yosemite aimed to create a more broad-based sensation of harmony than that of a "perfect picture." Here the second example, concerning bear management, is illustrative. In the early part of the twentieth century bears were killed and/or driven out of the valley. While undeniably a natural element of the environment, their presence was found disturbing and threatening to visitor experience.[11] Later, as the bears were irresistibly attracted to the food and garbage left by the increasing number of visitors, the bears became a spectacle, an attraction, in themselves. The Park Service stopped hunting the bears, but not out of concern for the bears themselves. Rather, the fact that bears provided recreational amusement meant that their removal would conflict with the wishes of visitors and concessionaires who profited from an entertaining environment. In the interest of avoiding this conflict, the Park Service grew to tolerate the presence of bears. Managers did raise objections, but they were primarily aesthetic ones. The spectacle of bears feeding at the garbage pits came to be regarded as improper on an aesthetic level. Therefore when a concessionaire offered to set up a clean feeding stand where bears could be observed without the stench of refuse, Park Service officials quickly approved the plan.[12] Later still, the bears became too familiar with their human neighbors. Although the bear-feeding platforms were eventually abolished, the bears had by that point grown more numerous and had become accustomed to human presence. With this the bears grew more insistent and aggressive, often breaking into cars, tents, and packs in search of food. Here the decisive question was not the "natural" quality of bear or human behavior. Managers knew that both the humans and the bears were behaving about as one would expect. This, indeed, was the problem. Their natural inclinations were resulting in conflict.

In the interest of creating harmony between bears and humans, managers today combine a vigorous informational campaign (telling visitors to store their food in bear-proof food lockers) with a law enforcement program of nightly patrols and direct and immediate intervention when a bear is spotted around a campground. While campers are encouraged to make loud noises to scare a bear away, police and park rangers may also use traps in a more intensive effort to manage the bears. Once a bear is caught, a semicircle of rangers will surround the trap, release the bear, and unleash a volley of riot ordinance, air horns, and bright lights as the bear runs for cover. In this way both bears and humans fall under a unified park policy: both will encounter law enforcement for any vio-

Bear warning near the John Muir Trail. Photo by the author.

Safety warnings in Yosemite Valley. Photo by the author.

lation, and both are subject to long-standing programs that aim to shift behavioral patterns. This ensemble of management techniques, including information, technology, and law enforcement procedures, manages nature and culture as an integrated whole.

Structure of the Built Environment

One-way, winding roads lead in and out of the valley. Their placement and design reflect a principle of harmony and the avoidance of conflict: the road leading in lies on the south side of the river; the road leading out occupies the north bank. Both roads consist of two lanes, meaning that motorists need not concern themselves with oncoming traffic and those traveling at different speeds need not experience frustration at being unable to pass. The curvature of the road prevents higher speeds. This design, in addition to reducing the risk of accidents and allowing visitors more opportunity to view scenery, forestalls the need to enforce the speed limit and removes the threat of police action.

Architecture in the valley reflects a concern for harmony through the use of camouflage. Wide, low-lying buildings made of wood and stone stand within groves so as to minimize their structural profile. Buildings are rarely visible from a distance—trees almost always intervene. In contrast, views of the major scenic features of the valley are maintained by cutting down trees that would otherwise block the view. When visible human structures cannot be avoided, their form maintains a natural aesthetic. Fences, made of wooden planks of irregular dimension, give the appearance of hand-split carpentry. Interiors of the buildings often exhibit exposed stone work, and supporting pillars in both the Ahwahnee Hotel and the food court at Glacier Point consist of tree trunks stripped of their bark, the remaining traces of knots, burls, and branches bearing witness to the trees' previous organic existence.

For all this, harmony is an incomplete task. In peak season, visitors driving out of the valley in early evening will find themselves in a line of traffic. Likewise, lines at the food courts in Yosemite Village offer little in the way of natural/cultural harmony: the pleasant views of the surroundings are accessible to seated customers only. Campers who arrive without reservations in summertime will end up sitting outside a small out-building next to a parking lot waiting for the announcement of last-minute cancellations. Those who bring their recreational vehicles may find themselves in a line with other RVs, the fumes of engine exhaust mixing with the stench of human waste as they wait to pump out their sewage. An experience of the harmony of nature and culture will most likely befall those who plan ahead and time their visit carefully to avoid the peaks of traffic flow and visitor density.

To the extent that it is realized in Yosemite Valley, "loving communion" within a natural "temple" depends upon a high degree of social management and planning. Within such an environment, social controls give nature its shape, hiding the signs of such control in the process. The harmony of nature and culture occurs through a sophisticated blurring of the boundaries between the two.

From Explicit to Implicit Spirituality

As previously noted, the official communication of the meaning of park experience falls under the rubric of "interpretation" and consists of a

highly programmatic enterprise of educating and edifying park visitors through lectures, tours, panels, exhibits, museums, and the like. While historically and functionally related to "education," interpretation has developed a distinct theory of practice adapted to environments such as national parks.[13]

One of the distinctive parameters for interpretation is time. In national parks, visitors have an extremely limited amount of it to spend, and for this reason interpretation gears itself to be effective within a time frame ranging from a few seconds to two hours, but rarely longer than that. This and other factors yield a different pedagogy from that of educational institutions that have an audience for a space of months and years. Rather than relying on extensive deliberation on large bodies of information, interpretation emphasizes, on the one hand, concision with regard to information and, on the other, evocation, implication, and suggestion with regard to meaning and significance. During the summer months when I conducted my research, Yosemite offered over fifty interpretive programs a week. Permanent park rangers conducted many of these programs, but each summer the park added seasonal rangers who also took responsibility for interpretation. While interpreters received training from senior staff, the specific content of the programs depended upon the individual rangers themselves. The diversity of interpreted environments, ranging from Yosemite Valley to the high country of Tuolumne Meadows to the Mariposa Grove of Giant Sequoias, combined with the diversity of staff to yield a high degree of variety within Yosemite's interpretive programming as a whole. Hence I offer not a comprehensive treatment of the content of interpretive programs in Yosemite, but instead survey, through selected examples, the general forms through which the spiritual harmonization of nature and culture took shape within park programming.

When the spiritual dimension of interpretation took explicit form, the reference generally occurred in quotation and without specific elaboration. The words of John Muir provide particularly pertinent examples. For instance, a sign directing visitors to Soda Springs, located near Tuolumne Meadows in the Yosemite high country, bears an epigraph attributed to Muir: "A Baptism in Nature's Warm Heart." In a similar vein, the sign identifying the trailhead for Cathedral Peak also begins with a quotation from Muir: "'This I may say, is the first time I have been to church in California.'—John Muir, after making the first recorded ascent of Cathedral Peak in 1869." Such citations, while finding no further elaboration on the informational signs on which they stand, express a spiritual mediation of nature and culture. The experience of bathing in a natural springs is here related to a ritual of social inclusion, a metaphorical washing away of sins that indicates the embrace of nature, God, and community all at the same time. Likewise, Muir portrayed the experience of wilderness mountain climbing not simply as an experience of solitude, but as a deeper form of communion: going "to church." These quotations thus expressed the paradoxical unity of nature and culture: a solitary individual who found in the farthest flights from society an experience of belonging and community. The state lets visitors know that out in nature, on their own and in public, they can go to church and be baptized. The state provides the ground for this solitary sense of communion.

In a more extensive forum, a weekly theater performance entitled "Wild Muir" contains a multitude of quotations from Muir. Performed at the visitor center auditorium by a single actor, Lee Stetson, the program begins with Muir as an apparition called back from the dead. Directly addressing the audience, the character asserts that the audience has called his "spirit" out, and that while he is rumored to be dead, his spirit lives on in Yosemite. Without ever defining "spirit" and the particular relations it may express, Stetson's framing of the performance echoes *Spirit of Yosemite* (which, shown daily in the room next door, also quoted Muir) in its evocation of natural and cultural harmony. In one way, Stetson's invocation of Muir's spirit shows a solitary individual communing with the grandeur of nature. At the same time, Stetson sets his performance within a cultural and communal frame: the audience has called this spirit out. To the degree that the audience is inspired to experience nature "on their own" in imitation of Muir, they link themselves not only to nature, but to Muir's legacy, a cultural tradition cultivated by the Park Service in its lionization of the "Father of National Parks." The individual appropriation of spiritual meaning in nature is thereby linked to the cultural legacy of the park as public space.

From a different angle, the interpretive programs dealing with the Ahwahneechee also expressed a harmony of nature and culture with religious dimensions. For instance, Julia Parker, one of the oldest surviving

Ahwahneechee, occasionally leads visitors on a program at the "Indian village" behind the visitor center. The village contains examples of the structures the Ahwahneechee would have lived in during the nineteenth century, along with examples of the typical flora that would have supplied food, baskets, and medicine. The exhibits show the integration of the natural environment with a particular cultural system. Moreover, that cultural system is not portrayed as some pure, romanticized utopia untainted by Western civilization. Rather, the exhibits emphasized the absorption of Euro-American customs and technologies, including firearms, metalworking tools, and non-native textiles, into Ahwahneechee culture right into the twentieth century. This picture of natural/cultural continuity leads, literally, into the Ahwahneechee gift shop at the exit of the tour.

Parker sets this journey into natural/cultural harmony within an explicitly religious framework. Before beginning the program that I observed, Parker asked our permission to sing a prayer to the four directions. She later explained that this introductory prayer, sung in her native language, allowed us to enter the roundhouse at the center of the village (the way was barred with a rope and sign) where she performed more songs and dances. At the end of the program, she stressed conservation: the need to take care of the park and the earth in everyday practices. This paralleled her earlier explication of Ahwahneechee religion, which she encapsulated in a single phrase: "Take from the earth with a please, give to the earth with a thank you, pray to the four directions."[14] Speaking privately after the program, Parker volunteered the observation that hers was an implicitly religious enterprise. She explained that she had been raised in an Indian boarding school run by the Christian Missionary Alliance, and that when she was young, she had planned to become a missionary. Regarding her present position, she continued, "But I guess I'm a missionary in a different way now," asserting that her interpretation of Ahwahneechee life as a harmony of nature and culture bore an implicitly religious character. [15]

Indeed, most often religion and spirituality play a strictly implicit role in interpretation. For instance, a number of interpretive programs fall under the category of science education and contain little or no explicitly religious language. Even here, however, the content of programming can have an implicitly religious character. To illustrate: Ranger Eric

Westerlund's programs span a wide range of scientific topics including the morphology of the valley, the dynamics of the meadow ecosystem, and animal behavior. In response to my question about any religious or spiritual dimensions to his work, Westerlund said, "I'm into Darwin. I like to see the natural processes and interrelationships behind what you see out here. To see natural selection at work." Such a view of nature, Westerlund continued, was for him spiritual, "if you want to call it that."[16] In discussing the looseness of the definition of "spiritual," Westerlund showed no strict investment in the term. Such willingness to label his program and its motivations as "spiritual" shows the flexibility of this category and also points toward the program's communicative potential with respect to visitor religiosity. I explored such potential by suggesting the structural similarities between Westerlund's Darwinian perspective and a certain theological approach to nature. I proposed that his perception of a central organizing principle behind the varieties of natural phenomena recalled the quest to see divine intelligence at work within nature. Both approaches emphasized a transcendent intelligence behind appearance, I suggested, an intelligence foreign to our own. "I think you nailed it," Westerlund responded.[17] He then went on to recall that nineteenth-century naturalists were theologians who tried to understand how God worked through the natural environment. By tying his scientific perspective to religious history and by being willing to describe such a perspective as "spiritual," Westerlund recognized an implicitly religious and spiritual dimension to his interpretation of nature.

Another ranger tied her spirituality even more closely to her work. Ginger Burley served as a lead interpreter in Yosemite, meaning that she was responsible for training other interpreters in addition to running her own visitor programs. Given her leadership role with respect to Yosemite interpreters as a group, I analyze her work in some detail.

When asked about any religious or spiritual dimensions to her scientific perspective, Burley responded, "Absolutely. It's as close to a religion as I have." And in relating her personal history and her abandonment of organized religion, she elaborated: "The best times of my life were happening out of doors, when I was observing things closely, when I was being focused. And that ability to focus and be at peace came more from being out of doors than it ever came from being in church. So it becomes my religion."[18] While both Burley and Westerlund attributed a religious quality to their devotion to science, they differed in the emphases of their comments. Westerlund stressed the cognitive aspect: understanding the connections that inform the natural order. Burley, on the other hand, emphasized the perceptual dimension of scientific investigation: the adoption of certain focal and behavioral modes that gave her the "peace" that she had been searching for in church.[19] In their experiential aspect, Burley suggested, the practices of natural observation and focus bore a religious character.

This emphasis on perceptual modes tied her religiosity most closely to her professional work. Burley asserted that she saw perfect consonance between her personal, spiritual attachment to the park and her public mission. When asked how this connection manifested in practice, she replied, "At the end of every program, when I'm summarizing or trying to give a direction to where I want people to go next . . . , the idea is to wake up some spark of interest or something that they can take home with them: the take home message . . . I want [them] to internalize it. I want them to compare the experience that we've had here in Yosemite with something important inside. And the word I use is sometimes 'spiritual connection.'"[20] Once again, Burley stressed the experiential dimension of scientific observation: a "spark" that arose "inside" and thus yielded a "spiritual connection."

Given the context of her personal history, the content of her professional work consisted precisely in sharing what she identified as religious in her own life (a "religion" that would manifest, in Burley's words, "when I was observing things closely, when I was being focused"). In her interpretive program as I observed it, she led visitors to a pond and engaged us in a series of exercises that forced us to focus on the life found in the mud and reeds at the pond's edge. After we had spread out and scooped out living things from the pond, Burley brought us together and offered observations on what we had found. Her concluding message infused these experiences of focus and observation with a call for moral and perceptual transformation. She encouraged us to work to preserve the environments we had just encountered, to respect the muddy, cluttered edges of ponds, to see them as alive and not as places that needed to be sprayed with insecticide or drained to make way for manicured lawns. In this way a spiritual connection to nature would work toward cultural transformation with respect to land management outside the park: a harmonization of nature and culture that could manifest along any waterway. And while in her program she never used the word "spiritual" to describe this transformative dynamic, her call for a certain ethic and aesthetic of land management bore an intention that she privately identified as "spiritual" in nature.

Burley's tacit treatment of the "spiritual" resulted not from lack of conviction but from conscious choice. She believed that her emphasis on experience furthered a goal of individual, interior change more effectively than extended argument. "I don't want to beat them over the head. I want it to be subtle and for the audience to come to a deeper understanding on their own. . . . I think subtle messages are more effective."[21] Through a more subtle presentation that sought to "spark" something "inside," Burley intended to communicate in such a way that visitors could appropriate or construct the meaning of her program on an individual basis. Such individual meaning construction, she suggested, yielded a sense of personal investment for the visitor, an attachment all the more profound as it arose "inside." Burley conveyed this with her aim to allow visitors to achieve "a deeper understanding on their own."

Burley did not choose such implicit communication, however, purely on the grounds of efficacy. Relating specifically to the religious or spiritual dimensions of Park Service interpretation, she recalled a conference presentation in which the speaker called for interpreters to be more "evangelistic" in their work. Burley continued, "And he took that word, and he separated it, and he told us what that word meant, and he asked us to be more evangelistic. And I totally agreed with what he said. But it didn't feel—somehow the word . . . it feels inappropriate. . . . But I'm not sure why. If we totally believe in what we're doing . . . maybe we should be [evangelistic]." While open to the possibility that her own methods may not have been faithful to the (religious/spiritual) source of their inspiration, she suggested that "preaching" would be out of place in the context of the park. In terms of the religious formulation of park interpretation, for Burley such impropriety remained purely contextual. She "totally agreed" with the speaker's aims and motivations while disagreeing on the suitability of the method in context. And in further considering methods of communication, she returned to her assertion that "subtle messages are more effective."

Through Burley's program, the muddy banks of a mountain lake lost the qualities of danger and discomfort that urban visitors might have associated with them and instead became a more familiar space of educational interaction: a place for children to go on an adventure in which they would learn how the lake itself formed a community. In her closing message Burley related this harmonious natural community to the cultural spaces of riverside homes: they did not need to be reduced to manicured lawns and sprayed with insecticide in order to make them enriching environments. Through this smoothing over of nature/culture distinctions, Burley intended to evoke a sense of spiritual investment in a certain way of managing land. Within the park, any consequent sense of peace and belonging depended upon state authority that preserved such environments. Outside the park, preservation of riverine ecosystems may likewise require state management in addition to public participation and consent, and it is the implied spirituality of Burleys presentation that prepares for the social realization of such a situation.

* * *

While explicit religious language does appear in park interpretation, as evidenced in the quotations of John Muir and the presentation of Ahwahneechee culture, an implicit religiosity can also inform interpretive programs without recognizable religious language and allow a wide range of topics to be addressed from and informed by a religious or spiritual viewpoint. And while by no means do the examples discussed above reproduce the breadth and complexity of interpretive programming in Yosemite, nevertheless these illustrations of implicit religiosity show the potential for religious communication in the "bread-and-butter" interpretative programs of the park.

This implicit dimension of interpretation yields the possibility of religious communication without the intent or conscious motivation on the part of the interpreter. Put simply, a visitor can find a nature program "spiritually enriching" without the presenter consciously seeking to evoke such a response. Such an observation, however, does not qualify such a religiously significant effect as an "accident," a random swell in the sea of American religiosity. Rather, the structures of public communication in the park harmonize with a spiritual logic, one that does not need to create nor stem from a common consciousness among park rangers and visitors. In short, spirit can operate without the name.

Unintended Spirit

Margaret Eissler's background did not fit the stereotypical mold for a park ranger. A classically trained musician rather than a biologist or forester, Eissler integrated her skills with the flute into a sunset "ranger walk" above Tuolumne Meadows in the Yosemite high country. Scheduled only during the summer months when evening temperatures were conducive to flute-playing, sitting, and listening, Eissler's music walk elicited reactions that, she asserted, visitors often labeled "spiritual."[22] Eissler did not offer this characterization by way of self-congratulation, but rather with a sense of mystification and, to some degree, frustration. She herself did not call her program "spiritual" and looked to me to help her understand why visitors often used this word.

The walk began at the base of Lembert Dome, a large granite swell that overlooks the eight-thousand-foot-high Tuolumne Meadows. When I observed this program, the summer months were drawing to a close, and colder temperatures were beginning to take their toll on visitor density and participation. The first time I participated in the program, only four visitors (including myself) joined Eissler in the grove of evergreens beneath Lembert Dome.[23] Our first steps took us up a path through the trees to a large, flat swath of granite only slightly elevated above the valley floor. Eissler instructed us to sit down in a semicircle that gave us a view, just out over the tree tops, of the meadow and impending sunset over the western horizon. She sat just below us, drew out an index card, and began by reading a quotation concerning "one woman's thoughts on the powerful experience of being on top of a mountain":

> In my dreams, the ones I have just before I wake up and have to go to work, I see myself on top of my grandmother's favorite mountain, standing as tall as I can on my tiptoes to see more; bowing to no one; taking big gulps of the thin air, the way you have to when you're up high, and you're tired, but feeling good, real good.

> When I do wake up, I say to myself what my grandmother used to say to me: "Don't bow to anyone, not in your heart." A mountain dream like that will carry a person right through a day working at that supermarket.[24]

Explaining that this program was going to be about the experience of high places, Eissler then asked us about our own experiences of climbing, about how it made us feel. Responses were varied. One visitor said "peace"; another "connection"; a third "insignificance." Then, asking herself the same question, Eissler gave her own, more detailed answer. And while she never used the word "spiritual," her answer sketched a trajectory that mirrors much of what park visitors have labeled "spiritual" as seen in this and other chapters.

Starting with her own body, Eissler stated that the "rhythm of walking and breathing" and the sense of "the body working together as a unit" yielded a benefit well before she reached the top. Moving out from this bodily perspective, she highlighted what she perceived along the way: the wildlife with its associated sights, sounds, and smells. Broadening out from these local perceptions, Eissler described the view from the top, stressing the great expanse of the visual field, the ability to place oneself "in relation to everything else," and, beyond, the revelation of "large patterns of the landscape" such as the former paths of glaciers and the characteristic rolling sweep of the Sierra Nevada as it rises from west to east. With this seemingly unbounded perspective on the environment, Eissler asserted, came the recognition that all is surrounded by space: "space above, space below, a huge sky, a huge land." These expanses gave one a new perspective, she suggested, one in which "what may have seemed very important a few hours earlier loses its significance" while "other things take on a far greater importance." Finally, after the evocation of an almost unbounded perspective, Eissler returned to a local, particular awareness: "the sounds that break against the backdrop of a vast silence: the breeze or howling wind, the clinking of rocks as you walk, and the buzzing of insects; all rhythms and sounds that reveal the life and natural processes that continue even in higher elevations." Through this chain of expanding perspectives, moving from internal, bodily consciousness to the revelation of geological patterns and the experience of unbounded space, and then back to local awareness, Eissler echoed what others said about the spiritual benefit of wilderness—that is brought a sense of individual embeddedness within an all-encompassing global whole.

This dynamic of individuality and universality thus served as the center of Eissler's program. After the evocation of the enormity of space, Eissler's presentation returned to the sensations of one's immediate surroundings. Here, she suggested that the significance of the breadth and expansion of perspective, even to the infinity of space, acquired a heightened intensity through its juxtaposition with individual, local perspective. The solitary individual who does not "bow to anyone" acquires strength, significance, and definition when silhouetted against that horizon of space. Eissler emphasized this point by having a visitor read a quotation: "For it is only framed in space that beauty blooms. . . . A tree has significance if one sees it against the empty face of the sky. A note in music gains significance from the silences on either side. A candle flowers in the space of night. Even small and casual things take on significance if they are washed in space, like a few autumn grasses in one corner of an Oriental painting, the rest of the page bare."[25] Combined with the opening passage describing how a woman's "mountain dream" inspired her to refuse "bow to anyone," the second quotation suggested that expansive space heightened individuality, clarified its significance, and brought its value, worth, and beauty into perspective. This stress on individuality, however, did not focus primarily on a solitary human being isolated in space. Rather, Eissler used these portraits to introduce a higher level of individuality: that of the earth.

After her evocation of various individualities (a person, a tree, a note, and a candle) and how they acquire their characteristics through the space around them, Eissler drew out a large coffee table book entitled *The Home Planet*, a collection of 150 photographs of the earth taken from space.[26] Connecting this book to the themes of her introduction, she explained that her program would take the visitors to "even greater heights and new perspectives." Leafing through the pages and displaying them as she talked, she noted that the photos were accompanied by quotations from astronauts reflecting on their perspective on the earth. While coming from a wide range of cultures and backgrounds, she said, all these astronauts were profoundly affected by their view of the earth

Evening sky above Lembert Dome. Photo by the author.

isolated in space. She then passed out index cards with selected quotations from the book and explained that we would read the quotations aloud "in an order that makes sense, that tells a story." Further, Eissler stressed, we as the audience would not merely listen to that story, but would play the role of the storytellers: "You will be the astronauts in space, telling the story, while I will play music from around the world between certain readings. So in effect I will represent life back on that beautiful blue marble."

After each set of quotations and musical accompaniment, we moved higher up on Lembert Dome, our horizons expanding as the sun set, the colors of the sky deepening and softening as we climbed. In this way the rhythm of readings and music integrated with the rhythm of walking and sitting. At the same time, the deepening themes of the readings correlated with the broadening of the visual field, setting the conceptual climax of the narrative against the visual crescendo of the sunset. Taken as whole, Eissler's program thus took on the structure of a musical performance, replete with rhythm, theme, and movement.

The final quotation from an astronaut selected by Eissler imagined nuclear catastrophe seen from space. In concluding her program, she explained that the reference to war was to be understood in the broadest sense: "war against people, was against the land, war against the incredible variety, the diversity of plant and animal species that share this planet and make it the precious blue green white jewel that it is." (This program was delivered in the summer of 2002, and Eissler had left unspoken the war in the immediate historical context: the run-up to the United States' invasion of Iraq.) Eissler then spoke most directly in her official capacity as a park ranger, explaining that Yosemite and national parks in general stood as "a statement of respect for place, for nature as it is—a peace treaty with the land." Tying together these evocations of care and attachment to the earth as seen from high places, she suggested that the distance and removal from the earth implied a care for it in its inherent qualities ("nature as it is"). Such a relationship took form in a political metaphor, a "peace treaty," which Eissler elaborated, saying that "people from all over the world come to visit," making Yosemite "an international park . . . a place where peace can be found, a reservoir of peace, an international peace park." Through the maintenance of "peace" and "nature as it is," she suggested, Yosemite and other national parks transcended U.S. boundaries and fostered a global social identity.

In summation, she paraphrased a former Sierra Club president and naturalist, David Brower: Yosemite was "a place that people come not just to view the scenery but to soak in the sacred relationships and connections that link us to all the physical and living aspects of the earth." And immediately following this invocation of "sacred relationships," she made clear the social import of her program: "Just as all of us together told the story of the astronauts, we must continue to overlook our differences and work together as inhabitants of the earth to safeguard this most beautiful and fragile home we all share. A view from a high place—the apron of Lembert Dome, a mountain peak, a space shuttle—makes it very clear what a fine home we have. It's up to us to keep it that way." Here Eissler tied the specific perceptual and experiential aspects of her program to its "sacred" and social significance. Through reading the words of astronauts from all over the world, gaining elevation as we hiked up Lembert Dome, looking at pictures of the earth from space, and listening to songs representing, not various national and cultural differences, but "life . . . on that beautiful blue marble," the participants in the program literally "overlook[ed] their differences" and "work[ed] together" to protect the earth in an expression of common love and attachment for the "fragile home we all share." Moreover, that love involved an implicit allegiance not to a particular nation, but to to a particular institution of the state, here embodied by the Park Service, which enforced the "peace treaty" with the earth.

How is this "spiritual?" On one level, Eissler's program showed a dynamic of individuality and universality that paralleled the spirituality of JMT hikers discussed in Chapter 2. Here the individualized connection to a universal reality took the shape of care for the earth as a natural/cultural whole. With this in mind, it is unsurprising that visitors might, without any conscious intention on the part of Eissler, have considered her program spiritual. And the line between spiritual and nonspiritual was extremely thin even for Eissler. Her frustration and mystification at the "spiritual" label did not prevent her from inserting the word "sacred" in describing the relationships between individuals and the earth. This word did not appear in her notes, and when I asked her after the program why she used it, she was again mystified: it was unintentional. I had interviewed her privately earlier that day, and we agreed that perhaps that discussion had sparked the religious indiscretion during the program. Such a slip shows that even her vigorous, conscious resistance to the label "spiritual" did not put her at a far remove from such an interpretation of her work.

Nonetheless, it was due to the fact that spiritual qualities remained largely unspoken that her program became even more spiritual. Precisely because she had not spelled out the religious significance of her program (her "sacred" slip excluded), visitors' religious investment in it, and in the space of the park, belonged to them individually. And as I noted previously, when religiosity takes a more personal form, one lacking in articulated conceptual expression and experienced more as a "feeling," it tends to take the label "spiritual." By leaving the meaning of her program broad and vague (care for the earth), Eissler allowed visitors to create a multitude of individual specifications of that meaning, and thus individual investments in the park.

And of course that investment has a social location. The natural and cultural harmony that visitors experienced as "spiritual" is provided by the state. The natural quality of the view depended upon state authority for its purity. This "peace treaty" with the land is maintained and enforced through the regulations that guide the Park Service. The peace and harmony that the earth need to survive do not come, Eissler's program suggested, simply from an individual feeling. Rather that feeling needs to be integrated into the ensemble of natural/cultural relations as an organized whole. In the parks, that organization is the state itself.

"Most Who Visit"

In the opening lines of *Spirit of Yosemite*, the narrator asserts that in Yosemite, "most who visit sense the presence of a spirit." Is the statement true? And if so, what does it mean outside of the context of the film? To answer these and related questions, I surveyed 150 visitors to Yosemite over a period of three weeks during the summer of 2003. In response to the questions, "Do you feel that there is anything religious/spiritual about your experience of national parks? Of this national park?" over three quarters of respondents (n=115) answered positively. Of these, roughly one third (n=40) preferred the term "spiritual" as opposed to "religious" as a self-description, and a similar percentage were comfortable with either term (n=43). As a total, therefore, slightly over half (n=83) of all respondents linked the term "spiritual" to their experience of national parks and Yosemite in particular. The intuition of the film, while perhaps ungrounded in the strict sense, appears correct.

Before exploring what, precisely, people meant when they called themselves or their experience "spiritual," I note that respondents to the survey exhibited several features that distinguished them from the general public. The vast majority, over 80 percent (n=122), was white, and 60 percent (n=91) listed an annual income over fifty thousand dollars, including 20 percent overall (n=31) who reported an income over one hundred thousanddollars. In line with these statistics, almost 90 percent of respondents (n=133) went to college, with 30 percent overall (n=46) achieving a postgraduate degree. In sum, and in contrast with the general public, the respondents to the survey were predominantly white, well-educated, and affluent.[27]

Income

	Frequency	Percent
No answer	15	10.0
less than 20k	14	9.3
20–50k	30	20.0
50–100k	60	40.0
over 100	31	20.7
Total	150	100.0

Highest Grade Completed

	Frequency	Percent
No answer	4	2.7
Pre-high school	3	2.0
High school	10	6.7
Some college	33	22.0
College	54	36.0
Postgraduate	46	30.7
Total	150	100.0

Race

	Frequency	Percent
No answer	4	2.7
American Indian or Alaska native	3	2.0
Asian	7	4.7
Black or African-American	2	1.3
Native Hawaiian or other Pacific Islander	1	.7
White	122	81.3
Other	11	7.3
Total	150	100.0

What can be said about the religiosity of the "knowledge class" that is so well-represented in national parks? In their influential 1985 work *Habits of the Heart*, sociologists Robert Bellah, Richard Madsen, William Sullivan, Ann Swidler, and Steven Tipton undertook a wide-ranging study of what they saw as core values in American culture. They explained how rising levels of education and affluence, with the consequent specialization of knowledge and career paths, tended to loosen attachment to conventional values and community ties. Those in this situation tended to perceive the effects of social organization as the result of their individual agency, a misperception the authors found threatening to the foundations of an enlightened political order and anxiety-producing for the individual left without clear standards for self-evaluation.[28] With respect to religion, the authors noted that this ethos of individualism demanded that one identify one's religiosity as self-originating and self-grounding, a situation that they illustrated with the case of Sheila Larson, who described her religion as "Sheilaism," and that they generalized as the tendency for individuals to describe themselves as "spiritual" rather than "religious."[29] While the authors were concerned about such an ethos spreading widely throughout the public sphere, they note how the divorce from community often involved an intensifying reliance on larger social structures, a "bureaucratic individualism."[30] The public sphere inhabited by the knowledge class, therefore, was one in which the broad structures of modern society remained as an unacknowledged foundation for the individuality of those who believed themselves to be the creators of their personal destinies and worldviews.

Writing at roughly the same time as Bellah and his coauthors, Robert Wuthnow drew out even more precise ties between class and religious individualism. In his 1988 study *The Restructuring of American Religion*, Wuthnow detailed the historical decline of denominationalism as the central organizing principle of American religion. He highlighted the dramatic increase in participation in higher education, particularly in the 1960s, and the emergence of a "new class" and with it a revolution in cultural attitudes. Citing public opinion surveys, Wuthnow documented stark increases in expressions of tolerance for blacks, homosexuals, and Jews, a greater willingness to accept women in positions of influence outside the home, and an increased concern for civil liberties. He connected what he saw as a "growing liberalization of American culture" both to the content of university education (such as greater familiarization with constitutional rights) and to the social structural changes brought about by having large numbers of young people moving away from their parents, spending a significant amount of time together in a new and uncertain environment, and proceeding on to professional and managerial jobs in new locales.[31] In terms of religion and the public sphere, Wuthnow found that these social and cultural shifts had led to a decline in the potential for religious discourse, of whatever stripe, to provide common ground for a sense of American identity. Instead, Wuthnow described a heightened reliance on freedom as the central legitimating myth of American culture. Consonant with rising prominence of a geographically mobile professional and managerial class, this freedom emphasized an individualism that found self-valorization in economic prosperity and placed faith in technology as a vehicle for providing freedom.[32] Moreover, according to Wuthnow, this kind of freedom informed a particular approach to religiosity, one that insisted on tailoring religiosity to one's individuality by drawing on a marketplace of religious possibilities.[33]

As mentioned in the previous chapter, Wade Clark Roof centralized this theme of the spiritual marketplace in his analysis of major trends in contemporary American religiosity.[34] Highlighting the formative influence of the Baby Boom generation, he noted how the 1950s and 1960s saw the start of a shift towards a language of the "self" and a therapeutic model in the fashioning of religious worldviews.[35] Citing the work of Ronald Inglehart, Roof tied this shift towards the self to the rising affluence of that time period, arguing that as basic needs were met, economic security fostered greater individualism and tolerance.[36] In this way the economic conditions of the Baby Boom generation, characterized by affluence as well as higher levels of education, provided both the impetus and the form for this movement towards a market-oriented religiosity in which the religious consumer could choose from a multiplicity of options, a religiosity that Roof called "spiritual," And while Roof took a less polemical tone than Wuthnow and Bellah and colleagues, his analysis resonates with the idea that major trends in contemporary religiosity tended towards a reduction of social effects to the level of individual consciousness and agency.

With this background in mind, one can see the relatively high levels of income and education found among visitors to Yosemite as conducive to a certain kind of religiosity, namely "spirituality," as well as to a certain kind of insertion within the public sphere, one that sees social effects as products of individual agency. The trope of "nature" is central to this spiritual reduction carried out in national parks, a reduction that tends to naturalize state authority.

To return to Yosemite visitors more specifically, over three quarters of respondents (n=116) called themselves "religious" and/or "spiritual." Given a chance to express a preference between the two terms, only 15 percent of the overall total (n=22) chose the word "religious." In contrast, nearly a third of all respondents (n=48) preferred the term "spiritual," while roughly 30 percent (n=46) were comfortable with either term. In order to link religious orientation to the experiential frames visitors bring to the park, the survey asked, "How deeply is your religion/spirituality connected to your appreciation for nature?" In answer, over half (56 percent, n=84) replied that their religion/spirituality was "very" or "absolutely" connected, while more than a quarter (27 percent, n=40) said the two were "somewhat" connected.

It is tempting to draw more precise conclusions from this general association of religiosity with attachment to nature. Following the suggestion that attachment to nature might have favored the language of "spirit," it is remarkable that 70 percent (n=34) of those who preferred the term "spiritual" said that their spirituality was "very" or "absolutely" connected to their appreciation for nature—a finding that is mirrored almost exactly by those who affirmed both "religious" and "spiritual" as self-descriptions. Those who called themselves "religious" as opposed to "spiritual" did not link their religiosity to nature to the degree that those who accepted the term "spiritual" did.

In sum, these results show a tendency among visitors to associate nature with religiosity and/or spirituality. To investigate the range of meanings that could be encompassed under terms such as "spiritual," "religious," and "nature," respondents were asked to elaborate, in writing, on the connection between their religion/spirituality and their experience of nature and national parks.

Even among the roughly 15 percent (n=23) who identified themselves as neither religious nor spiritual, several (n=9) showed a willingness to characterize their park experience as religiously and/or spiritually significant. For instance, one respondent who affirmed no religious affiliation and characterized religion/spirituality as "unimportant" for her life left open the possibility of a religious dimension to her experience. She wrote, "I have a deep appreciation for nature but do not believe in a spiritual being. Does that count as religion?"[37] Another said that his experience of nature and national parks operated at "possibly some spiritual level."[38] A third respondent wrote that if she had any religion or spirituality, "it would be deeply connected" to her appreciation for nature. In answer to the question, "Do you feel that there is anything religious/spiritual about your experience of national parks? Of this national park?" she replied, "Yes very connected—inspired." When asked to elaborate on her answers, she explained that her father was paranoid/schizophrenic and thought he was Jesus, and that this caused her to shy away from religion. Nevertheless, she said that Yosemite was a very special place for her, and that she "would go crazy" if she was prevented from coming to places like this. She had gotten engaged the previous day at the top of Half Dome, and when pressed by her fiancé, she accepted the term "spiritual" as a self-description.[39] These answers indicate that even those who did not identify themselves as religious or spiritual, who attested to no religious affiliation, and who considered religion/spirituality "unimportant" or "not very important" in their lives, nevertheless could leave open the possibility of religion and/or spirituality as relevant to their experience.

For a large majority of respondents (77 percent, n=115), a connection between religiosity/spirituality and nature in the parks was not simply a possibility but an affirmed reality. In contrast to the lack of connection to religious tradition within hiker spirituality, a significant number (25 percent, n=37) of Yosemite visitors explained the meaning of their experience by referring to a creator whose existence was made evident by nature in the park. Referring to the religious dimension of her experience of national parks, one woman wrote, "God created it, shows his amazing power."[40] Another affirmed, "The sheer beauty and interconnectedness of nature in this setting bespeaks God's awesome power and love. I appreciate him more each time I experience nature in a setting such as this."[41] Within perspectives such as these, the experience of nature could become "proof" for particular truth claims. For example, one respondent wrote: "I don't really see how anyone could experience Yosemite . . . devoid of the understanding of the creator who made it all."[42] Another used the language of mathematics to argue for a creator God, noting that "the chances of human life even existing are astronomical (1 / [$1x10^{213}$])."[43] Such expressions cast the religious/spiritual significance of nature as a second-order phenomenon: The immediate experience was significant for what could be inferred from it. Visitors here inferred a singular, supernatural creator consonant with that of the scriptures of Christianity. In contrast to the interviews with the largely "unchurched" JMT hikers, therefore, these answers of Yosemite visitors resonated with a biblical tradition and highlighted belief as a central feature of religiosity.

While such "traditional" religiosity characterized one quarter of the Yosemite answers, the majority of visitor answers (57 percent, n=86) employed the themes of perspective and perception. These answers highlighted "feeling" as opposed to specific tenets of belief. The theme of perspective refers to the shifts visitors described in the way they viewed themselves and their relationship to the environment. This theme, appearing in 38 percent (n=57) of the surveys, included a sense of "connection" with the surroundings, a deepening relationship to "self," "soul," or "spirit," an appreciation for solitude, and evaluations of the wilderness/civilization distinction. In terms of differences from wilderness hikers, Yosemite visitors employed the theme of connection much more frequently than did the former. I return to this below. Also, while the vast majority of wilderness hikers employed a wilderness/civilization distinction, only a small number (n=12) of Yosemite visitors employed a similar distinction in describing the religious/spiritual aspect of their experience.

Under the broad theme of perspective, 20 percent of all respondents (n=31) explained the religious/spiritual dimension of their experience in terms of "connection," writing in a therapeutic language that often focused on the self. For instance, one woman, who described herself as "spiritual" as opposed to "religious," explained her perspective: "My sense of spirituality is based on feeling a connection with nature. Being with animals in their natural setting is important to me. Animals open my mind and deepen my senses and allow me to appreciate things around me that I would have overlooked. Animals slow me down and make me understand what is important.”[44] Note the use of “sense,” “senses,” “feeling,” and “being with.” All these terms describe an immediate, experiential relation, one that is primarily bodily and perceptual rather than rational and cognitive. Even the reference to understanding applies not to an objective truth claim, but to a sense of value, to understanding “what is important.” Another respondent, who preferred the label “spiritual” (identifying her religious tradition as a “strictly earth based spiritual point of view associated w/ [and studied] Wicca now I feel more tendency towards Spirit and Energy [nameless]”), echoed this sense of immediate, felt connection: “Being connected to nature brings me back to a centeredness within myself where I can more fully see and feel the universe within myself. I can see spirit in all of nature and I can see and feel it vibrating at a higher speed and connecting to this somehow brings me to a higher spiritual plane.”[45] Not only did this respondent “see” her connection to the universe (where “see” could mean “understand”); rather she also came to “feel” the universe inside herself, experiencing it as a vibration that provoked a spiritual movement. Such emphases on feeling contrast with the “traditional” view of nature as evidence for the existence of God.

Of course, such contrast did not preclude the theme of connection from appearing alongside that of faith in a creator God. A “spiritual” and non-churchgoing visitor wrote that “it is all very moving to think that ‘God’ created all of this. . . . Being out in nature, feels like being ‘home’ or at one with all of the universe.”[46] Here, and in combination with immersion in a “natural” environment, the belief in a creator evoked a spiritual feeling of belonging. Another respondent, a Methodist who preferred the term “religious” as a self-description, wrote that “when in nature I appreciate the natural beauty of God’s work. I immediately feel connected to his presence.”[47] Here again, faith in a creator God went hand in hand with emotive and aesthetic reactions. However, even with the co-presence of these themes that stressed belief and feeling, respectively, one can see a recognition of the distinction between them. This same respondent, who described a sense of immediate connection to God, continued, “But I do not feel this connection to be important to my religious views.”[48] While one might expect that feeling the presence of God would represent the peak of faith, this respondent suggested that this sense of connection was incomplete without a proper attitude that one would carry outside of that experience. As I will show, many respondents attached no such qualifications to their description of their religion/spirituality.

In describing religious and/or spiritually significant shifts of perspective, a number of visitors (17 percent, n=26) highlighted the interiority of their experience, a shift in the way they perceived themselves. A respondent who identified himself simply as "spiritual" wrote, "Being with nature rejuvenates my spirit: reconnects me with self."[49] One "non-denominational Christian" who was a seasonal staff member wrote, "I absolutely feel a spiritual connection with the Parks that I visit, including my stay here @ Yosemite. Working here in the park has offered me time to really explore not only the park, but myself as well."[50] Another "spiritual" respondent drew a direct connection between the removal from civilization and spiritual self-discovery: "National parks, like natural surroundings in general, hold a place of spirituality due to the isolation I feel from distractions of 'life.' I cannot describe in detail what aspect(s) of nature create this for me. Perhaps the removal of the ordinary; the uniqueness of a moment that will not be experienced again (an animal asleep; a moon over Yosemite w/snow dusting the walls shared w/a great Friend the day after I buried my father; etc.). I have come to find that though I do not completely understand the 'why,' it is in natural surroundings that I am closest to myself and to my soul."[51] These and other answers reinforce the idea that the parks not only provide visitors with nature, but through the opportunities for solitude provide them with deeper contact with their selves as well.

This last respondent suggested that such spiritual self-reflection occurred not simply through the revelation of nature as a pregiven state but also through the art of creating contrasts with respect to "civilized" life. Furthermore, the recognition of a wilderness/civilization distinction came to expression in a smaller number of answers (n=12), but the descriptions of the religious/spiritual import of this distinction resonates with several of the broader themes described above. A younger respondent (age twenty-one), describing herself as "spiritual" but without any religious affiliation, wrote, "Nature (being outdoors) helps me to understand life while sometimes trying to understand can be very difficult if you are always in a city area surrounded by people who don't care about anything more but getting to work."[52] This respondent characterized civilization primarily as a social environment rather than a physical one. The drawback of civilization came from the fact that it made prolonged reflection an alienating activity that separated one from the rest of society. Nature, in contrast, removed that social environment and thereby facilitated the process of self-reflection. Focusing more specifically on the perceptual dimensions of the environment, a Catholic respondent echoed such a view: "Being here without distractions such as TV, computers, cell phones give[s] me the opportunity to think freely. I can simply be still, alone in my own thoughts, alone with myself. My mind can be quiet so I can listen to anything my Lord may be trying to tell me."[53] This respondent suggested that civilization tended to monopolize the sensory environment in such a way as to constrict the possibilities for self-reflection and communion with God. Such a perspective treats the nature/civilization distinction in terms of media, and characterizes nature as allowing an opportunity to focus without new communications continually demanding attention. Finally, another respondent highlighted the broader social significance of the differences that separated nature from civilization. An Episcopalian who considered herself "religious" rather than spiritual wrote, "I feel that the pagans had the right idea in worshipping God in nature rather than in man-made structures."[54] Here the experience of nature relativized a commitment to religious tradition, suggesting the superiority of social traditions that conformed themselves to nature rather than the reverse.

In the answers discussed above the themes of connection, self-reflection, and the wilderness/civilization distinction often overlap with one another. Taken together, they express a tendency to see a spiritual shift in perspective with respect to the way that visitors understood themselves, their environment, and the relation between the two. Such broader shifts in perspective went hand in hand with changes in more concrete, perceptual aspects of visitor experience as well. Here again, visitors tended to express their spirituality in terms of feeling and personal experience rather than in relation to specific religious traditions.

Under the theme of perception, encompassing 43 percent (n=64) of visitor answers, two broad categories may be identified. The first speaks to one of the management paradigms described in Chapter 1 and can be called "recreation." Here visitors highlighted the beauty of the environment as well as the sense of peace, harmony, quiet, and rejuvenation that it gave them. The second category differs more in degree than in kind. When visitors spoke of the awesomeness, power, and energy of the park, I classified their answers as "sublime." These two categories dominated the description of the spiritually significant perceptual aspects of park experience. In contrast to JMT hikers, Yosemite visitors did not speak as often about more broad-based and ingrained changes in the perception of time, distance, and response to sensory stimuli. Here again the distinctiveness of the two environments and the length of time visitors spent within them may adequately explain the difference in answers.

Under the theme of recreation, addressed by 31 percent (n=46) of respondents, visitors expressed appreciation for the physicality of their experience. One respondent, a lapsed Catholic who described himself as neither religious nor spiritual, was most explicit: "The ability to interact physically with the beauty and grandeur of the world as god created it is the most satisfying and closest I ever feel to god. Joy derived in this manner; from sight, from physical exertion, using my body in harmony with the world, is the best of all."[55] Again, different themes overlap. Here faith in a traditional creator god emerges from bodily experience, both passive (seeing "beauty" and "grandeur") and active ("physical exertion"). But a spiritual appreciation for recreational experience could also come without reference to God. A Scientologist wrote that "being in communication with plant and animal life, particularly where they are the dominant life forms, provides a break from routine, is relaxing and allows one to leave refreshed. Places like Yosemite provide a wide sense of space where one can experience sensations on a much grander scale than an urban environment."[56] Here the visitor described the religious/spiritual dimension of his experience as an effect of contrast, resulting from a "break from routine" and anticipating a return to that routine in a rejuvenated state. The visitor presented this contrast as a psychophysical process, an engagement in "communication" and an experience of "sensations" that changed not just perceptions, but perceptual tendencies. Such refocusing of one's perceptual lens could take a more self-reflective turn as well. One visitor, describing himself as both religious and spiritual although without any official religious affiliation, highlighted the gentler aspects of the perceptual environment of the park: "I experience God in one way through nature. It's almost a direct communion. I feel peaceful and quiet when I allow myself to experience the natural world." [57] For this visitor, nature provided the conditions for both self-reflection and communion with God. The two melded into one another by way of an environment that provided peace, quiet, and the opportunity to remain "undisturbed," as he further elaborated. Again, this bodily religious/spiritual experience arose through a contrast, where nature was seen to work its effects as much by what it lacked (conflict, noise, disturbance) as by what it contained. In sum, while drawing on themes ranging from biblically based faith to appreciation for a nature/civilization distinction to abstract self-reflection, the religious/spiritual dimension of these answers focused on feeling—on emotion and perceptual attitude.

While the theme of recreation involves the gentler aspects of park experience, the theme of the sublime, shared by 23 percent of visitors (n=34), concerns a grander scale. Under this theme visitors expressed a sense of awe and of being overwhelmed, or spoke in superlatives regarding the energy or power they felt in the park. As one might expect, such expressions could evoke thoughts of a transcendent being to parallel the experience that went beyond the bounds of ordinary experience (n=13). One respondent, describing herself as both religious and spiritual and her affiliation as "Lutheran/Episcopal," wrote, "Visiting this park reminds me that the creator of all living things is magnificent! The trees, rocks, and earth speak to my soul in a way that transcends current time and thoughts."[58] Here the physical aspects of the park spoke to the visitor in her transcendent interiority (her "soul") and in a way that implied a transcendent being above and beyond nature. The extraordinary aspect of the environment therefore found a mirror in the individuality of the visitor and in the singularity of a God who created "all living things." More often than not, however (n=21), visitors described an encounter with the sublime without such reference to a traditional God. A spiritual, non-practicing Presbyterian wrote that he was "a scientist who is awe-inspired by the beauty of the natural world." He described his spirituality: "My spiritual relationship to nature has changed from a relationship of supernatural/human orientation to a mankind *in* nature. A reverence for nature and your place in nature is far more pertinent/relevant to humankind than a relationship of blind faith to a supernatural 'being.'"[59] The experience of awe thus found its spiritual correlate in a relationship to nature by itself, a relationship, the respondent implied, grounded in reason and guided by practical concerns. Another respondent evoked the sublime by using a much different approach. Describing himself as spiritual and affiliating broadly with "Eastern religion" (with "lots of Native American beliefs tied in there"), he wrote that "everything 'speaks' of so much energy and beauty. It feels so awesome." He elaborated by saying that he found his spirituality everywhere, but mainly out of doors. The sublime energies of nature therefore provided fuel for the individualization of his spiritual path: rounding out his religious affiliations with Eastern and Native American religion, he wrote that "years of talking and listening and traveling and thinking and praying and writing have shaped the rest."[60] Taken together, these evocations of power and awe show that people of widely divergent religious/spiritual persuasions could find reinforcement for their beliefs and traditions in the same environment and with similar characterizations of their experience.

Whether in terms of beauty and serenity or power and energy, visitors to Yosemite gained religious/spiritual uplift through their sense experience. While visitors could self-consciously tie such experience to larger intellectual or social commitments, such links were not necessary for visitors to recognize their experience as religiously or spiritually significant. For many, the feeling of peace and energy was enough to satisfy them. More broadly, those who affirmed a more specific religious orientation, the most common being that of faith in a creator consonant with biblical tradition, found the park experience supportive of their beliefs. But the subtler shifts in perspective and the sensory impact of the park could also work independently, as it were, appropriated by individuals without reference to tradition. The status of this level of experience is debatable: Is it religious? Pre-religious? not-quite-yet religious? The preference for the term "spiritual" suggests that visitors recognize that such experience was religiously significant and yet distinct from religiosity at the same time. However one evaluates this fine distinction and/or paradox, it meshes with the public aspect of the park. Park officials have designed and managed the environment to facilitate certain kinds of experiences in the hopes of investing visitors in the park. The surveys show that those experiences and investments carried a strong religious and/or spiritual charge.

* * *

This chapter emphasized the harmony of nature and culture under the rubric of "spirit," in contrast with the accentuated difference between nature and culture that informed the spirituality described in the previous chapter. The reader will note a thematic tendency within the production and expression of spirituality: interpretive silences, invisibility of civilization, harmony of nature and culture. The connections among citizen, state, and nature come to expression indirectly, through strategies of implication rather than assertion. Such indirection figures as a constitutive feature of the secular management of spiritual experience.

4

Muir Woods

The Living Cathedral

Located just north of San Francisco on the Marin peninsula, Muir Woods National Monument consists of an old-growth redwood stand, many of its trees reaching over 250 feet in height. The largest trees stand in a flat valley floor nestled between the steep slopes of Mount Tamalpais, a 2,500-foot peak overlooking both the Pacific Ocean and the San Francisco Bay. Visitors arriving at the park find two parking lots just outside, a knot of urban life in an otherwise pastoral scene. Due to the high visitation of Muir Woods, such concentration of artificial structure is unavoidable, and managers seek to mitigate the effects of rows of automobiles and clumps of visitors by creating a series of stages for entering the park. From the second, more distant overflow parking lot (regularly filled during the summer months), visitors are directed to a small, paved opening into the forest. Lined with rough wooden fencing similar to that seen in Yosemite National Park, this small side trail ducks under thick foliage and follows the creek that flows down from Muir Woods.

This small excursion into nature empties into the main parking lot and the public bathrooms at its edge. Crossing the lot, one arrives at a small, half-open corral lined with boulders, bushes, benches, and rough fencing. In the center stands a small wooden building with two ticket windows. To the right, attached to the first building but set back farther into the trees, sits the visitor center: a modest hexagonal room lined with books and surrounding a relief model of the park under a glass case. Outside, the Park Service often staffs a small table with a ranger, seed cones, and bark. Lines at the ticket window can extend almost to the parking lot, and for those who are waiting, this mobile exhibit relieves frustration and begins to articulate the park visit. Finally, having paid the three dollars, and with park map in hand, one veers left to face the park entrance proper. On either side of the wide asphalt path, sturdy log pillars support a wooden crossbeam. Hanging from this beam a large plank is adorned with the name "Muir Woods National Monument." Beyond, a boardwalk leads into the forest.

At this point the flickering negotiations between nature and civilization—the parking lot, side trail, bathrooms, nature petitions, and entrance station—burrow underneath the green of the redwood canopy. The forest cannot be seen from "outside"—trees, bushes, and hillsides intervene. But in the shade of the high, overarching canopy, ground cover dissipates and shrinks in size. With the resultant opening of horizontal views, the massive trunks of the redwoods are fully exposed. The girth of these trees (with a diameter at chest height that can reach twenty-two feet) draws the eye up towards the sky-dappled vault some two hundred feet above. Necks and heads begin to crane upward. Foot traffic slows and moves in stutters. Attention to destination and companions now gives way before attention to the environment.

This passage into the park proper yields a curious incongruity. Having entered the definitive enclosure of the forest, visitors encounter an openness within the space of the park. Up to this point visitors and their attention have been channeled linearly, following a line from the parking lot to the entrance station. But now paths and lines of sight scatter within the bounds of the valley. To the right, up a terraced stairway, one can see a patio with a gift shop and snack bar beyond it. Up ahead and to the left, a wooden bridge crosses the creek and turns into a winding path through the forest. Straight ahead, the boardwalk leads to a round deck that empties onto two more paths, one leading up to the restrooms and circling back to the patio and gift shop, the other leading deeper into the forest. All around and only partially obscured by foliage, the wooden structures and the reddish-brown turf of the redwood floor extend into a bounded horizon.

With the confluence of paths and the presence of restrooms, gift shop, and snack bar, this part of the park maintains a high visitor density. This means noise and conversation, a counterweight to the quiet of the forest. Park managers take advantage of this sacrifice of a certain natural quality of the park to present their more formal and artificial exhibits. The round deck houses a miniature arboretum, its contents devoted to the redwood family around the world. On the outer edge of the deck, a cross-section of a redwood displays two thousand years of history in its rings. The formality of these exhibits might be seen to clash with the aesthetic of the park as a whole, an aesthetic that depends upon experiencing the trees in their native habitat and organic state. But such a clash is minimized by the placement of these exhibits within the most densely trafficked area of the park, where visitors are already paying more attention to each other and to the concerns of eating, buying, and visiting the restroom.

The concentration of visitors, noise, and circulation heightens and intensifies at the entry to the woods themselves. Stepping off from the deck to begin the loop trail up the valley, visitors cross a second threshold, a sound barrier where the noise of scuffling feet and conversation suddenly deadens and dissipates. Located between steep slopes, lacking virtually any bird population, and with a canopy over two hundred feet high, Muir Woods both absorbs and shuts out sounds that would otherwise be more prominent. The placement of the trails takes advantage of this acoustic feature of the forest. While the transition from one sound environment to another would be more gradual if not for the knot of paths, structures, and visitors just inside the forest dome, the concentration of noise near the entrance creates a sharp contrast to the quiet of the path that brings visitors to the center of the forest. Visitor behavior shifts accordingly. Separating themselves from the traffic circulation around the gift shop and restrooms and encountering the relatively steep drop in auditory sensation, visitors begin to speak in more hushed tones. Sporadic whispers replace loud exclamations. Further, as visitors begin to move in a more unidirectional flow (traffic around the loop tends to run in a counterclockwise direction), they need not pay as much attention to other visitors. This yields greater opportunity to stop, look up, or walk without the worry of a collision. With the relative stability in the forward field of vision along the path, attention is drawn more easily into the expanse of the valley and to the breadth and height of the redwoods within it.

Continuing farther up the path, one reaches the center of the park: Cathedral Grove. This grove contains the largest and tallest trees in the park, and its configuration provides the most distinctive vertical views in Muir Woods. Here visitors stand and look straight up into a high vault, the trunks of the redwoods converging like giant spokes into a center of needles, cloud, and sky. The redwoods depend upon a regular shroud of fog: the needles catch the moisture and drop it onto the forest floor below. While on clearer days the sunlight creates long, scattered beams through the canopy, foggy days provide an even more pervasive quiet in the depths of the forest floor, the muffled tone broken only by the restrained movements and conversation of visitors and the occasional tap of a water droplet falling from the dome above. The width and height of the tree trunks recall pillars that one might find in a cathedral, and the cool quiet within the forest cements the resemblance. Just as cavernous church interiors provide cool relief from the noise and heat of the city outside their walls, so too do the redwoods offer a calming endpoint to the journey from the Bay Area metropolis. A plaque in the middle of Cathedral Grove stresses this peaceful quality and highlights its religious aspect. Quoting a letter inviting the inaugural United Nations delegates to visit Muir Woods in 1945, the plaque reads: "Here in such a 'temple of peace' the delegates would gain a perspective and sense of time that could be obtained nowhere in America better than in such a forest. Muir Woods is a cathedral, the pillars of which have stood through much of recorded human history."[1]

More than any other feature of the park, the sensory environment of Muir Woods illustrates the management of spiritual experience by the Park Service. While interpretive rhetoric makes use of brief but strategically placed invocations of religious language, the shaping of visitor spirituality begins long before visitors reach Cathedral Grove. Whether through sound, sight, or the combination of the two, Muir Woods works its effects environmentally, largely avoiding demands for focus on particular points or ideas and instead promoting a roving eye and ear. This action of the park—its atmosphere—fosters a sense of envelopment rather than point-to-point relation: it is an organization of the environment that allows visitors to relax their perceptual devotion to tracking, concentrating, and completing sequences of tasks. As the analysis in this chapter will show, this atmosphere elicits one of the most common words that visitors used to describe the spiritual aspect of their experience: "peace." When given the opportunity to elaborate on this sense of spiritual peace, visitors seldom went beyond mentioning the quiet of the forest, the escape from their daily routine, or the solitude provided on the upper trails. This failure by visitors to pinpoint a number of discrete causes for or manifestations of their spirituality does not indicate vagueness about spirituality as a religious mode. As the preceding description has illustrated, the non-concentrated awareness that visitors call "spiritual" arises with a series of carefully articulated management practices. The complexity and specificity of spirituality do not, therefore, lie in common "feelings" that visitors express. Those feelings are designed, at the level of shared experience, to lack a complex structure. The catalysis of those feelings, however, shows a sophisticated and planned management of visitors' religiosity.

A History of Public and Private

In its historical origins, Muir Woods National Monument illustrates the ambiguous relations of public and private dimensions of land management.[2] Before its designation as a national monument in 1908, the present-day confines of Muir Woods belonged to William Kent, a native of the Bay Area who had gained a reputation as a reformer in Chicago city politics. Returning to the Bay Area, Kent purchased the remote forty-seven acre redwood stand that would later become Muir Woods. Located within a steep, relatively inaccessible valley on the southern slopes of Mount Tamalpais, Kent's property would have remained his private preserve if not for the catastrophic earthquake that hit San Francisco in 1906. This disaster, including devastating fires that followed the quake itself, destroyed much of the built environment around the Bay Area. With the need for wood and opportunity for profit that came with the rebuilding effort, Kent's property took on a value foreign to what originally attracted him to it as an idyllic forest retreat.

Many of the redwoods that had surrounded the Bay Area had already been logged by 1906. Kent's property had been spared not for its beauty or grandeur but because its location presented significant logistical problems for any logging effort. The earthquake and fires, however, changed the fundamental economic equations that had protected Kent's land. Shortly after the fire, Kent was approached by a local businessman, James Newlands, who wished to purchase the lot as part of a larger commercial operation. When Kent refused the offer, Newlands tried to take the land from him by other means.

On the surface, this story appears to be running along a simple line of public/private conflict. These ancient redwoods, threatened by private enterprise bent on consumption and destruction, will fall under protection of the public who value the trees in their living state. Closer analysis, however, reveals a more complicated picture. Prior to 1906, San Francisco's infrastructure consisted of a patchwork of public and private entities supplying various services. While the earthquake constituted a natural disaster of great proportions, the subsequent fires resulted largely from the failure of the social infrastructure. The lack of coordination among various agencies and, more directly, the inability to provide enough water to fight the fires led to destruction that far exceeded the damage caused by the quake itself. In the aftermath of this natural and social catastrophe, the establishment of a reliable water supply for the city took center stage. Within this context, the efforts of private enterprise to address these needs became more than simple business opportunities. Rather, such efforts took on a quality of public service.

These social and political developments put the history of Muir Woods in a new light, for James Newlands represented the North Coast Water Company that intended to turn Kent's property into a reservoir. Not only would the land produce profits by providing water to San Francisco, but as a bonus those redwoods could be logged and sold at the high market value generated by the reconstruction effort. The depiction of this enterprise as private exploitation of a business opportunity is accurate. However, the local political climate gave rise to a different view of Newlands's efforts, one that recognized the reservoir as a public good and Kent's attachment to the redwoods as a private concern.

It was in this context that Newlands, having been rebuffed by Kent, initiated legal proceedings to claim the land to further the public interest. San Francisco's need for a reservoir, Newlands argued, outweighed Kent's right to dispose of his private property as he saw fit. Newlands, who in addition to his company's wealth boasted an array of political contacts, saw a good chance of success in taking Kent's land by legal fiat. The political environment showed increasing favor toward San Francisco's drive to regularize and centralize its social services, and Newlands's efforts fit closely into conceptions of the public good that were rising to dominance at the time. The legal fight would unfold in local and state courts and would pit the public interest in a reservoir against the private wishes of an individual citizen. In such a context, Kent's attachment to his redwoods, however laudable as a reflection of his personal convictions, would fall on the weaker side of a public/private conflict as it rolled toward resolution.

But "public" and "private" were, then as now, malleable categories. An experienced politician, Kent saw an opportunity to preserve his land by way of a higher power: the Antiquities Act of 1906. Under this new federal legislation, any land within the public domain could, by executive decree, achieve protected status as a "national monument." Intended to preserve small areas of prehistoric and scientific value, the law was written in language broad enough to encompass lands of many different types. Put bluntly, the legislation required nothing more than the stroke of the U.S. president's pen to bring public land under protected status. With Theodore Roosevelt in the White House, a president who had shown great willingness to preserve land from commercial development, Kent saw that he could keep the redwoods in their organic state by donating the land to the federal government. Having arranged the transformation of his land into a National Monument, Kent had turned the tables of public and private. Now Newlands would no longer represent the public good against the private interests of an individual citizen, a battle to be waged in local courts. Rather Newlands would have to sue the federal government in federal court. Now a contest between the local interests of San Francisco and the national interest as expressed in federal law, Newlands's fight took on the character of a private concern: local and legitimate rights pitted against a higher, more authoritative conception of the public good. With the rise of such substantial obstacles, Newlands negotiated a retreat. He purchased an alternative tract of land from Kents and built his reservoir there.

This history shows that public and private do not rest as preestablished spheres or domains. Rather they are categories invoked, applied, and rearranged in the service of particular management regimes. In order to preserve his private interest, Kent turned his land into a particular form of public property. Most certainly he lost significant rights and options through such a maneuver. But he also established certain of his private interests as public ones, and national ones at that. In this way Kent gained a huge measure of protection for his intentions regarding his land. As a national monument his land took on symbolic value: it represented prehistoric nature, national heritage, and the public good itself.

These new meanings, or at least newly emphasized meanings, transformed the land into a park that provides visitors with their own identity, their place in the world. The rhetoric and design of the park aim to stimulate an individual connection with universal realities. This most all-encompassing sense of connection and belonging locates visitors in nature. But this sense is eminently social as well, referring to national origins. Both these senses of belonging and connection depend upon the state, the structure of organization that gives nature and America to the visitor. Further, the unity of this organization of individual and nature finds expression as spiritual experience.

Interpreting Individuality

To turn to religiosity and the public/private dynamic in contemporary times, it is useful to consider the most public and manifest communication of meaning in the parks: interpretation. Interpretation must be understood within the sensory context of the park. In its aim to situate the visitor within the environment, interpretation acts more as a guiding hand than as a self-sufficient manufacturer of meaning. Only from this perspective can one appreciate the power of the religious messages contained in Park Service rhetoric, a power that implicitly links individual experience with the state organization of the environment.

Recall the entrance station to the park. There, visitors receive a brochure, including a park map, an overview of redwood ecology, and a brief park history, but most continue on into the forest with only a cursory scan of the documents. On the round deck just inside the forest, visitors encounter the first interpretive exhibits they are likely to spend time viewing: the miniature arboretum and the cross-section of a large redwood. These exhibits convey the global significance of these trees. The entire world is represented through a selection of different redwoods, with maps of the globe marking the habitat of each species. An expansive historical narrative finds expression in small captions pasted onto the heartwood of the cross-section. The visitors milling around these exhibits, therefore, experience the trees in abstraction, as symbols of space and time on a global scale. In other words, the redwoods are not simply "here and now" within the space of the visit; rather, they link the visitor to the natural and cultural expanse of the world as a whole.

With the establishment of this global symbolic framework, visitors then proceed along the path toward the center of the forest. As mentioned earlier, this section of the boardwalk individualizes visitor experience. Dense, amorphous traffic circulation yields to a more linear pattern with greater space between visitor groups. This creation of relative solitude coincides with and intensifies the drop in the sound level created by the trees and the topography. Thus the rational and cognitive dimensions of the interpretive exhibits, symbolizing universal realities, preface a sensory and perceptual experience that takes on a more individual quality. This dynamic of the global and the particular, the universal and the individual, comes under a unifying religious metaphor upon the arrival in the center of the park: Cathedral Grove.

Within the grove an interpretive panel, mentioned briefly above, illustrates the religious aspect of this dynamic. The panel contains a black and white picture of an official gathering in the grove: a podium, surrounded by men in military uniform, stands before rows of seated guests in formal attire. The panel explains that in 1945, a group of international delegates met in San Francisco to discuss the establishment of the United Nations. After the death of President Franklin Delano Roosevelt in that year, the delegates were invited to Muir Woods to attend a memorial service. The panel explains: "Organizers of the event hoped that the beauty and serenity of Muir Woods would inspire the delegates to pursue the president's program for world peace as they met to establish the United Nations." Two quotations accompany the interpretive text. The first comes from Dag Hammerskjold, who in 1955 visited Muir Woods as secretarygeneral of the United Nations. Echoing the interpretation of Muir Woods as a place of peace, Hammerskjold is quoted as saying, "Persons who love nature find a common basis for understanding people of other countries, since the love of nature is universal among men of all nations." And linking this concern for peace more directly to the religious aspect of Cathedral Grove comes a section of the previously cited letter from Harold Ickes, secretary of the interior in 1945: "Here in such a 'temple of peace' the delegates would gain a perspective and sense of time that could be obtained nowhere in America better than in such a forest. Muir Woods is a cathedral, the pillars of which have stood through much of recorded human history."

I will return more specifically to the metaphor of the cathedral, but first note how the interpretive panel within the grove highlights the individual/universal dynamic. In recounting the memorial service for President Roosevelt, this interpretive panel sets the sensory environment of the forest ("the beauty and serenity of Muir Woods") within a world historical framework (the establishment of the United Nations and the quest for "world peace"). The panel links a particular environment (Muir Woods) to the general environment (the world). Further, through the stress on "beauty," "serenity," and "peace," the panel links the particularity of the environment to the individuated sensory experience created by park organization. In this way an individual experience of "peace," one facilitated by the organization of solitude in the sensory environment, is linked to the world in both space and time. The political dimension of this individual/universal link is further stressed in Dag Hammerskjold's remark. An individual experience ("persons who love nature") is linked to a project for universal political unity ("common basis for understanding"), one that transcends national identity and affirms the global state entity of the United Nations.

Note how this politically colored dynamic of individual and universal is religiously colored at the same time. Ickes's references to "cathedral" and "temple" impute a religious sanctification to the unifying political project of the United Nations. The panel does this not only through rhetoric, but through visual presentation as well. The photograph shows thick redwood trunks surrounding finely dressed delegates seated in rows before a podium, with a uniformed musical ensemble behind the podium. The "cathedral" metaphor activates the religious iconography of the photograph: the grove is a temple, the trunks are pillars, the delegates sit in rows as if in pews, the podium stands before them as a pulpit, and a uniformed choir sits behind the podium. The "natural" resemblance to a cathedral is echoed by a social organization of space similar to that of a worship service. In this way the panel affirms, both rhetorically and visually, the union of the religious and the political.

This iconography echoes the link between individual sensory experience and universal symbolic significance that informs the park environment more broadly. Ickes stated that in Muir Woods the delegates would gain "perspective" and a "sense of time" in furtherance of "peace." This is exactly what the preceding sensory and interpretive environment (from the round deck to Cathedral Grove) intends: that visitors frame their individual sensory experience within a perspective of world space and time. The interpretive panel encourages visitors to experience the same dynamic that those international delegates encountered: a sense of peace that is not merely individual, but operates at the most universal levels of political and religious significance. Through such a dynamic, the interpretive panel suggests, religion, nature, and the state form a fluid harmony.

Such use of religious metaphor echoes John Muir's characterization of Yosemite Valley discussed in Chapter 3. To recall: in advocating the designation of Yosemite as a National Park in 1890, Muir wrote that the valley "looks like some immense hall or temple lighted from above." Further, Muir stressed the unifying aspect of this religious metaphor. He wrote that in this temple, "Nature [has] gathered her choicest treasures . . . to draw her lovers into close and confiding communion with her."[3] In Cathedral Grove, the interpretive panel adds a more direct political dimension to such sentiments of religious and natural unity. But while the reference to the United Nations, an organization formed well after Muir's death, obviously invokes a different political context from the one in which Muir was writing, nevertheless Muir himself also made direct links among religion, nature, and the state.

In the large fold-out map and guide for the nature trail through Muir Woods, only one religious reference appears, in the form of quotation from John Muir that reads:

> Any fool can destroy trees. They cannot run away; and if they could, they would still be destroyed—chased and hunted down as long as fun or a dollar could be got out of their bare hides, branching horns, or magnificent bole backbones. Few that fell trees plant them, nor would planting avail much toward getting back anything like the noble primeval forests. It took more than 3,000 years to make some of these trees in these western woods—trees that are still standing in perfect strength and beauty, waving and singing. . . . Through all the wonderful, eventful centuries since Christ's time—and long before that—God has cared for these trees, saved them from drought, disease, avalanches, and a thousand straining, leveling tempests and floods; but He cannot save them from fools—only Uncle Sam can do that.[4]

Here Muir proposed a partnership between God and the state in the protection of the forests. To stress, this is a partnership: Muir did not equate God with the state by any means. But the survival of the forest, Muir suggested, required that the two act in perfect accord: God would assert his sovereignty in the domain of nature (over "drought, disease, avalanches . . . tempests and floods"), and the state would assume sovereignty over the domain of the human (the actions of "fools"). In this way, Muir's words set individual freedom as the limit of God's sovereignty.[5] At the same time and in the same movement, this theological formulation also defines the sovereignty of the state: extending over individual freedom and ending at nature. Here individual freedom and nature mark the boundary between, and thus constitute, the sovereignty of God and the state.

While Muir's words establish a divine/political partnership, they do not invoke nationalism. "Uncle Sam" does not refer to America as a nation or to "the people" as a cultural unit. Rather, "Uncle Sam" represents the American government—the state, the system of order that regulates relations within the nation. The reference to "fools" reinforces this distinction between nation and state. While a nationalist might portray the reckless pursuit of recreation and wealth as departures from a singular, communal, cultural identity ("un-American" behavior), Muir stressed the individual, plural, and chaotic character of such actions. According to Muir, "any" individual could destroy these ancient creations. As a group, these "fools" did not act in concert but as an uncoordinated amalgamation. The pursuit of pleasure and profit here has a mindless character that calls for regulation, not a foreign character that calls for expulsion or transformation. In sum, Muir's words apply to individuals acting in a disorganized manner in the pursuit of instinctual and/or economic desires, and these form the basis for his call for the coordination of divine and state sovereignty.[6]

Taken as a whole, the interpretive panel, the brochure for the self-guided trail, and the environment per se serve to naturalize and universalize the state authority that governs the park. Consider the regulations that channel visitor behavior, including prohibitions against walking off the trail, eating outside designated areas, playing music within the park, and a host of other proscriptions. Through the facilitation of spiritual experience, these proscriptions become reflections of nature rather than dictates of an alien authority. By investing visitors in solitude, park managers legitimize the management of visitors' bodies so as to keep them out of each other's way. By generating spiritual associations between the quiet, serene environment and world peace, park managers gain implicit support for their disciplining of park visitors, making disobedience an assault on nature and on the harmony it can elicit among humans. In this way the symbols of state authority, embodied most notably in the paramilitary uniform of park rangers, take on the sign of nature and make the state the protector not only of the forest, but of harmonious living at the broadest level. The set of associations described above link embodied solitude, the experiential environment, and public, institutionalized authority. Through this linkage, private, individualized spirituality takes on the quality of public religion.

The religious dimension of park interpretation, while central, exhibits a principle of economy. "Ranger talks," given several times daily, tend not to use religious language. The bulk of interpretive discourse, including programs, the nature guide, and the panels together, concerns redwood ecology. The modest amount of space devoted to religion, and the consequent lack of complex elaboration, facilitates the individual construction of religious meanings. As suggested by the analysis of the individual/universal dynamic, such modesty and simplicity are intentional. The Park Service has no intention of creating a communal consciousness among park visitors with regard to religious meaning. It does, however, intend to facilitate a multitude of individualized spiritual connections to the park, deepening visitor commitment to conservation of the space and, implicitly, to the state authority that regulates such conservation.

Visitor Spirituality

In analyzing visitor experience in Muir Woods, a comparison with the Yosemite surveys provides a useful starting point. First, one should note that certain differences in the two park environments shape visitor experience in fundamental ways. Muir Woods offers no overnight accommodations within the park, meaning that almost all visitors complete their visit within the space of a few hours. While there are several miles of trails that climb the steep slopes of the mountains, the vast majority of visitors stay on the main 1.5-mile loop trail along the flat valley floor. As mentioned earlier, this most easily accessible area of the park also contains the largest trees. The combination of spectacular attraction, flat terrain, and proximity to San Francisco (a forty-minute drive) leads to high visitation: the park is open 365 days and receives over 800,000 visitors yearly.

In terms of demographic characteristics, one finds modest but telling differences that separate Muir Woods visitors from those surveyed in Yosemite. Recall that in comparison with the general population of the United States, Yosemite visitors were, according to my survey (discussed in Chapter 3), predominantly white, well-educated, and affluent. Surveys of visitors to Muir Woods, gathered just outside the entrance and visitor center during the summer of 2003, found some of these tendencies to be even more pronounced.[7] Thus, of the 150 respondents, roughly 83 percent (n=124) identified themselves as white—a statistic virtually identical to that of Yosemite visitors. Also similar to Yosemite, 60 percent of Muir Woods visitors (n=90) reported an income over fifty thousand dollars in the previous year. However, responses in Muir Woods were weighted toward the higher end of the scale: 31 percent (n=41) reported an income over one hundred thousand dollars, as compared to 21 percent (n=31) for Yosemite. As for level of education, statistics showed a similar weighting towards the higher end: 39 percent of Muir Woods respondents (n=58) had postgraduate education (compared to 30 percent for Yosemite (n=46)). While sharing many of the same distinctions from the general public, therefore, Muir Woods visitors showed an even stronger tendency toward affluence and higher education than did visitors to Yosemite.

In terms of attitudes and sense of identity, the two visitor populations had additional similiarities. Two thirds of Muir Woods visitors (n=100) accepted the term "spiritual" as a self-identification, with 37 percent (n=56) preferring the term "spiritual" to "religious" and 29 percent (n=44) indicating that they were comfortable with either term. These statistics correspond well with responses in Yosemite. Also in line with Yosemite responses, Muir Woods visitors show a strong attachment to nature: over three quarters of respondents (78 percent, n=117) indicated that "encounters with nature" were "very" or "absolutely" important in their lives. And in connecting religiosity with nature, the tendencies of

Income

	Frequency	Percent
No response	18	12.0
Less than 20k	9	6.0
20–50k	33	22.0
50–100k	43	28.7
Over 100	47	31.3
Total	150	100.0

Highest grade completed

	Frequency	Percent
No response	1	.7
Pre-high school	1	.7
High school	5	3.3
Some college	30	20.0
College	55	36.7
Postgraduate	58	38.7
Total	150	100.0

Race

	Frequency	Percent
No response	3	2.0
Asian	3	2.0
Black or African-American	5	3.3
Native Hawaiian or other Pacific Islander	1	.7
White	124	82.7
Other	14	9.3
Total	150	100.0

the two visitor populations again correspond: over half of Muir Woods visitors (53 percent, n=79) said their religion/spirituality was "very" or "absolutely" connected to their appreciation for nature, while a significant minority (29 percent, n=43) said the two were "somewhat" connected. In total, therefore, 81 percent of visitors (n=123) were willing to ascribe a considerable degree of significance to nature when describing their religiosity, and even among those who consider themselves neither spiritual nor religious (n=25), a considerable minority were willing to ascribe religious/spiritual significance to their park visit (n=7).[8]

Religious/Spiritual Person?

	Frequency	Percent
Religious, not spiritual	20	13.3
Spiritual, not religious	56	37.3
Spiritual and religious	44	29.3
Not spiritual, not religious	26	17.3
No response	4	2.7
Total	150	100.0

The breadth of possible meanings associated with "spiritual," "religious," and "nature" makes more specific analysis impossible at the level of categorical responses. Hence I turn to the comments section of the survey that fleshes out these terms and their associations. While visitors use religious language in a wide variety of ways, certain trends do appear. In terms of aesthetics, visitors tend to privilege the language of emotion, perception, and "feeling" when expressing the religious/spiritual significance of their experience. Further, and as seen in the previous chapter, this tendency finds expression in the theme of perspective, and specifically through a spiritually significant sense of "connection." Both the perceptual and perspectival dimensions of visitor spirituality show the influence of the managed environment.

This influence can be found at an exceedingly modest level. Recall that the term "cathedral" served as an overarching metaphor in the interpretive presentation of the forest. This religious association was sometimes echoed in conversation within the forest. For example, while photographing the central grove, one visitor exclaimed to a companion, "We're in the cathedral now!" Another couple sprawled over a bench, the woman lying on her back with her head in the man's lap. "Beautiful, isn't it," I commented, referring to the beams of sunlight streaming through the foliage. "Just found heaven," the man replied. Such easy adoption of and appreciation for religious metaphor show the fluidity of religious communication in the park. The momentous and world-encompassing religious rhetoric of park interpretation may serve simply as a light and suggestive frame, one adaptable to an offhand remark or the casual bliss of an afternoon in the park.

Only a few visitors (n=5) made explicit reference to such a metaphor in their surveys, but their responses show the wide range of religious backgrounds to which such rhetoric could appeal. One couple who identified themselves as both religious and spiritual, claiming "scientific creationism" as the tradition to which they belonged, singled out the allusion to religious architecture: "When we're here, we feel we're in the cathedral of God: the trees are pillars, the leaves, stain[ed] glass."[9] Another respondent made a similar observation, although here stressing a negative dimension. Preferring the term "spiritual," he identified himself as "ex Catholic, now a pagan" and explained, "This is my religion. . . . This is God's church. I've seen a ton of beautiful churches and none come close to this."[10] Moreover, visitor uses of religious language did not need to be strictly tied to park interpretation. Consonant with but moving beyond the structural metaphor, for example, one "spiritual" visitor, identifying herself simply as "Protestant," said, "We were about two hundred yards in and I said to my husband, 'This is better than church.' So peaceful."[11] Here the visitor compared subjective experience rather than objective structures. Visiting Muir Woods, she asserted, was better than "going to" church—an environment that is not simply architecturally superior, but more subjectively affective. Further, such sentiments did not need to be associated with a disavowal of organized religion. One respondent, who preferred the term "religious," echoed the "spiritual" sentiments: "I feel more connected in a peaceful park camping than I do at my church on Sunday morning."[12]

Finally, in another expression of tension with organized religion, a visitor from the Bay Area said that his brother calls Muir Woods "his church." I asked the visitor if he would say the same, and he paused before answering. In his survey he indicated a preference for the term "spiritual" as opposed to "religious," and when asked to which religious tradition he felt he belonged, he wrote "Buddhist, Christian, student of life." Perhaps this open-ended religious affiliation made him shy away from the term "church." He replied: "I'd say it's my temple, just to be different."[13] Such comments reflect the power of religious metaphor across religious differences. Through the name "Cathedral Grove" and the judicious emphasis on its religious associations, park interpretation resonates with perspectives ranging from scientific creationism" to "spiritual" Protestantism to "Buddhist, Christian, student of life." Here a semantic core of modest size informs a wide range of religious perspectives.

Regarding the aesthetic dimensions of visitor spirituality, one may first note the relatively modest and traditional expressions of religious appreciation. These can be found largely in references to the biblical narrative of creation, a theme that appeared in 25 percent (n=38) of Muir Woods surveys and at a rate nearly identical to that of Yosemite visitors (25 percent, n=37). For instance, when asked if there was anything religious and/or spiritual about her experience in the park, one respondent who identified herself as a Baptist wrote "sure." She explained simply, "Wildlife is a part of God's creation that I can appreciate and enjoy."[14] A Roman Catholic responded similarly, writing, "I enjoy nature as God created it and prefer to be outdoors instead of indoors."[15] A Unitarian respondent elaborated on such sentiments: "The grandeur of this park plus the complexity and beauty of nature always make me think of a God, a creator, who designed our world."[16] While this last response points to a more rationalistic experience, citing "complexity" and design, verbs in all three responses like "appreciate" and "enjoy," and nouns like "grandeur" and "beauty" point to an aesthetic evaluation of the religious significance of the park. With their references to God and creation, these responses invoked a traditional theological context based in Genesis and thereby expressed an indirect experience of God, through an encounter with God's works. This indirect quality may explain the use of the generalized aesthetic evaluation "enjoyment." Without going into great detail, these tradition-oriented responses bespoke a more distanced appreciation of nature as an expression of relationship between God and humans.

In contrast to these responses, expressions of more direct aesthetic experiences of God in nature (n=15) were not accompanied by references to creation, a creator, or evidence for God's existence. For instance, one respondent who identified herself as "I guess Protestant, but mostly 'Gen-X spiritual'" wrote that "to look at/be in nature is to talk with God."[17] Another "spiritual" respondent who identified herself simply as "Protestant" echoed this sentiment: "This is one of the best places to see God."[18] An Episcopal respondent, identifying herself as both religious and spiritual, wrote, "I feel God in most all of nature."[19] Such responses emphasized a concrete perceptual encounter, not simply an "enjoyment" of nature, but rather direct engagement with God. Such responses did not rely on biblical narrative. Rather, they derived their authority from individual experience itself, from "feeling," and used terms that expressed more immediate engagement: talking with, being with, seeing.

And of course the indirect (creation-oriented) and the direct (sensing God) aesthetic experiences need not be seen as mutually exclusive. One respondent, describing himself as "religious" and a Protestant, put the two modes of experience side by side: "I feel all God's creation should be taken care of and viewed for its beauty. It makes me feel close to God when I'm in nature. I can speak to him more clearly."[20] Here the more distanced appreciation, an abstract ethical position that "God's creation should be taken care of" and a genteel aesthetic injunction to view nature "for its beauty," prefaced a statement of a feeling of closeness and an ability to communicate clearly with God. One United Methodist respondent expressed the juxtaposition of direct and indirect encounter in seemingly paradoxical terms: "This experience (visiting Muir Woods) was very spiritual for me. The beauty of nature is GOD! I was alarmed at some of the park dedications to people / from people. For nature is GOD'S creation—not connected to man at all even if his money helped preserve it."[21] On its face, such a response may seem logically contradictory. Here nature was God and God's creation at the same time. A Presbyterian respondent, describing herself as both "religious" and "spiritual," stated the contradiction most directly: "I feel that nature is the representation of God to us and also a gift to us from God. Out of doors is where I feel closest to God."[22] These responses indicate that tension between direct and indirect encounter with God was not universally self-evident among visitors. The respondents encountered

God through/as "the beauty of nature," an experience that yielded a feeling of closeness with God. Such responses indicate that any particular theological commitment does not correlate with any specific aesthetic experience of God. In this way feeling, perception, and appreciation for "beauty" resonate across a range of official and institutional theological differences and syntheses.

These emphases on embodied sensation highlight the theme of perception that appeared in 38 percent of the surveys (n=57), a figure again comparable with the responses gathered in Yosemite (43 percent, n=64). Such emotive and perceptual appreciation manifested in a general preference for the language of "feeling" as seen in testimonies such as "I have strong spiritual feelings when I am out in nature"; "[Nature] allows me to feel connected and as one with the earth"; and "Spirituality is about feeling and appreciating beauty and energy."[23] Within this theme, responses that did not mention God (n=28) tended to discuss emotive and perceptual experience in greater detail than those that did. For instance, one respondent who identified with no religious tradition wrote, "The redwoods, to me, have a very deep and spiritual meaning. The energy flow influences my emotions as I walk among them. Nature . . . reflects our inner feelings and beliefs."[24] Another who followed "[her] own belief system" wrote, "Feeling close to nature, the sun on your face, the smell of the woods provides my own spiritual guidance."[25] One couple who preferred the term "spiritual" and identified themselves as "Jewish Buddhist etc." found the connection between sense experience and spirituality to be self-evident. When asked if there was anything spiritual about their experience they wrote simply, "Yes—waves in the babbling brook and the light through the trees."[26]

In other respects, responses in Muir Woods displayed similar characteristics to the theme of perception as it appeared in Yosemite. In describing the spiritual dimension of their experience, a large proportion (42 out of 57; 74 percent) used language consonant with the recreational paradigm: "beauty," "peace," and "harmony." A smaller but still significant proportion (29 out of 57; 51 percent) wrote in superlatives of the awesome and overwhelming power of the environment, thereby invoking the theme of the sublime. Again, it is important to note that while these themes could easily appear in tandem with expressions of traditional biblical faith, they were just as, if not more likely, to appear without any such reference, even at the most general level of invoking the terms "God" or "higher power" (28 out of 57; 49 percent).

While differing in the degree of descriptive specificity, these examples of the theme of perception nevertheless suggest continuity at the level of aesthetics. Further, such continuity that glides over theological differences found echoes at a higher level of abstraction, namely, within the theme of perspective. Appearing in 35 percent (n=52) of Muir Woods responses, and again paralleling the prevalence of this theme in the Yosemite surveys (38 percent, n=57), a sense of a spiritual shift in perspective was expressed through a variety of subthemes. But, and again paralleling the case of Yosemite, one of these subthemes predominated: "connection" (23 percent, n=35). Whether referring to God or spirituality, visitors again and again used the word "connection" to describe the religious/spiritual aspect of their experience in Muir Woods. Furthermore, this term not only provides a thematic foundation to visitor responses, but also a logic of integration, one that ties together the various emphases discussed above (such as focus on God versus focus on the individual, reason versus emotion/perception, direct experience versus indirect experience).

This multifaceted integration centers on the link between the individual and the universal. To begin with a more traditional theological formulation, one can see the theme of connection in relation to creation. One Lutheran respondent wrote, "Being outdoors in nature reminds me of how small we really are in relation to all of god's creations. It reminds me to enjoy the simple things that god gave. So I would say when outdoors, I feel more spiritual connection."[27] Here an aesthetically informed perceptual experience—human smallness in comparison to the redwoods—recalled biblical narrative. The experience "reminds" the respondent of a particular story in which the world was a gift from God to humans. The respondent linked her individual experience to a universal one. From the perceptual impression of smallness with respect to the particular environment of Muir Woods, the respondent linked herself to all humanity ("we") in relation to the totality of nature ("all of god's creations"). These links of aesthetics, memory, and narrative on a concrete level, and humanity, nature, and God at a more abstract level, found expression under a single, all-encompassing category: "spiritual connection."

Moving away from direct reference to biblical creation, one can find the focus on linkage in the words of a "spiritual" respondent who identified herself as a Southern Baptist, Catholic, and Buddhist. She wrote, "My wholeness as a human being cannot be separated from my faith. My faith cannot be disconnected from nature. I cannot be whole unless I am in connection with the earth. From it I learn to care for myself, my fellows, and my world. Nowhere else is God's perfect web of life so intimately available."[28] This series of connections began with the individual and branched out to the most universal level. The respondent's "wholeness as a human being" stood distinct from but inextricably linked to her "faith," which in turn connected with "nature," the whole of which connected the respondent to the "earth." The respondent emphasized the progressively expanding character of this series in her summary statement, "From it I learn to care for myself, my fellows, and my world." Similar to the set of connections evoked in Cathedral Grove, these connections range from individual to society to world, the whole of which found expression for this respondent as an intimate contact with universal reality: "God's perfect web of life."

Such connection between the individual and the universal need not focus on a specific conception of divinity, either. One "spiritual" Buddhist expressed her sense of connection: "I believe a higher power is connected to beauty in nature—it provides a sense of peace and tranquility as well as a sense of being connected to a larger more meaningful universe."[29] In specifying a "sense of peace and tranquility," the respondent emphasized an internal, emotive, and individual experience. At the same time, this internal orientation led outward to "a larger and more meaningful universe." The middle term that allowed such a dual orientation consisted of an unspecified "higher power" linked to "the beauty of nature." This power working through beauty thus catalyzed an individual/universal harmony. Another respondent, a practitioner of Siddha Yoga meditation, expressed a similar idea in free form prose: "Feeling of connection to nature/the earth and connection of nature/trees being grounded/deep rooted and myself connecting with my inner self."[30] Here the respondent described two vectors of connection—one linked to "nature/the earth," the other linking "myself" to "my inner self." Thus the two vectors were oriented toward the universal and the individual, respectively. Here the particularity of the redwood environment served as a middle term: the "deep rooted" quality of the redwoods served as an analogy for the connection of self with self within a more universal whole.[31] Finally, a respondent who attends a "'new age' church—religious science" made this emphasis on individual/universal connection even more explicit: "Connecting to beauty and to nature returns me to my essence—my home—my place in the universe." Elaborating on this response, she continued: "I agree with John Muir that connecting to nature is one way of connecting to the universe. I do energetic healing and I find that being in natural settings rejuvenates me and returns me to harmony within myself and with all there is."[32] Once again, this respondent stressed how an outward orientation ("connecting to beauty and to nature") reached inward at the same time ("returns me to harmony within myself"), in a dual orientation that connected the individual with the universal: "All there is."

While having a variety of religious affiliations, respondents described shifts in perception and perspective along similar lines. Such an observation does not imply that the content of their comments is similar. Rather, it shows that while the content of their spirituality differs, the grammar of spirituality, its logical structure, retains its form across the comparison. Structure is not essence. Language matters: the invocation of "God" and "creation" placed certain respondents within certain narrative traditions that separated them from those who eschewed theistic language. But the shared grammar of spirituality implies a different and higher level of social integration.

While differing in terms of religious self-identification, the respondents expressed commonality as individuals relating to universal realities that transcend their particular viewpoints, a solidarity that found expression in a number of responses as "spiritual connection." Given the generality and abstraction of this spirituality, its role as a principle of social organization may appear unimpressive. But when seeing this organization as one of difference as opposed to a shared identity, one begins to appreciate the social logic of spirituality. Precisely in avoiding the complicated and rigorous demands of communal identity, ideas about spirituality forge what, following Edmund Husserl, one might term "intermonadic community."[33] Strictly speaking, this is no community at all. Rather this term expresses a principle of overlapping noninterference. Through the rhetoric of spirituality, individuals of the most varied stripe express a sense of connection to an all-encompassing and transcendent social unity in the same place and at the same time, but without having to confront any differences that separate the visitors from each other, indeed, without having to engage each other at all. Such an expression of social unity is not logically contradictory, for this unity is structural and not essential.[34] According to the logic of the individual/universal dynamic, "spiritual connection" insists upon the individual differentiation and plurality of all that is tied together within the universal. Such individual differentiation requires a semantic core of great breadth and capacity, and this is exactly what the category "spiritual" provides.

What does this sense of spiritual connection between the individual and the universal have to do with the state? Note that this sense of connection refers to a certain organization of experience rather than a specific, embodied entity; visitors affirm a sense of place within a particular order. When visitors express a feeling of belonging or harmony within an environment such as Muir Woods, they express an investment in the state organization of the park. While the order of the park is recognized as nature, it cannot be easily distinguished from the order mandated by the state through the Park Service. By facilitating a sense of spiritual connection between individual visitors and the universal reality of nature, the state garners implicit allegiance for its structures of authority that wear the cloak of nature.

In sum, these surveys illustrate how the religious logic of park management (individuating sensory experience and setting it within a universal symbolic framework) finds expression as spiritual experience among park visitors. The themes of calmness, tranquility, peacefulness, and all-encompassing spiritual connection reflect implicit allegiance to the state structures that organize the environment. Of course, there is no necessary correlation between the park environment and the spiritual experience of visitors. One could, and many visitors did, assert that the experience of the park had no religious or spiritual significance. But the structures of the park environment, and particularly the interpretive environment, show a high degree of resonance with the religious and spiritual responses of park visitors.

Communicating the Incommunicable

For all the links between park interpretation and visitor comments, the word "spiritual" did not appear in the texts available within the park. This absence bespeaks the power of the separation of church and state that governs official rhetoric. The references to "cathedral" and "temple" occurred within a quotation and echo the name of the grove. Likewise the proposed partnership of God and the state also occurred in a quotation drawn from the park's namesake. In this way religious allusions were presented not as authoritative pronouncements from park management but as objects of cultural heritage—as explanations or elaborations of names, historical events, and founding figures. This oblique character of official communication shows a strong sensitivity to the legally mandated distinction between educating and preaching. Further, one should not lose sight of the power of social propriety in maintaining church/state separation. In response to questions and suggestions that I posed, park rangers indicated that certain avenues of religious expression would be simply out of place. One ranger, for example, said that in the course of an interpretive program, it would feel "inappropriate" to be "evangelistic," no matter how noble or secular the cause.[35] Given both the legal and the social context, therefore, how do ideas about spirituality avoid these barriers to communication? Put another way, and anticipating the argument below, how is spirituality channeled by these barriers in such a way as to affirm the public character, and state authority, of the park?

To answer these questions I interviewed rangers and volunteers in Muir Woods, both formally and informally, and arrived at the following conclusion. The religious significance of the park travels across the church/state barrier through a paradox. That is, the incommunicability of the park's spiritual significance informs the spiritual experience of park visitors most fundamentally.[36] This incommunicability does not reside in any mysterious essence of the park. Rather, this incommunicability refers to the requirement that visitors experience the meaning of the park "on their own." If the spiritual significance of the park were contained within a communication, then one of spirituality's defining characteristics—namely, its quality as an expression of a person's individuality and uniqueness—would be destroyed. Yet the task of interpretation is to connect the park to the visitors in their individuality. In short, making the park visit personally meaningful for the visitor requires that visitors experience meaning without that meaning being communicated. Put in the form of a paradox, interpretation requires communication without communication.

This paradox is illustrated most clearly in my interview with Marcus Combs, an interpretive ranger in Muir Woods. Combs was something of a rarity in the Park Service: a local resident who managed to obtain a career-level post in a park near where he grew up. While identifying himself as a Christian (adding for emphasis "I go to church, I believe in Jesus Christ. And I believe a lot of people here worship the creation and not the creator"), Combs expressed a preference for the category "spiritual" over "religious" when discussing the communicative task of interpretation. His words indicate the centrality of incommunicability for spirituality and interpretation: "A lot of people come up to me and say this is a spiritual site or a moving site. And some people will feel that they don't know what it is [inaudible]. And as an interpreter, I feel that I'm not allowed or not supposed to say that. In fact I wouldn't want to say, 'Here you are in a spiritual place.' The idea is self-discovery, because that's half the joy, if not most of the joy, of the site [which] is walking in and discovering for yourself what it is for you to be here."[37]

Combs emphasized the individuality of spiritual experience in several ways. First, he portrayed visitors as taking the initiative in expressing spiritual views. His description implied that the spiritual significance of the park spoke directly to the visitors, evoking linguistic expression without the verbal prompting of rangers. Given the social structure of the park, where visitors are almost never placed in situations that encourage them to speak with other visitors outside of their own group, spiritual experience would thus take on a private and intimate quality. The adjective "moving," with its connotations of an internal, emotive experience, further shaded this spiritual expression in the direction of individuality.

Second, and in line with the focus on individuality, Combs stressed the incommunicability of spiritual experience. Visitors feel something that they label "spiritual" and then seek clarification: they express their inability to articulate their experience and implicitly call for help from the ranger. Here Combs denied this call in three ways: legal ("not allowed"), social ("not supposed to"), and personal ("wouldn't want to"). Justifying this trifold injunction of incommunicability, Combs centered on individuality explicitly, highlighting the perceptual, perspectival dimension of experience. Tying his refusal to communicate to the mission statement of the park (to provide for "enjoyment"), Combs stated that the "joy" the park provides lies in individualized action ("self-discovery"), stressing embodiment ("walking in") and self-reference ("for yourself"). This self-reference should be specified: Combs did not state that individual visitors discover, on their own, "what the place means." Rather, Combs stated that visitors experience individuality itself: "what it means for you to be here." This more complicated phrasing locates meaning not in the place but in the relationship of the place to the visitor and thereby sets up a structure of self-reference. From Comb's perspective, this is the true or privileged meaning of the park: relating the individual to his or her individuality in that space.

Given this assertion of the incommunicability and individuality of spiritual experience in the park, one might assume that there was little left for the ranger to do. However, this is not the case. In fact, the incommunicability and individuality of experience are built into a theory of interpretation. Elaborating on his role as an interpreter, Combs continued:

> "My job as I see it is to explain some of the questions for these trees that make them so majestic. Why are there fire scars? How can they survive this? How can they survive so long? What is it about them? And answer those things, and sometimes through those things you can get across what we call the tangible/intangible. . . . It's a thing where you want to affect the visitor mentally—or I should say emotionally or intellectually—so when they leave they will feel a part of the place. And half that they discover on their own just through walking through the woods. And just a little push here or there. Just a question you might lead them with will guide them . . . in the sense of 'this is a place with something special. [inaudible] It's peaceful.'"[38]

Combs's initial description of his role focused on explanation, on communicating factual information, about the trees. However, according to him this presentation of information was not value-neutral. Rather, it had a specific intention: to "get across" the "tangible/intangible." Here Combs expressed the meaning of interpretation in the form of a paradox. Combs did not say that his interpretation has any specific meaning. If he had expressed such a meaning, then the tangibility of factual information would yield the tangibility of a specified meaning, and the intangibility of the park would be destroyed. Instead, Combs communicated the paradox itself. In other words, Combs communicated the incommunicable. Through this paradox, Combs suggested, the park communicates individuality to the individual.

Combs's portrayal of this communication of experience resonates with the broader interpretive environment. Recall that while Combs asserted that "half" the experience came just from walking in the woods, he continued to say, "And just a little push here or there. Just a question you might lead them with will guide them . . . in the sense of 'this is a place with something special. [inaudible] It's peaceful.'"[39] Such leading questions have been discussed earlier in this chapter, notably in the context of the interpretive brochure that addresses the visitor, saying, "Lift your eyes. Can you guess why this is called Cathedral Grove?" Following this question, the brochure made no direct explication of the religious significance of the grove. Rather it discussed the role of fog in redwood forest ecology, stating, "To reach such majestic heights, these giants require a special spot amid the coastal fog belt."[40] Combs echoed this structure in his comments, saying that while he refused to communicate the "spiritual" significance of the park directly, he saw his role as explaining what made these trees "majestic" by asking and answering questions concerning fire ecology, questions that led the visitor to a sense of "something special." In both these cases, asking and failing to answer directly questions of spiritual or religious significance placed the call for an answer in the individual visitor. At this point the visitor was not, however, in a neutral position.

As a tourist destination, Muir Woods puts most visitors in a new, unfamiliar place. Interpreters can count on the fact that when feeling a call to answer questions of religious or spiritual significance, visitors will search their immediate environment for those answers. In the case of the brochure, the allusion to religious architecture comes on the same page as the quotation from John Muir that constructs a partnership between God and the state in promoting conservation. For both the brochure and for Combs, any induced call for spiritual meaning could draw on the name "Cathedral Grove" and the memory of an experience of church, as do several surveys discussed earlier. These associations resonate with the perceptual dynamics of the environment, such as a sense of smallness and majesty, which are in turn intensified by other interpretive exhibits such as the redwood cross-section and the broad temporal scale it evokes. Combs offered a specific example that echoes this latter exhibit: "And it's describing that we are an old growth forest, and what that means. One of the things I'll say is, 'If you took everything in this valley that somebody has placed here, and you took it away in your mind's eye, you can very easily picture what this valley looked like a thousand years ago. And you know what? Some of these trees were here a thousand years ago.' And just leave a pregnant pause there and let them think about that. And there's a little push there about how special the place is." So while one cannot "control" how visitors may answer questions of spiritual significance for themselves, interpreters can construct and/or anticipate the environment to which visitors will appeal for such answers. As Combs put it, "You tell them that and they'll make up their minds. They'll get the connections, that something is at work here." Summarizing the incommunicability that informs interpretation, Combs concluded: "So there are certain things you can do without saying anything that will maybe make them use their senses, make them think, or make their minds go in different directions."[41]

This strategy of incommunicability stimulates individualization. Lacking clear and explicit official pronouncements of meaning, individuals must attribute any meaning to their own reflections, experience, and identity (connecting these to nature and/or the park, but not to a recognized social agent). Differences may arise in the specific meanings that individual visitors formulate. Or not. But the operative effect remains the same: an attribution of meaning arising from one's own individuality.

This individualizing aspect of park experience universalizes at the same time, and in this way the social function of "spirituality," namely, finessing the religious differences within the visiting public, becomes clearer. This more social focus informed my interviews with Ranger Heather Boothe. Boothe had intended to become a teacher before she joined the Park Service. While she had visited Muir Woods as a child and had positive associations with the park, her choice to become a ranger evolved out of her teaching experience: she had always found "experiential learning" to be the most stimulating aspect of her work. Combining her personal attachment to the outdoors (she stated: "These are places that calm me and de-stress me and whenever the world is getting a little wild I find myself going to nature") with her desire to teach across a range of ages and abilities, Boothe was eventually drawn to a career in the Park Service. Boothe asserted that she was not religious "in the traditional sense of the word" and preferred the term "spiritual" to describe her attachment to the park. Echoing Combs, she highlighted incommunicability in spirituality and interpretation, focusing particularly on the social and universalizing function of spirituality:

> "It's an equalizing thing. Because someone who's Muslim, someone who's Buddhist, someone who's Christian, someone who's—I can think of so many other religions—Wicca, they're all going to come here and feel a spiritual connection. And whether they attribute that to their God or gods, or whether they're an atheist and they just feel the power of it, it's completely irrelevant which church they worship in. When you walk into the Cathedral Grove, you know why it's called that. It's something that we don't have to explain to anyone, that it's a very powerful place."[42]

Here Boothe addressed the diversity within the visiting public. At the level of religion alone, she suggested, one could not even name all the worldviews that might inform visitor experience. Through the experience of the "spiritual," however, all those differences became "completely irrelevant." "All" who came would feel a "spiritual connection," and in this way visitors were "equalized." Of course, Boothe did not suggest that "spirituality" would *replace* the particular religious identities of visitors—that visitors would, in and for themselves, become identical in their spirituality. Rather, visitors were "equalized" for park management. By rendering religious diversity "irrelevant," "spirituality" addressed the complexity of the social body and provided interpreters with a manageable task. Echoing Combs, Boothe highlighted the incommunicability that made such an operation possible: "We don't have to explain."

To reiterate: interpretation communicates individuality through paradox. There is something special about the park, but it cannot be specified. This "tangible/intangible," the unspecified special, makes further specification of significance, perforce, individual. The park's social structure, which discourages visitors from communicating meaningfully with other visitors outside their own group, means that the construction of meaning takes on a private and intimate quality. Yet at the same time, that meaning is embedded in an experience of public and universal space. Without self-sufficient meanings provided by the Park Service and absent any other community grounded in that particular space who might give meaning to the park, the individual meanings provided by visitors become *the* meaning of public space. That is, the difference between private, individual meanings and public, universal meaning is, by design, unobservable. From the perspective of visitors, this dynamic unity of individual and universal constituted the "spiritual" aspect of the park. Boothe suggested that this dynamic also constituted a national, social unity at the same time. She explained,

> "If you look at as how many Americans today don't belong to a church, don't have a formalized spiritual outlet, but the national parks are something that most Americans are very proud of. What's on our stamps? What's on our brochures? What do we advertise to other countries when we're trying to invite them to come to our nation? Our national parks are almost always in there. This is a source of American pride and it's something that Americans worship in that way. That they've come to say, 'I don't go to a church, but I might go to my national parks because it's something that I feel this connection to that is part of who I am,' whereas in the past or for some people in this country belonging to a church is who you are. So it's a different form of worship.[43]

The difference of this "form of worship" lies in individuality. In contrast stands more traditional, "formalized" communal identity ("belong[ing] to a church"), an identity Boothe characterized as absent for many Americans. Lacking such identity, she suggested, Americans have turned to a broader level of social unity, a national one that has become local and particularized in the form of national parks. Here the attachment centers on pride and thus privileges individuality. In general and historically, pride in a social possession may take the form of a collective consciousness in which one sees or feels as an echo of social others. Here, however, Boothe characterized American pride in singular, and thus more personal and individual, terms. Switching from the first person plural ("we," "our") to the first person singular ("I"), she characterized parks as "something that I feel this connection to that is part of who I am." Here the sense of effervescence, the welling up of "spiritual" feeling, was not collective. The "spiritual" park visit was thus unlike a religious ritual such as an initiation ceremony or a festival in which the dynamic relation of the individual to a broader whole collects or gathers together the participants. Rather, this spirituality singularized and individualized its participants. In this respect, however, it would be a mistake to characterize this spirituality as antisocial. As Boothe asserted, the individualizing function itself provided a source of social unity. This unity of individualization and socialization occurred through paradox, through a non-"formalized" "form of worship," indeed, a nonreligious religiosity that bore the name "spiritual."

While Boothe portrayed spirituality as public religion, seeing the parks as a national church, her emphasis on the individuality of spiritual experience gave nuance to this national dimension. Specifically, this paradoxical union of private and public meaning, expressed by visitors as a sense of spiritual connection to universal realities, has invested visitors in the state that has provided the structure of communication in the parks. To the degree that visitors have invested themselves in this structure of communication (which creates the incommunicability that fosters individuality and an unspoken link to the environment), they have invested themselves in a certain structure of authority. That authority blocks rangers from treading on the individuality of spiritual experience. It requires that certain communications remain subdued and that certain meanings remain unspoken. When visitors invest themselves in this feature of the environment—that vague "certain something" that yields a sense of individual connection to a universal whole—they invest themselves in the state as the structure of communication (and incommunicability) in the park. In this way the public religious dimension of spirituality, particularly in its individualistic aspect, orients itself toward the state.

* * *

Silence, invisibility, harmony, incommunicability—here are yet more, and more clear, indications of the secularity of this management of spirituality. The secular takes shape not as one side of the distinction religion/not-religion, but rather as a set of conditions for managing this distinction in indirect ways. Integral to this management is the public/private distinction that park managers, and the Park Service in its mission, treat in a way that connects public and private and allows for the one to find reflection of itself in the other. Such connection and reflection form the bedrock of much official rhetoric concerning the national park ideal.

5

Theorizing Religious Individualism

This book has proceeded along two tracks. On the one hand, it has sought to illuminate how the National Park Service has managed the parks so as to foster spiritual experience. On the other hand, it has sought to show how visitors have experienced the parks as spiritually enriching environments. But the presentation of these two tracks does not fully explain the connection between them. To do so I begin with a question: Why would the state foster spiritual experience?

By way of answer, one may first examine some possible intuitions. One could surmise that, in a democratic society, the state requires no motivation to serve the needs and wants of the populace. From this perspective, state officials need only recognize that park visitors find spiritual significance in these spaces. Upon such recognition, such officials would then simply follow their mission of public service in order to foster such experience. However, such an account leaves much unexplained. First, it does not account for the particular shapes that spirituality takes in the parks. Why would park officials prefer the language of spirit and spirituality, or eschew explicit articulation of spiritual value even as they attempt to cultivate an experience of it? Second, such an intuition assumes that the spiritual experience of visitors is primary and that the Park Service simply reacts to this experience. However, this study has revealed the heavily managed character of the experience of "nature" in the parks. Such management precedes the spiritual experiences of visitors and contributes to the shape that such experiences take. Of course this is a dialectical process: park managers adjust their programs based on the feedback of visitors. But to regard one side of that relationship as primary would ignore the dynamic nature of the relationship between visitors and management.

This book assumes that this sophisticated and, to some degree, coordinated effort to foster spiritual experience must serve some self-interest on the part of the state. While this may sound insidious, the same idea can be expressed in the language of public service. The status of these areas as national parks implies that they are intended to serve the public good and not simply the interior and private satisfaction of individuals. One can argue, and state officials do, that the state is a vehicle for the public good and therefore the promotion of its "self-interest," distinct from the interests of any number of private entities, is a perfectly legitimate goal. And yet, to a certain degree, the state facilitates experiences that are meant to remain interior and private. Indeed, this appears as a central goal as expressed in a motto of the National Park Service: "Experience Your America." It does not say "our" America. Why use second person rather than first? How may such an emphasis on individuality contribute to the collectivity of the state and/or nation? And what does religion and/or spirituality have to do with this?

Alternatives to Tradition

When Ken Burns's and Dayton Duncan's six-part documentary history on *The National Parks: America's Best Idea* aired on the Public Broadcasting Service in 2009, it garnered over 33 million views, the companion book took a place on the New York Times' Bestseller list for seven weeks, and subsequent sales and rebroadcasting disseminated the work even farther.[1] In the preface to the book, Burns explains a central theme of the project: "If the genius of America has been to liberate humankind by permitting its citizens to govern themselves, it has also helped to free them in another perhaps more important way by permitting its believers to worship God as they saw fit. Where our European ancestors required a formalized dogmatic devotion in cathedrals made by men, we Americans would more easily find God—or Science or Art, if that is your way—in Nature."[2] For Burns and Duncan, and for numerous figures interviewed for the project, this freedom for self-government and freedom to find God in nature are intimately related in national parks. In these public spaces, individuals could come and find themselves, individually and personally, at the same time and in the same movement as they found God, Country, and Nature. Writer Terry Tempest Williams, interviewed for the project, stated, "No American ideal resonates more powerfully than the national park. Equality is expressed through humility. Liberty is expressed through the simple act of wandering. . . . I think each American can look into their own hearts and tell you, 'This is *my* national park. . . .' [The parks] are a covenant with the future, saying, 'This is where we were, this is what we loved, and now they are in your hands. We entrust these sacred lands to you.'"[3] Precisely because the parks have been kept as spaces that are free for exploration and equal in terms of access, Williams suggested, they have become theaters of American identity and ideals. For Williams and many others in the film and book, this dynamic stands at the heart of the sacred quality of these spaces.

One must not take the popularity of this project as reflective of a consensus among its viewers regarding its message. The journal *Public Historian* published a roundtable of critical responses to the film, noting its reliance on conventions of the natural sublime, narratives of American progress, and its consequent exclusion of alternative narratives and approaches.[4] But while the film may dwell within conventions, inhabiting them ever so skillfully, those conventions have not been fully understood within conventional theories of religion.

To understand what kind of religiosity Burns and Duncan and many in this book express and promote, one cannot rely on a model that centralizes religious organizations and traditions. Scholars of religion have recognized the need for alternative models, and one that focuses on nature appears particularly appropriate in this case. Historian Catherine L. Albanese's *Nature Religion in America* grew out of her recognition that much religious belief and practice in American history had escaped analysis largely because of the narrowness of the definitions of religion that scholars employed. Offering a more expansive theoretical lens, she sees in nature a symbolic center that Americans throughout their history have used to negotiate their relation to ordinary and extraordinary dimensions of life.[5] Scholar Bron Taylor has developed a theoretical approach that is equally fresh, if in some ways more narrow, in his *Dark Green Religion*, in which he investigates the conceptual foundations for a religion of nature "in itself," thereby eschewing a focus on religious attitudes towards nature in traditions that hold other entities or concerns at their core.[6] Anthropologist Leslie Sponsel's *Spiritual Ecology* focuses on the intersections between on the one hand, religiosity broadly conceived and, on the other, concern for the environment. His preference for the term "spiritual" rather than "religious" indicates his intent for the greatest inclusivity, and his work covers a broad historical range, a number of religious traditions, and nontraditional religiosity.[7] Historian Lynn Ross-Bryant focuses specifically on national parks to illustrate Americans' attachment to nature, applying traditional categories of religious analysis such as pilgrimage, myth, and ritual.[8] These works and others go far beyond self-identifying religious institutions, and the focus on nature in various guises applies to a central concern of spirituality in the parks. However, while applicable, none of these works focus on the particular relation of nature and state within the national park ideal.

Another alternative approach for studying spirituality in the parks comes in recent scholarly literature on secularism. Studies have noted a rise in the religiously unaffiliated, and the preceding chapters have noted the preference among many to self-identify as "spiritual" rather than "religious."[9] Given this tendency as well as the general separation of church and state that informs the state management of public spaces—combined with the prominence of religious language and logic in descriptions of experience in the parks—the question of the religious dimensions of the secular becomes particularly salient. A number of works have taken this approach. Scholars such as John Modern, Tracy Fessenden, Courtney Bender, and Kathryn Lofton have investigated how a variety of flights from, denials of, alternatives to, and replacements for "religion" in America over the last two hundred years show deep and complex connections to traditionally held religious concerns. In investigating the rise of networks of communication, the creation of a generically Protestant culture, the social entanglements of "individualistic" religiosity, and the religious dimensions of a media empire, these scholars have shown how secular culture has not eliminated religion so much as changed its form.[10]

How has religion changed form under conditions of the secular? The increasing complexity of society has given rise to difficulties in representing what society is. In this sense, the rise of the secular was not just a rejection of religion but also a way of talking about the limitations of any overarching narrative to encompass all of an increasingly complex social order. The formal rejection of religion (separation of church and state, rule by the people rather than a divinely sanctioned monarch, insistence on empirical evidence and purely rational explanation in the determination of truth, and so on) did not give rise to a new answer to the question of what society/reality/the-world is; instead, it elicited a multitude of narrower answers that left large epistemological spaces blank.[11] Religion reappears as an echo and shadow in these unmarked spaces, but an echo and shadow that displays both form and power.[12]

Questions of atmosphere, inverted or paradoxical presence, and invisible or camouflaged operations get to the heart of the theoretical concerns of the present study. In broad terms, these works on secularism have asked how religion continues to maintain power, form, and relevance in its various inversions, subversions, and modifications. This book continues in a similar vein, focusing on the various logics of obscurity that serve as vehicles for power at the ground level.

Concern for religion found a prominent position in the foundational expressions of democratic ideology. In the eighteenth century, French social theorist Jean-Jacques Rousseau advocated a religion of simple, general doctrines that supported morality, public order, and governmental authority rather than a sense of exclusive group identity.[13] He called this a "civil religion," and although not explicitly adopted by any regime or society, the sentiments he expressed became influential among the political classes of democratic societies from his time forward.

Within the American context, it was not until late in the twentieth century that Rousseau's thesis was taken up explicitly and proposed as a way to explain contemporary realities of political life. Writing in 1967, sociologist Robert Bellah analyzed the invocations of God and their linkage to collective destiny within American presidential inaugural addresses. He also noted the ritual formality and symbolism associated with patriotic celebrations of Memorial Day and Veterans' Day. He argued that these amounted to a "civil religion" that stood "alongside of and rather clearly differentiated from the churches [as] an elaborate and well-institutionalized" religion that supplied the American nation, at least potentially, with the kind of social cohesion that Rousseau had envisioned under his understanding of the term.[14]

But while this thesis has stimulated huge amounts of discussion and scholarly work, it has also proved immensely problematic—so much so that Bellah has abandoned the term. Shortly after the publication of Bellah's civil religion thesis, scholars noted a variety of ways in which the term could be understood.[15] Further rumination only expanded the range of possible meanings, so much so that empirical work was equaled or outbalanced by definitional questions.[16] A key issue had to do with the different models of citizenship that a civil religion might be said to foster. A republican model, one championed by Bellah, drew on a civic piety— a collective faith in the nation and the common valuation of certain central ideals. A liberal model, valuing individual freedom from collective norms that were not absolutely necessary for public security, militated against such a civic piety. Insofar as American political culture left the tension between such models unresolved, civil religion, with its intelligibility for only one side of the tension, remained implausible as a unifying religious force.[17]

This problem, however, went much deeper than the divide between republican and liberal models of citizenship. A deeper definitional issue arose out of the distinction between religion and politics more generally. Once one expanded the definition of religion to include phenomena outside of the institutions traditionally associated with the term, it became difficult to draw authoritative boundaries for the concept of religion. How could one postulate religious dimensions to the "other" realms of social life without denying the differentiation of modern society (in terms of separation of church and state, scientific method that does not depend on revelation, global economic markets that transcend national, ethnic, and religious boundaries)?[18]

To deal with these quandaries certain scholars have advocated another term that proves most central for this study: "public religion." Championed in 1979 by historian John F. Wilson, this term grew in part as a critique of the older term "civil religion." Wilson, while admitting the religious nature of the phenomena analyzed under this latter term, disagrees that civil religion was similar to what can be found in religious institutions conventionally understood. Rather than a discrete, "well-institutionalized" religion "alongside" of others, Wilson proposes public religion as a meta-religion, one that can be said to float among a myriad of institutions and practices. It might be more appropriate to identify this in terms of "religious dimensions" of American public life, he suggests, ones that can recognize the sacredness of society, sanctify certain cultural values, legitimate a particular political order, or endow America with a divinely sanctioned mission. Analyzing these different dimensions, he suggests, requires sensitivity to the particular domain of public life to which they apply, whether that of society, culture, politics, or theological discourse, respectively.[19] Wilson argues that while it would not suffice to treat such dimensions as parts of a unified and discrete religious system, their religious aspect and their prominence within American culture do demand scholarly attention.

Going beyond the American context for public religion, Jose Casanova focuses on the distinction of public and private. Building on Jeffrey Weintraub's work, Casanova counters the blanket assertion that secularization has relegated religion to the private sphere.[20] Instead, he argues that religion's place and influence within the public sphere depends on which conceptions of the public/private distinction one adopted. While he equivocates on the public role of denominations, he lists a number of conditions under which "disestablished" religions act in support of a secular public order. He also states that private religious communities can be seen to contribute to a public religion of "civil society."[21] Finally, he argues that the view of religion as a product of purely private sentiment and free choice, and the consequent view of the public world of work and law as rightfully absent of religion, are what religions have constantly struggled against and renegotiated. Bolstering his argument with a number of case studies, Casanova asserts that, whether for good or ill, modern religion played an active and influential role in the public sphere.

In his presentation, Casanova sees little public significance in individualistic religiosity. Only when "individual mysticism" is organized under denominations does it take a public face.[22] Meanwhile, the liberal model of citizenship, with its fostering of "individual privatist religions," is positively inimical toward the "republican civil religions" such as those that Bellah proposes.[23] Casanova suggests that individualism has significance for the public sphere only when individuals join communities of some sort. This study, however, has shown how a state institution actively fosters individualistic religiosity and does so as part and parcel of its mission to serve the public good. I suggest, therefore, that Casanova and Bellah miss the ways in which a liberal model of citizenship, precisely through the encouragement of "individual privatist religions," lies at the base of a public religiosity expressed in national parks under the terms of "spirit" and "spirituality." But how can such a religiosity foster social cohesion?

Here Wilson's theses on public religion can provide a guide. While Casanova focuses on organizations and communities in his analysis,

Wilson presents communities as only one of four elements to which one could apply the concept of public religion. In his comments on ritual, he notes how voting, paying traffic tickets, presenting a passport, and countless other engagements with governmental agencies constituted "symbolic acceptance of the system" and "a direct ritual acknowledgment of the authority on which society is based." In this context he mentions national parks. Pointing to the social network that shapes the individual or family adventure into wilderness, he writes, "What may look and feel like individual independence asserted against the culture turns out to be dramatization of a deeper cultural identity." Here he addresses how the apparently individualistic nature of a national park visit implicitly affirms the legitimacy of the public appropriation and management of land, the social worth of the sporting goods industry through participation in "a culture of proper equipment," and ideals of public service through the reliance on volunteers in case of emergency. This often unacknowledged public shaping of private experience indicates that "citizens are bound to the society in countless ways quite below the threshold of normal self-consciousness."[24]

If the link between public power and private experience is not contained in "normal self-consciousness," then where is this link, and in what does it consist? Benedict Anderson theorizes that national identity is an act of imaginative construction, and one that often operates implicitly. In analyzing the emergence of nationalism, Anderson shows how a national self-consciousness can arise from a semantic context rather than an explicit formulation. In other words, individuals who did not know each other can assume a common identity in order to explain their participation in a particular social structure. Once the structure has arisen, for whatever technical and/or historical reasons, a sense of collective identity can arise as the implicit context of that structure. This context is not pregiven; nor does it need to be an object of intentional construction. Rather, collective identity can be thought of as the shadow cast by new social arrangements. From this perspective, those who participate in a social endeavor *imagine*, ex post facto, an answer to the question, "Why are we here together?"[25] The grounds for that imagination, however, exist outside of any explicit thematization.

What shadow is cast by the social arrangements in national parks, and what do religion and/or spirituality have to do with this? I propose that the imagined community fostered by park programming could be more accurately termed an imagined individuality. Park visitors see their experience in the parks, and especially their spiritual experience, as a manifestation of their own individuality rather than that of a specific religious tradition or of the Park Service that governs the space. This sense of individuality requires much social work to become plausible and must overcome a variety of factors that might counter it. Visitors tend to take the same routes, listen to the same programs, see the same sights, and share the same ignorance of the local environment. Yet visitors do not tend to express their experience of the parks as one that they share with a body of visitors, or with any larger group whatsoever. Despite their commonality with other visitors, visitors describe their experience as one step in a personal narrative, not a communal one.

This imagined individuality provides a different kind of community than what Anderson discusses in his work on nationalism. Rather than the republican model of citizenship that postulates a *res publica*, a "public thing" in which all may participate collectively, this individuality informs a more liberal model of citizenship that emphasizes individual freedom as the guiding principle of social life. Theorists of civil and public religion have given short shrift to the possibilities for a liberal model, at least insofar as it could manifest in the lives of individuals in their day-to-day experience.[26] This study, however, has shown how spirituality in the national parks reflects and feeds into a liberal ethos.[27]

Liberal and Public

At the base of park management principles lies the recreational paradigm, expressed most eloquently in Frederick Law Olmsted, Sr.'s, 1865 report to the Governor of California.[28] In arguing for the value of natural spaces held open to the public, Olmsted concentrated on the cultivation of individual human bodies. He saw Yosemite as a space where individuals could develop perceptual and aesthetic faculties that might have atrophied within a repetitive work environment, and he linked the stimulation of those faculties to the public good through a metaphor of America as a body. Only when its individual members, the citizenry, demonstrated a balanced constitution could the body of America as a whole achieve health and strength.

In Olmsted's formulation, public value arose out of the individual benefits each visitor received through his or her "free use" of the parks.[29] Those benefits—namely, improved perceptual faculties—did not need to yield any particular representation of collective unity that visitors would recognize as a group. It was enough that these faculties be more highly and more evenly developed by and among individuals. These qualifications provide the liberal dimension of the public good that Olmsted asserted to be a product of a free and wise government.[30] Olmsted saw the parks as places where each individual could develop his or her potential, a potential that converted into actual enjoyment in aesthetic experience. Through the development of faculties, Olmsted suggested, the individual and American society as a whole realized the benefits of freedom.

The heritage management paradigm stands in contrast to this liberal orientation. Park officials such as Roger Toll suggested that the recreational development of the parks could limit and conflict with the symbolic value of national parks, thus pitting two types of public good against one another. He argued for a balance between the two, for when kept in a more pristine, natural, undeveloped state, the parks would give visitors an "original" America and thus a sense of collective unity. Such symbolic value of the parks accords with the republican concern for the *res publica*, the "public thing" to which citizens would feel bound, and through which they would feel bound to one another. The religious overtones of Toll's promotion of the heritage management paradigm signal what Bellah, with attention to its republican dimensions, would come to describe as civil religion.

But Toll did not assert the supremacy of the heritage paradigm over recreational concerns. Rather, in terms of practical application, he saw potential for a happy union. Within the span of recreational opportunities that parks could provide, he privileged hiking, and in particular solo hiking, as most conducive to an appreciation for a common heritage. He wrote that such a "pilgrimage on foot," away from the clutter and noise of cars and crowds, would result in "inspiration . . . [and] awaken thoughts deep and abiding," all of which would contribute to "the building of a better, stronger race."[31] Given the context of the passage, these "deep and abiding" thoughts would concern a collective heritage. At the same time, the cultivation of perceptual and aesthetic faculties would contribute to the public good along lines similar to those proposed by Olmsted under the recreational paradigm. Managing the parks to encourage hiking and solitude, he suggested, would thus provide for recreational and symbolic benefits at the same time.

This latter concern for heritage inaugurated a specifically religious notion of public value within state literature. Already, though, Olmsted saw the cultivation of individual bodies as the building and maintenance of a collective body of America—an idea at least implicitly religious in its metaphysical claims. Hence, these recreational and heritage paradigms do not show a difference between nonreligious and religious attitudes, but a difference between liberal and republican notions of the public good, both of which use religious logic to make their claims. Thus, the operative distinction is between republican and liberal expressions of public religion.

Religious conceptions of the public value of national parks took on a different dimension under the systems paradigm. The broad scope of this paradigm saw the public value of the parks in the patterns of connectivity that extended well beyond individuals, their experiences, and even the land itself. In terms of religion, this paradigm can be seen from two different perspectives. On the one hand, the ecological systems that sustained a park could be seen, as Newton Drury argued, as evidence of God's original design. So rather than recalling a specifically national origin, preservation of natural systems allude to a deeper, more ontological foundation. On the other hand, preservation of the social systems in which the parks participated, including economic, political, and spiritual dimensions, resulted in a diffuse yet significant form of symbolic capital. By preserving a balance between natural purity and recreational development, Conrad Wirth argued, the parks supported tourist economies, put a positive face on government activity, and contributed to the spiritual well-being of American citizens.

In conceiving of the parks as complex environments that involve a number of social and natural functions, none of which can necessarily be reduced to one or another in terms of tangible equations, exponents of the systems paradigm have presented it as a higher synthesis of the earlier paradigms. The emphasis falls on balance and harmony among management goals, rather than singling out particular goals as all-important. With respect to public religion, the systems paradigm can regard symbolic attachment to the nation, to the *res publica*, as a worthy goal. Likewise this paradigm can support the more liberal notion that cultivating individual faculties of natural (and social) appreciation contribute to collective well-being. But with its emphasis on the relation of different management goals to one another, all-encompassing religious language dropped out of official rhetoric while economic metaphors took a more prominent place. This shift reflects not the absence, but the occultation of religion and/or spirituality as a goal of public management. Such occultation, with a concurrent and surreptitious encouragement of spirituality, has subsumed the spiritual value of the parks under the broader symbolic capital that the parks are said to constitute and/or to produce. Further, such occultation accords with a more liberal model of public religion by allowing visitors to attribute their spirituality to their own agency, indeed, to their own individuality.

How do these textual expressions of public religion inform the contemporary experience of park visitors? A focus on wilderness and the long-distance hikers along the John Muir Trail allows a comparison between, on the one hand, the "natural purity" that many park officials have seen as most conducive to a socially unifying public religiosity and, on the other, the religious experience of park visitors in more developed areas. And while marked differences separate the experience of long-distance hikers from that of visitors to Yosemite and Muir Woods, I argue that the public religiosity fostered by these various park environments displays liberal features.

With respect to the John Muir Trail, consider the recreational dimension of hiker spirituality. Hikers saw the spiritual impact of their experience in terms of the way it re-created and reoriented the perceptual and aesthetic habits that governed their non-wilderness lives. The distinction between wilderness and civilization served as a touchstone to which they turned to explain the spiritual dimension of their experience. On the one hand, they characterized civilization as a pattern of mundane experience often infused with impatience, ignorance, and alienation. What's taking this stoplight so long? What's in this water I'm drinking? Who are these people passing by me? Wilderness, on the other hand, offered a refreshing contrast: no traffic to get in the way, a more immediate connection to the environment, and a natural social bond with fellow hikers in the face of a common situation. Even given this characterization, hikers did not anticipate a return to civilization with dread. Rather, they felt that wilderness had reoriented and rejuvenated the faculties through which they would encounter civilization. They thus anticipated (and likely recalled from previous journeys) a renewed sense of patience, ease, and privilege with respect to the social infrastructure that would surround them upon their return.

The hikers I interviewed did not offer a nationalist perspective in the way that Olmsted did. However, the recreational paradigm, and liberal, progressive politics more broadly, do not necessarily depend on the recognition of public value on the part of private citizens.[32] Rather, the key ingredient is liberty. As long as citizens come to the parks and recognize themselves as free, the contributions to the public good will accrue regardless of whether citizens link that sense of liberty to a particular public entity. Or, expressed in terms of the self-interest of a social system, when the state becomes the guarantor of a particular kind of freedom, citizens become implicitly, structurally dependent on the state for their quality of life. In the public, state-managed space of wilderness, hikers attested to a sense of spiritual liberation from the burdens of civilized life. In this way their spirituality takes on the character of a liberal, progressive public religion.

While the recreational paradigm stemmed from a liberal and progressive orientation, the heritage paradigm drew more heavily on republican sentiments, on a recognized concern with and commitment to a common social possession: the *res publica* or "public thing." In this regard, hiker spirituality is notable for the almost complete absence of a sense of heritage. The heritage paradigm sees national parks as the symbolic representation of a collectivity extending out into the past and future. Nature, from this perspective, gives visitors a sense of connection with those who came before, while at the same time promising continuity with those who would come after. This theme arose in only two of the hiker interviews, and in one of those the sentiment was tempered by a liberal orientation.[33]

In contrast, there are subtle but significant affinities between hiker spirituality and the systems management paradigm. Rather than positing a singular notion of the public good, the systems paradigm recognizes a plurality of potentially incompatible ways of valuing national parks, meaning that the Park Service needs to strive for a harmonious balance through diverse and flexible management strategies. This paradigm can be seen to serve a more liberal, progressive agenda in its emphasis on pluralism. The systems paradigm recognizes that visitors come to a national park with a variety of backgrounds and interests, and managers therefore serve the public by maximizing the range of choices available to visitors as they shape their own individual experience. There is a liberal dimension to the way hikers reflected on the effects of this paradigm. Hikers saw wilderness and civilization as patterns of perception and perspective. Not simply relieved of the burdens of civilization under the recreational model, hikers found the movement from one system to another as spiritually liberating. Thus their sentiments can be characterized as a spiritual perspectivalism, with hikers finding spiritual value in the very contingency and temporality that now informed their approach toward life. Again, hikers saw such realization as an effect of nature. But the fact that this revelation of nature depended upon state management renders a public quality to these spiritually liberating effects.

In wilderness the liberal aspect of the state is an effect of absence. The state operates not as a *res publica*, a public thing associated with particular objects and symbols. Rather the state "appears" as the absence of private enterprise, as a largely invisible force that keeps private enterprise from encroaching upon the land. This powerful absence of the state endows it with both a natural quality and at the same time, a liberal quality. The spiritually liberating effects of nature, constructed as the absence of civilization, depend upon a form of government that prevents elements of the private sphere, such as individuals seeking solitude and businesses seeking profit, from interfering with one another.

What about a significantly different public environment such as Yosemite Valley? Here, as shown in Chapter 3, one certainly does not find wilderness. Up to thirty thousand people can visit the valley on a given day. With the consequent development and infrastructure, one can hardly assert an absence of civilization and its governing agency. Still, this environment displays a similar dynamic of nature and civilization shadowed by the obscure presence of the state. And here again, one can find the encouragement and expression of a public religiosity that tends toward a liberal orientation.

In the more developed areas of Yosemite, the Park Service strives to present a harmony of nature and culture rather than the absence of the latter. This endeavor modifies the guiding principle of wilderness management rather than presenting a strict contrast. In Yosemite, acts of camouflage hide the difference between nature and culture, allowing the two to blend smoothly into one another. The effect is similar to that of wilderness, for this strategy naturalizes state authority and liberalizes it at the same time. But it does so by trading on the pastoral dimensions of nature, ones that becomes manifest in an atmosphere of tranquility rather than one of radical difference from civilization. This kind of nature offers freedom not primarily through "escape," but through a range of programmed entrees into the natural/cultural harmony of the park. Visitors reflect this liberal ethos in their portrayal of their experience, and in particular the spiritual dimensions of their experience, in terms of personal, unimpeded connections within a peaceful environment.

Working within a more restricted space, park managers in Muir Woods create icons of natural/cultural harmony through their maintenance and presentation of the redwoods. There is little possibility of camouflaging the boardwalk, although the weathering of the wood proceeds down that path. But through the coordination of pedestrian traffic management, building placement, and the perceptual environment, park managers facilitate episodes of relative solitude and peace. Visitors can walk and stand without paying much attention to other visitors, and their eyes are often guided into visual fields absent of human presence. Again, the recreational management paradigm provides visitors with a sense of freedom, but in this case it is freedom from the demands of the perceptual environment of civilization. Visitors often express such release as an encounter with a nonalien, nonalienating environment. They get in touch with their "selves" and/or their gods, and feet themselves in harmony with their surroundings. This kind of freedom, in which visitors encounter their environment as a part or reflection of themselves, again reflects a liberal ethos in which the state provides the conditions for individual self-realization.

Visitor Self-Understanding

How did visitors understand their park experience as it related to collective identity? To explore this question, I engaged in a series of interviews with twenty visitors from Yosemite and Muir Woods who had participated in earlier surveys I conducted.[34] In addition to dealing with visitor spirituality in more detail, these interviews addressed the question of collective identity directly by asking interviewees to explain the National Parks motto, "Experience your America," and to consider how their experience may have influenced their attitudes toward America and/or its government. I then asked visitors how the spiritual dimension of their experience may have influenced those same attitudes, and to what degree they saw such experience as an effect of park management. Because of the limited number of interviews, the responses cannot be considered as representative of survey respondents as a whole. I offer an analysis in order to outline the forms through which visitors elaborated on the public dimension of their park experience.

Responses to the Park Service motto can be most generally classed along a scale of approval/disapproval. Twelve out of the twenty interviewees suggested positive appreciation for the message that the motto conveyed. These positive evaluations can be further classed into two related themes: heritage and nationalism. In terms of heritage, a theme invoked by four interviewees, the responses echoed park officials. Thus, one respondent saw the motto as an imperative to "see how beautiful the country once was for the people that came here first."[35] Another said, "To me it means experience America before we have paved it over. The example of Yosemite park . . . you go there and there's just meadows and trees and you can see the hand of man occasionally because you'll see an orchard where somebody once had a farm, and there are some roads. But it's wild, and that's the way all of America used to be. . . . That's why I think it's important to keep our parks and all parts of our country, so we can see what it was like."[36] Here the management techniques of camouflage reinforced the sense of a collective past. Recall the high population density of Yosemite Valley. There, despite maintaining an infrastructure capable of handling thirty thousand visitors a day, the Park Service succeeds in creating an impression of wildness, one that these respondents link to a sense of national origins.

Another dimension of collective identity evoked by the motto of the national parks concerns the theme of nationalism more directly. This theme, addressed by eight of the twelve who positively evaluated the motto, came in two varieties. Four interviewees stressed what I call, following historian Alfred Runte, "scenic nationalism."[37] The other four invoked what I call "republican nationalism."

"Scenic nationalism" refers to the claim that parks, through their beauty, evince the national superiority or grandeur of America. One respondent said, "There's not another country in the world that has even a fraction of the natural beauty of America. . . . It's an amazing thing and an amazing place. And it is in our country. It's almost unfair that it's all here."[38] While such sentiments refer to a sense of national superiority with respect to other countries, they can also take the form of a more freestanding evaluation. As another interviewee put it, "I think, what a country. It's beautiful. That's a natural phenomenon, the national parks. Do I feel more American when I look at it? No. But I just think what a great country we have. What a beautiful country. What a beautiful land."[39] Again, one may see the hand of management in these evocations of nationalism. Admittedly, I spoke with no park rangers who indicated a desire to evoke such national pride. But whether park managers intended it or not, their work in maintaining framed scenes of balanced composition and spectacular scale can evoke, as they do here, a sense of collective possession and self-affirmation.

Sentiments of republican nationalism, shared by four interviewees, stressed the public aspect of the parks most directly. Here the beauty of the parks reflected not only on America in general, but on its system of government. As one respondent put it, "Our country has plenty of flaws and there's things about it that are easy to criticize, but the fact that these areas are set aside and made available to all is—not just to a few privileged ticketholders or whatever, but they're there and accessible to everyone—I think is in keeping with the spirit of our country. When I look at that motto and what it means and how it's carried out, I think it's consistent with . . . the ideals of our founding fathers and how the country was established."[40] Here the management of the park does not remain in the background. The beauty and grandeur of the park is not just a passive reflection of national greatness, but an active reflection of collective will and discipline. These lands have been "set aside" and "made available," making the encounter with beauty a testament to the republican virtues of equal access, which are embodied in the management and authority of the state. In this way the action of the state that regulates access to nature (and prevents the private and exclusive appropriation of such lands) yields an experience of liberty. Another respondent stressed this when she explained the motto as meaning "the freedom to be able to go to places, and they've been set aside and maintained for us. That there are places that we can go to."[41] While this respondent did not mention the beauty or grandeur of the parks, the very fact that they are public lands was enough for her to find collective affirmation of her experience of the parks. This respondent implied that the pervasive influence of private property was mitigated by the state, which guaranteed that some (highly valued) space would remain free from exclusive claims.

Of course, not all responded positively to the motto. Of these six interviewees, one put the blame on visitors themselves for not showing enough respect for the space.[42] Another felt that the natural atmosphere of the parks created the discrepancy. She stated that, for her, "America" made her think of small towns and community, neither of which she found in the parks.[43] But there was a cluster of responses that shared a common theme in resisting what they perceived as the message of the motto. Rejecting its nationalist tone, these four interviewees instead proffered a global social identity. One respondent reacted to the motto by saying that "it seems so xenophobic. It's a park, and nature is global. It's not [just] ours. So I would not relate to that at all."[44] Another stated that "I like to think of our parks as being part of the world, because I don't like all those boundaries."[45] Here the sense of the public quality of the parks extended to all society, and the notion that the parks belonged only to Americans suggested a private possession, one that deprived the rest of the world of what rightly belonged to it.

Notions of a global social identity also appear in the interpretive panel in Muir Woods, discussed earlier, which this respondent may have encountered in her visit. Both these perspectives display a liberal dimension, with the emphasis on universal human rights that Wuthnow and Casanova highlight as elements of liberal thinking.[46] But whereas the authors concentrate on the sense of an all-encompassing social identity, the environment in Muir Woods locates the seat of such identity in individual experience, an experience that belonged to all who took advantage of the freedom to encounter nature in such a setting. To return to the responses to the motto, the counter to a nationalist ideology serves as a reminder that state management is not monolithic in its interpretive messages, and can in fact spur more critical reflection on the public value of the parks. From such a perspective, the celebration of a "national treasure" can thus reflect on the system of government in a negative way—more as an attempt to manipulate than as an effort to serve. One respondent explained: "I think there are equally beautiful spots throughout the entire world, and I don't know if that's a sales point they want to make. I think it may be a selling point to push the national parks on us, and maybe the American public needs to have that. . . . I don't need to have it."[47] This respondent suggested that the symbol of America was tapped as a kind of capital for creating investment in the parks. But as this respondent later noted, and as many others affirmed, the appearance of nature was a predominant and adequate means for achieving such investment.

Of course my request for visitors to explain the meaning of the motto may have carried with it a certain nationalistic bias, given the wording of the motto itself, so to get at visitors' more personal opinions, I asked how their park experience may have influenced their attitudes towards America and/or its government. Here I found respondents split. Twelve out of twenty found that their park experience had influenced their attitudes towards America or its government in some way, while seven did not.[48] For those who indicated that they had been influenced, eight reported positive feelings, three offered negative evaluations, and one expressed ambivalence.

For those whose park experience had strengthened their sense of the value or greatness of the larger social entities involved in the parks, the positive evaluations echoed the sentiments of nationalism and heritage discussed above. One respondent said, "In America we're free. We have the opportunity to see things like that. There are places that don't have that opportunity. They have the same type of things there but you don't have the freedom to go there or it's not kept well."[49] This nationalism, one grounded in the equal access provided by the parks, also reflected more specifically on the government. Evoking a sense of heritage, this same respondent stated, "I feel proud that we've saved the land and preserved it for years and years and years to come for our kids and grandkids right on down the line. And somebody had a lot of foresight—our presidents and government in general the last couple of hundred years have done some bright things."[50] Here the continuity of the nation over time, a theme discussed in some detail in Chapter 1, found expression in this person's sense of the natural appearance of the park (it was "preserved") and evoked a sense of pride. Further, this creation of a socially binding legacy was tied to a progressive political program. I have already noted how the park movement in general has been recognized as a feature of progressive politics.[51] Given the identification of such politics with an agenda to create long-term resources for improving public welfare, one can see this respondent's linkage of national heritage to a progressive political orientation in his perception of "foresight" within the government. Such an evaluation shows how the appearance of nature becomes a source of pride in America and in its government.

While this respondent's positive sentiments conflated the nation and its government, other respondents made a distinction between the two. An interviewee who found that the parks contributed to a sense of global identity expressed negative sentiments toward America. She said, "The way I feel about America right now, I want to leave the country. I'm so disgusted with the politics. . . . I don't even like to think of our national parks as part of America." With reference to the motto, she said, "I don't like it. America is also the ghettos and all the darkness too. It's not just the gorgeous beauty."[52] But even with the strength of these negative evaluations, this respondent found room for collective self-affirmation in the historical role of the state in the parks. She said, "One of the things that I think about when I go to a national park is—I believe it was Franklin Roosevelt who put all the people to work. That makes me feel good. I'm walking around thinking this is great that this man did this, that so many people contributed to making the paths and the trails—all of that. That's a good feeling."[53] This respondent found affirmation of a progressive political orientation in the appearance of the parks, in their aspect as developed spaces. Even with her sense of a global social identity, there are suggestions of a more localized republican orientation in her sense of collective welfare provided through state activity.

Another respondent who made a distinction between America and its government saw the park experience reflecting on the former and not the latter. Having attested to a scenic nationalist reading of the motto, this respondent found the parks to be immune from her own sense of the negative aspects of American identity: "The national parks are something that you certainly can't adulterate, so even if we have a government that may give me to some extent a negative feeling about myself as an American because of our government's policies, national parks are still a positive image of the American."[54] Here the appearance of nature in the parks conferred on America a certain purity, one that could not be tainted by the actions of the state outside the park (she cited "foreign relations" as the aspect of America that had wounded her sense of national pride).

Even when park experience resulted in a negative evaluation of America or its government, this did not necessarily reflect failure in the communication on the part of management concerning the public value of the parks. One respondent indicated that the sense of heritage conveyed by the parks involved a tragic dimension: "It makes me sad that that's the only places where wildlife can be the way they used to be. It makes me sad that we've done what we've done to the rest of the country."[55] While she certainly found that the parks reflected poorly on America as a whole, she did express the conservation ethic that park management strives to inculcate. Another respondent who found that the parks reflected negatively on American society focused on the perceptual environment of civilized life. He found that the parks reminded him of how "whacked" the American lifestyle was—how it was informed by a hectic (and soulless) greed. Parks gave him a greater sensitivity to that negative path that America made so available, and they provided an alternative that, he suggested, brought him closer to God.[56]

One should not ignore those instances when the communicative mission to create investment in the parks may have missed its mark entirely. For one of these two respondents, the experience in Yosemite reflected negatively both on the park and the state more generally: "The cops there have a bad attitude towards climbers. . . . They didn't make me proud that the national parks were organized and run by our country at that point."[57] The second respondent in this category could not get past the commercialism that had bothered her during her visit. Referring to the parks she said, "They're beautiful places, but they represent the capitalism in America as well as the beautiful part of America."[58] Such responses indicate that the assertion of authority in the parks, whether in the management of recreational activity or in the regulation of social infrastructure, is not without its risks of meeting resistance.

Finally, and perhaps this is just as important for understanding the pubic value of the parks, we can consider the seven respondents who rejected any connection between the parks and social identity. For them nature could serve to block any potential association. I asked one respondent who had expressed a sense of encountering heritage in the parks if his experience had influenced his attitudes towards America. He responded in unequivocal terms: "No, not at all. One is one thing, and one is another. . . . I think of national parks as natural areas."[59] Others offered only grudging respect for the government that maintained the appearance of natural parks. A respondent who attested that the parks evinced a global sense of identity said that she would not associate her experience with America, "other than maybe being happy that our government is actually providing a place, a sanctuary, a natural habitat. . . . I guess I should feel some gratitude about that, but I had not thought of it in terms of exactly that. It seems like it's not just ours. It's the world's."[60] Another respondent displayed a similarly qualified recognition of the positive role of the state, even as she expressed sentiments of scenic nationalism: "I say, oh what a wonderful country, but I don't connect it with the government. It seems like I'm taking it for granted. You assume it's always going to be there. It's there when I want it. It's a very thoughtless way."[61] While offering some appreciation for society more broadly, these responses show the limits of the associations between park experience and collective identity. A sense of encounter with national origins need not increase feelings of patriotism, and the claim of the country's superlative beauty need not indicate a stronger sense of American identity. (Of course, the association of nature with the world as a whole shows an extremely diffuse sense of social belonging.)

These responses show that visitors were generally open to associating their park experience with some form of collective identity. In terms of the themes of heritage, scenic nationalism, and global belonging, the key to this identity resided in the natural appearance of the parks.[62] This point is particularly salient with respect to the religiosity of visitors, for this natural quality was the critical element of the spiritual experience to which visitors attested.

Among interviewees, the religious and/or spiritual approach to nature could take the form of a traditional expression of faith, as it did for nine out of twenty. One respondent pointed to "the whole thing that God created that is just so amazing."[63] Or, as explained by another interviewee, "There is something about being in a national park, and you can see what God created without—with very few effects of man diminishing things, that it truly is more spiritual and more and more drawing you closer to God."[64] And again in parallel with the surveys discussed earlier, a number of respondents (nine out of twenty) found spiritual significance without reference to a creator, focusing more closely on the perceptual and perspectival shifts that park experience evoked.[65] Here references to God could take a broader form with no identifiable location in tradition, as it did for this "spiritual," religiously unaffiliated respondent: "To me I think that when you're out in nature like that, you're one with God. It's totally the closest I ever feel to him or her or whatever that spiritualness is. I just always feel a connection because it's quiet and it makes you be quiet within yourself. So you get to really spend some quality time within."[66] Whether this sense of quiet referred to the concrete perceptual environment, a general perspectival shift that informs self-reflection, or a combination of the two, the primary emphasis lay in an experience recognized as individual and personal. Again mixing the perceptual impact of the park with more abstract shifts in perspective, another respondent stated that "I'm not alone in this, a lot of people feel connected with something powerful and great and mighty. You can describe it as God if you want to. It's a feeling of awe. And also with the ocean—you just feel like there's something so powerful and so wonderful. It's very healing. It puts everything into perspective."[67] This respondent located her spirituality in a powerfully emotive and embodied experience. As for its social dimension, she left it up to the listener to fashion it as he or she chose. But here, too, the individuality of her experience located her socially: she said that she "is not alone in this." Her offer to leave open the identity of the transcendent thus became an orientation toward others, part of a social code that labels her as a tolerant individualist. Or, more to the point, she displayed through her words a liberal sense of collective identity, one that did not reside in a sense of bonding with a group, but in an experience that each person had the freedom to interpret in her or his own individual way.

These links between individuality and a perceptual/perspectival spirituality have been outlined in the previous chapters. It is worth stressing the links between spirituality and the managed environment that these more detailed follow-up interviews illustrate. Note the implication of a managed environment in the phrasing of one of the above respondents: "You can see what God created without—with very few effects of man diminishing things."[68] This respondent stopped short of asserting a state of "pure" nature in the parks, and in correcting himself, he suggested that by restricting development, management was important in allowing him to feel closer to God. In elaborating on his spirituality, he commented on the importance of a person's perceptual environment, particularly the way that the concrete demands on his attention within civilization ("there's traffic and there's people and there's pollution and there's the roads and your job") distracted him from a spiritual focus. Even though he suggested that the parks offered a contrast to such an environment, the fact is that parks contain much of what distracted him in civilization. The difference, in addition to his release from the obligations of work, lies in the effectiveness of management in minimizing the sensory impact of traffic, and people, and roads.

Hints of the influence of management on spirituality can be seen in references to the atmosphere of the parks. One respondent said, "I just feel that national parks are just such a beautiful example of God's handiwork and God's creation. And even just driving into a park, somehow you can just feel that; it's like you can breathe it in the air and you can hear it in the sounds around you."[69] Recall the design of the road leading into Yosemite, how it eliminates the need to deal with oncoming traffic and minimizes the attention demanded by traffic moving in the same direction. This respondent's reference to breathing and hearing a manifestation of God is thus not a purely metaphysical claim. As I have suggested earlier, these metaphors of embodiment suggest an appreciation for the way the park is organized as a perceptual environment. This respondent suggested as much in her elaboration of her spirituality: "A lot of times we let the little things in life get us down or pile up. And when you're standing in someplace that's really majestic and just really beautiful, all that little petty stuff, like whether the mail came on time or not, just doesn't matter. And so it's much easier then to focus and clear your mind of the clutter. You really just get back in touch with your spirit and with God's sense of beauty."[70] Traffic, of course, constituted some of the "little petty stuff" that this interviewee found as a distraction from spirituality outside the park. When management operated in such a way as to minimize this kind of distraction, it opened avenues toward self ("your spirit") and God ("God's sense of beauty") at the same time.

A more prolonged reading of the interviews provides further examples of how the construction of a natural appearance shapes spiritual experience in the parks. While these connections have been treated earlier, I have not yet addressed the way visitors evaluated the possible connections between the social environment of the parks and their spirituality. To pursue this, I asked visitors if park management may have played a role in shaping their spiritual experience. Out of twenty visitors contacted for the follow-up interviews, eight suggested that park management had played a role in shaping the spiritual dimension of their experience, while twelve declined to make such a connection.

Those who answered the questions positively made clear that the Park Service played an indirect role in shaping the spiritual aspect of their experience. The behavior or attitude that rangers modeled could have that effect. One respondent pointed to the spirituality of rangers themselves: "We get newsletters from different national parks—they do feel a sense of reverence themselves, even if they don't identify it directly as spiritual. There seems to be a reverence approach to park management."[71] As a member of the Yosemite Association, a nongovernmental organization that arranges volunteer work and other activities to promote the mission of the park, this respondent probably had more knowledge of rangers than most visitors. Still she pointed to rangers' public work of management rather than their private opinions in identifying the influences on her own spirituality. Another respondent saw that rangers could influence spirituality by "showing respect for the land, by keeping it clean and not allowing people to trash things . . . so you're not distracted."[72] This respondent stressed that the landscape itself provided the object of her spiritual attention. But she noted how important it was to keep those objects free of the clutter that could otherwise impact her spiritual experience. A third respondent pointed to the importance of perceptual management directly. As the director of the creative arts department of an evangelical church, he chose an analogy that was appropriate given his background: "It's like when you walk into a cathedral, your immediate response because of the whole orientation of the cathedral your focus is drawn upward, and I think that that intentional design affords a focus. And I would say the same is true in a lot of my experience in the parks. . . . The park . . . is designed to focus our attention on the grandeur. And . . . for me it promotes worship because the other stuff is out of the way."[73] As perspectives such as these demonstrate, the Park Service manages spirituality obliquely by directing attention in unobtrusive but powerful ways. Such management is primarily nonverbal, an act of managing perceptions rather than shaping concepts.

Those who denied any association between spirituality and management highlighted the more solitary nature of park experience. For some, the rejection of a possible connection stemmed from the fact that they had not spoken with rangers or heard them say anything they recognized as religious. These respondents did not offer a picture of management that conflicted with that portrayed above. Rather, they suggested an understanding of social influence that had more to do with face-to-face interaction and language. As one respondent said, "There were a lot of talks. There was a lot of stuff that you could definitely go and get as much info as you wanted and have that experience. I just wasn't looking for it. So for me, I just didn't tap into that at all. Nor would I have wanted to, because that's just not where I look for my spirituality. I'm much more like, 'Hey you and me let's sit down on a bench and go for it and talk . . . and get your perspective.'"[74] This respondent understood her spirituality to reside within a sphere of interpersonal privacy and intimacy, one in which social influence was attached to names, faces, and specific episodes. Further in line with this emphasis on privacy, she had earlier in the interview highlighted the importance of being quiet and alone for feeling a sense of spiritual connection. Given the extent to which pedestrian traffic is managed in the parks, such solitude does not occur strictly by chance. Indeed, this respondent expressed appreciation, even amazement, at the way she could find solitude in Yosemite despite the high number of visitors she knew were there.

Other respondents invoked solitude to deny management influence more explicitly. "It's more your independent self. . . . I think it's more what we do than what anyone provides," said one respondent.[75] Another said, "I think the most profound spiritual moments . . . are the quietest times when you look around you and you see all of it and you say, 'Wow.' You can't really lose yourself in it until you've been left alone long enough out there. I would have to say that I don't see how management would have contributed or dissuaded."[76] Again, this respondent's denial of the influence of management does not disagree factually with those who attested to such influence. Rather he put such a focus on solitary encounter with the environment that he refused to recognize the social construction of the possibility for such an encounter.

The overarching questions of these interviews concern the connection between park management and spiritual experience: How do they connect and how does the relationship construct social identity? While these interviews demonstrate a variety of responses, as a whole, they suggest how the appearance of nature in the parks translates into nationalist sentiments and approval of state authority. Nature becomes a symbol of the nation and of the efficiency and worth of certain types of state activity, particularly as regards a progressive political program. However, for some, the natural appearance of the parks undercuts a nationalist message and instead stands as a symbol of the world.

At the same time that nature points towards society, it also points toward God, spirit, and self. From the perspective of biblical tradition, nature provokes thoughts of a transcendent being whose history is recorded in and accessible through scripture. In the more open-ended evocation of immanence in perceptual and perspectival shifts, nature symbolizes a larger unity of self and world. In both cases nature serves as a religious and/or spiritual symbol, evoking transphysical entities either outside ("God") or inside ("spirit," self) of the concrete particularities of the environment.

Given these emphases on collectivity and the metaphysical, what can one make of park spirituality as public religion? The perceived location of spiritual experience within the private sphere, within intimate relations between visitors and God/spirit/self, reflects on collective identity through freedom. In creating the opportunities for solitude, for freedom from social interaction, the parks facilitate metaphysical investments on the part of visitors. Such investments sometimes reflect directly back on the nation and the state that provides the opportunity for such investment, as some visitors saw. At other times visitors perceived their metaphysical investments as purely private and/or natural affairs. Even here, however, the structural dependence of this private, individual, spiritual experience on state-managed nature is apparent. While visitors may not explicitly associate this shaping of their private lives with the action of the state, the state nevertheless appears to be highly useful to fostering activities and feelings that its citizens value. In terms of public religion, such state-nurtured spirituality can feed into a background assumption that, despite all the management and authority to which citizens are subjected every day, they are still free.

Such an analysis complements the theoretical perspectives outlined at the beginning of this chapter. Scholars have only lightly sketched the outlines of liberal public religion and the role of individualism within it. This book's treatment of spirituality in national parks suggests that the fashioning of religious individualism proceeds under the conscious and sophisticated guidance of the state, and that these individualized experiences inform, in varying degrees, visitors' sense of allegiance and belonging to larger social entities. These allegiances cannot be fully captured through the conscious affirmations that visitors have offered in these follow-up interviews. Part of the sensation of freedom may require that the hand of management, and of the nation and state behind it, not be felt directly. For this reason I suggest that in national parks the state wears nature as a glove. Visitors are spiritually attached to the feel of this glove, making their attachment to the hand, and to whatever guides it, a natural predisposition.

Conclusion

This book began as an attempt to understand the statement "This is my church." The preceding chapters have found that the structures of this church are both massive and invisible. Soaring cliff walls fill the eye, and yet their status as a site for divine communication, personal integration, and societal belonging lies, to cite a founding figure in Park Service interpretation, "behind what the visitor can with his senses perceive."[1] Rather than rendering the invisible visible, this volume has focused on that invisibility itself. Indeed, I have argued that the inability to define this church is part of its foundation. The lack of precise borders for this church gives it a certain universality, an all-encompassing quality that slides over the innumerable differences that characterize the visiting public. At the same time, the vagueness of this church has allowed visitors to claim it within their own individual experience. Belonging to everyone publicly and to each individual privately, the invisible church of national parks is the site for an American public religion. This religion recognizes a shared and sacred heritage both within and beyond the visible forms of nature, a heritage that reflects, in the words of Ralph Waldo Emerson, the "secret experiences" of each individual visitor.[2]

Visitors asserted that this church conveys a sense of peace, harmony, and individual connection to a universal whole. This book has shown how this sensibility arises as an effect of power. The national parks are managed environments. Each vista point, curve of the road, and recreational opportunity is an extension of a structure of authority, and each is designed to reinforce that structure through the management of experience. When visitors stand in awe before a grand panorama, enjoy the cool, quiet embrace of a redwood grove, or find time for self-reflection while walking on a smooth, well-marked trail, they do not simply connect to nature as something "out there" nor simply to themselves as something "inside." Rather they invest in a certain way of experiencing, one that is maintained by the state that carves out these panoramas, keeps the forest quiet, and evens out the trails.

This disciplining of subjectivity is subtle. The Park Service organizes the environment in such a way as to imbue it with a higher, abstract value. That value is, by necessity, intangible. It refers to nature, spirit, heritage, America, God, the state, and others, but without being stated explicitly or conclusively. This intangibility, the suggestive or unspoken character of this value, allows visitors to mark that value as their own. By forging the last link in the chain of associations created by park management, visitors arrive at a sense of interconnectedness and peaceful belonging that reaches into their individuality. This book has shown that visitors identify that sense as spiritual. Through spirituality visitors invest in the environment and themselves at the same time. The particularities of objects acquire an abstract value that is then appropriated by individuals in such a way as to differentiate them from one another. The investment created by this process is not only a "precious personal possession," but is in fact investment in the social (state-run) system of experiential production.[3]

This disciplining of subjectivity in the parks recasts some of the underlying logic of liberalism with respect to the exercise of power. For liberalism, a just social order depends upon a balance between individual freedom and responsibility to the collective. With respect to religion, this balance manifests in a tension between "spirituality" (that is, individual, private, interior orientations) and "organized religion" (or collective, traditional, institutionalized doctrines and behaviors). In analyzing spirituality as a liberal public religion, I have sought to expose the finesse with which liberalism exercises power within these tensions. In short form, I have shown how the concrete construction of individual freedom (as in the conditions of a walk in a park) carries within it and camouflages the workings of power in ordering collective life. This is not to say that the exercise of power in this way is unjustified or unjustifiable. But the self-justifying quality of this exercise of power tends to cast any opposition or difference with respect to that exercise as an ultimately arbitrary assault on a universal good. The implicit assumption of such a perspective is that those who oppose such exercises of power cannot be reasoned with and can only be forced to comply.

This operation legitimizes a history of dispossession. With respect to native populations this has been documented, and efforts within Yosemite have sought to mitigate this dispossession, at least in the case of the Ahwahneechee.[4] But "America's Best Idea" centered on a dispossession of private interests more generally. Outside of parks, seeking fortune and pursuing enterprise through private development of land has been regarded as a sacred right, one belonging to Americans by birth.[5] The incredible feat of the national park idea consisted in a sharp reversal and inversion of this ideal. It was precisely the removal and prohibition of private development that became an expression of an American ideal and a means for preservation of America itself. Under the circumstances, Richard Sellars's critical history, pointing out how the ideal of "conservation" has been subverted by private enterprise throughout the history of the parks, misses a crucial point.[6] It is in no way surprising that public mandates for conservation would be subverted by private enterprise. What calls for explanation is precisely *why conservation would hold any power whatsoever* in the management of so much land. An instinctual answer, and one reflected in much conservation rhetoric, would contend that the history of the destruction of nature naturally led to a general consciousness of the importance of conservation, and this led to the creation of parks, among other things. This book contends that the pervasive naturalness of that way of thinking is a product of the disciplining of subjectivity, not its cause. In other words, that's the secular talking.

The perceived naturalness, and therefore invisibility, of operations of power in the public sphere is integral to the secular ethos. Such naturalness also informs ideas about religion. Even the relatively innovative and critical theories of "nature religion" in various guises fall curiously silent when faced with the task of analyzing public power. Despite the urgency Bron Taylor feels about the state of the environment, his concept of Dark Green Religion focuses largely on the expressions of individuals in their private capacities, offering their opinions freely and operating within private organizations.[7] Leslie Sponsel's work is even more focused on rhetoric and literature rather than institutionalized practices.[8] A glaring example of this blindness to power is Susan Power Bratton's work on spirituality on the Appalachian Trail. Despite her acknowledgment of the history of public management of the trail, including the various exercises of power required for its establishment, she focuses on the private beliefs and assertions of hikers throughout the work.[9] Catherine Albanese's work on nature religion does center on power, but it is a power that is taken and wielded by individuals acting within and against larger structures. She writes, "The failure of nature religionists to institutionalize well, if at all, means that—for all our longing for precision—we will find them in a somewhat murky world."[10] But nature religionists did institutionalize well and quite publicly: see the National Park Service. As discussed earlier, the invisibility of this religious institutionalization stems not from a failure of people, even officials in the course of their public service, to use religious language to describe their activities in the parks. Rather it stems from a secular ethos that defines preservation of nature as a human, collective, public necessity while religion is a product of personal choice and belief.

Singling out these authors, more innovative and critical than many, may be unfair. This failure to address religion as an integral feature of the public sphere afflicts scholarship on religion most generally. The study of religion by and large regards it as a private affair, living in the experiences of individuals and groups, and relating to larger public structures as something outside of what religion is in itself. This theoretical choice reflects what often goes without saying (and without much reflecting or analyzing) in the shorthand description of what religious studies is: the secular study of religion.

Recognition of this pervasive secular ethos has driven certain scholars to critically address the issue. John Modern's history of secularism in antebellum America treats its atmospheric, obscure, and embodied character.[11] Tracy Fessenden's work focuses on the paradoxical construction of America as a simultaneously religious (Christian) and secular nation.[12] Courtney Bender lays out the network of institutional entanglements of (supposedly individualist) spiritual practice in a specific locale, entanglements that find spectacular illustration in Kathryn Lofton's study of Oprah Winfrey's personal branding.[13] All these authors revise any notion of the secular as a natural, self-evident category that can be clearly and cleanly separated from religion. This book contributes to such appraisals of the secular, focusing on space, power, and the state.

While offering important innovations in critically analyzing secularity, these viewpoints have not been fully taken up within the general discourse. The present analysis of experiential production in the parks illuminates key features of secularity that have received relatively little treatment. Scholars have studied the secular largely as a concept, a set of arguments and beliefs, a system of evaluation with rules for inclusion and exclusion of claims for the purpose of generating consensus. The idea that a secular worldview is a "natural" one, a default and norm that relies on no contentious/optional claim of supernatural/transcendent realities, has been treated in much of the literature as precisely that: an idea.[14] Such studies have failed to address the construction of the experience of nature, and thus have failed to address the construction of secular subjectivities with respect to aesthetics, embodiment, and the microphysics of power. This study has addressed precisely this lacuna in scholarship in the case of national parks in America. The resulting portrait of the secular, as particular to its context as it is, shows how the "ideological" exclusions that inform the secular can take socially productive form, and with this portrait any simple binary of religious and secular becomes problematic. As a state institution and also by virtue of secular custom and mores, the Park Service is forbidden from "preaching," attributing their actions to divine authority, and promulgating religious doctrine. But through strategies of implication and management of aesthetics, the Park Service can, and does, facilitate connections among state, citizen, and environment that are experienced as "spirituality" while avoiding the church/state barrier.

The subtlety and sophistication of this operation of power should not obscure its magnitude. This book has shown that the state can kick people off land, prohibit others from coming in, blast roads and trails, consciously manipulate animal populations, landscape the landscape, and set up a whole complex of national self-representation with buildings and speakers and media and signage—all of it in such a way that the audience, the "owners" of this land, swallow it whole, leaving them with the sense that the resulting environment is "nature" and that their individual experience of it gets them in touch with their inner selves and ultimate reality. *That* is power—liberal, individualist, progressive, spiritual, and secular power.

One might object, if this is power then it is a pretty nice form of power. For the visiting vacationer, this may be true. For the original inhabitants and locals who would like to live in and with the land in ways incompatible with a pristine nature resort, not so much. But there is a larger issue at work. As Talal Asad has shown, the secular is a construct that legitimates the projection of power around the world. What constitutes valid forms of political organization, whose voices are recognized, what kinds of behavioral standards can be respected, which statements are treated as reasonable and worthy of dialogic engagement—all these are governed according to standards that are often taken for granted as natural and conducive of freedom and authenticity: secular norms. But other cultures and societies around the world, particularly the ones that have been colonized by freedom-loving secularists, make different assumptions about the nature of being and the social order. And when countries/societies/cultures/religions and their individual participant members are regarded as violating the natural order that respects individual freedom and authentic being, they might get not just a calm argument from a park ranger trying to get them to stay on the path. They can become subject to violence.[15]

This violent dimension of the secular ethos relates closely to the failure to recognize the social, embodied construction of subjectivity. As Charles Taylor has argued, a foundational feature of secularity is the idea not only that the world is purely natural, but that religious claims are purely optional, not grounded in "reality" but in free will.[16] And when religious claims come into conflict with secular ones, not only are the religious claims regarded as out of touch with reality, but they are also *therefore* regarded as being immune from any efforts to change them. If the religious will not listen to reason, they can only be manipulated by force, so the secular argument goes.[17] But when nature, freedom, and reason are seen as products of particular social arrangements that engender subjectivities, then conflicts between the religious and secular can find alternatives to violence for their resolution.

By no means do I intend to place the blame on the parks or the Park Service for creating conditions for secular intolerance. Secular subjectivities can manifest a variety of behaviors and political orientations. And parks and their rangers should not be expected to endow visitors with all the tools for enlightened citizenship. Critical reflection on the social construction of one's own subjectivity plays a vital role in such citizenship. A more critical awareness of the depth and sophistication of this cultivation of a secular mindset might lead to a better ability to relate peaceably to those whose subjectivities have not been cultivated in the same way. And that relation is strongest and most just when it is self-critical even as it criticizes others in the name of freedom and authenticity.

Some may find the intermeshing of nature spirituality and state power disturbing. But for most park visitors, the combination goes down easily. This book has shown how, under the guidance of the state, nature comes alive in a variety of pleasing ways. Recognizing the mechanics of this process may be unsettling, particularly in seeing how the government constructs nature. But such disquiet can be seen as the price of asserting freedom and individuality. It may not be a bad thing to be disturbed by one's ideals even as one embraces them, and in the case of national parks to allow oneself—willingly, self-critically, and with some trepidation—to be guided by the invisible hand of the natural state.

APPENDIX

Research Methods

CHAPTER 2: THE JOHN MUIR TRAIL

The data for this chapter is drawn from formal, recorded interviews with thirty-six hikers, supplemented by informal conversations with approximately a dozen other hikers over the summers of 2002 and 2003. To gather these interviews, I first stationed myself at Red's Meadow, a small cluster of private establishments outside of Devil's Postpile National Monument near Mammoth, California. The private campground in Red's Meadow is located close to the John Muir Trail/Pacific Crest Trail (the two trails run concurrently at this section), and the general store and restaurant are logical stopping points for hikers, as well as popular spots for day trippers or car campers visiting Devil's Postpile, nearby Rainbow Falls, and several lakes where one can fish. I also conducted interviews at the southern end of the trail at Whitney Portal, a similar cluster of businesses underneath Mount Whitney outside of Lone Pine, California. My hope was to interview a number of hikers twice, but timing and logistical difficulties limited that number to five.

Fallen arches and a strong tendency to pronate capped my comfortable hiking range at about five miles. Given the pain and risk of further physical damage, I decided not to hike the John Muir Trail (JMT) myself. Only once did I accompany a hiking group along the trail, setting out along an alternate route for the JMT that led up Fish Creek to Iva Bell Hot Springs. This three-day sojourn was the longest period I spent "hiking the trail," and even so the experience was quite different from what that of the JMT hikers. Required to maintain a light pack, keep moving, and get to the next resupply point, the two hikers whom I accompanied were in a situation quite different from mine: I had a one-day return journey to an established campsite with a variety of amenities. Overall, therefore, I was not "living with" the hikers.

Given these conditions, I cannot call my study of JMT hikers "ethnography." Had I lived with them, I would have had to move with them, and I simply could not. While the status of fellow hiker was unavailable to me, I did have an alternative that gave me a certain integration into the world of long-distance hiking. I became a "trail angel." "Trail angel" is a term used among long-distance hikers to refer to those who do not hike the trail, but who place themselves along the trail in order to offer aid and support.[1] As my project encouraged me to stay for prolonged periods at points along the trail, and as my research ethic calls for some contribution to the well-being of my subjects of study, becoming a trail angel was natural and almost unavoidable. I asked hikers coming off a long day's journey to spend some time helping me with my project. In the spirit of reciprocity I offered any aid that I could provide, such as food, firewood, first aid, or a ride to the nearest town if needed. As simply as that, I acquired my (so-called) heavenly status.

My interviews with hikers generally occurred around a picnic table. I used a digital recorder and a boundary microphone. In order to set the hikers at ease, and also because of the limited light outdoors where the interviews occurred, I decided not to ask hikers to fill out a written survey. I likewise largely refrained from writing or reading from a questionnaire, opting instead to conduct the interview extemporaneously. The survey below therefore served as a guideline that I followed from memory. Towards the close of the interview I would attempt to fill gaps that had not been covered in the course of conversation, most often addressing demographic questions. In these ways I hoped to preserve the "natural" atmosphere as much as possible, thereby maintaining the enthusiasm of the interviewees by not interrupting their out-of-doors experience.

In terms of interview style, I chose to keep the interview as close to a conversation as possible, hoping to address the questions below in the natural course of the exchange. Much of my participation therefore consisted of comments and follow-up questions concerning issues the hikers had raised. I often followed tangents, hoping to move the interview to an area where the hikers would respond with the most enthusiasm. The advantage of this method lies in the degree of spontaneity and passion it can evoke on the part of interviewees. The disadvantage lies in the failure to ask all the same questions of each respondent, leading to a lack of comparability among interviews.

The idiosyncrasy of each interview cannot help but affect the analysis. In order to stimulate further response, I often offered my own analyses and observations. These assertions of my own voice cannot be separated from the "raw data" of hiker responses. Given the great variation among the interviews, as well as my role in shaping each conversation, the conclusions I draw cannot be considered as "found objects" belonging exclusively or even primarily to the subjectivity of hikers. Rather I draw on these interviews to address a set of theoretical problems generated largely outside of the world of long-distance hiking.

Interview Guidelines for John Muir Trail Hikers

1. Why did you come to the park? What were you expecting?
2. What struck you most about your experience here?
3. How often do you spend time in nature (daily, weekly, monthly, ______ times per year)?
4. Where are your favorite natural areas found (private property, local beaches, city parks, national forests, wilderness areas, national parks, etc.)?
5. How important are encounters with nature in your life (unimportant, not very important, somewhat important, very important, absolutely important)?
6. How has this place influenced your appreciation for nature, for what nature means to you?
7. Do you consider yourself a religious/spiritual person? Do you prefer either of those terms?
8. Please name the religion, if any, and if appropriate, to which you currently adhere (please be as specific as possible; i.e., Southern Baptist, Roman Catholic, Reform Jew, Protestant evangelical, none, etc.).
9. How important is religion/spirituality in your life (unimportant, not very important, somewhat important, very important, absolutely important)?
10. How deeply is your religion/spirituality connected to your appreciation for nature (not connected, not very connected, somewhat connected, very connected, absolutely connected)? Please explain.
11. How has this place influenced your religious/spiritual views of nature?

12. What is your zip code or the country of residence where you currently live? _____
13. What is the highest grade of school or year of college that you have completed? ______
14. Are you single, married, living with a life partner, or widowed?
15. In what race would you place yourself? Select one or more of the following groups.
    a. American Indian or Alaska Native
    b. Asian
    c. Black or African American
    d. Native Hawaiian or other Pacific Islander
    e. White
    f. Other: _________
16. What is your age? _____
17. Which one of the following best describes your employment situation?
    a. Working full-time for pay
    b. Working part-time for pay
    c. Self-employed/consultant
    d. Currently seeking work/unemployed
    e. Permanently disabled
    f. Homemaker/caregiver
    g. Student
    h. Other
18. How many children under the age of 18 are living in your household? ___
19. Which of the following income groups best describes your total household income in 2002 before taxes?
    a. Less than $20,000
    b. $20,000 to $49,999
    c. $50,000 to $99,999
    d. $100,000
20. What is your gender, M / F ?

CHAPTERS 3 AND 4: YOSEMITE NATIONAL PARK AND MUIR WOODS NATIONAL MONUMENT

Data gathered for these chapters arose out of a protocol much different from the one used for long-distance hikers. In order to gain the permission and cooperation of the Park Service, I had to limit myself to certain areas and methods within the space of the parks. In Yosemite, the Park Service approved the administration of a formal, written survey (see below) to be conducted outside the visitor center in Yosemite Valley. I was instructed to bear a clipboard and a name tag, and to identify myself in a way that clearly distinguished me from a Park Service employee. I placed myself near some benches off to the side of the main walkway leading from the bus stop up to the visitor center (given the parking situation, visitors could reach the visitor center only by walking a good distance or by taking a shuttle bus). As each busload got off, a crowd of visitors started to make its way up the walkway. Standing at the edge of the walkway, clipboard in hand, I endeavored to make eye contact with the closest visitors. After greeting the first responsive visitor/s, I would ask if they might fill out a survey. I would then inform them of the nature of the survey and its purpose. If the visitors agreed to cooperate, they would sit on one of the nearby benches. Visitors were given the option of completing the discursive response (see question 13 below) in conversation with me, after which I would record verbal notes into my digital recorder. In this way I gathered 150 written surveys over the course of several weeks during the summer of 2003.

In terms of gaining a representative sample of park visitors, this method of gathering data has a number of limitations. One might reasonably assume that those who have visited Yosemite before, especially those who visit with some regularity, would avoid the crowds and buses that a trip to the visitor center entails. Likewise those who seek a more wilderness-type experience might not make such a stop.[2] Even those who intend a more "civilized" visit might not make it to the valley. With the crowds and heat in the valley, especially in the summertime, the high country of Tuolumne Meadows becomes an attractive alternative. Likewise the Mariposa Grove of Giant Sequoias, over an hour's drive to the south but still within the park, is an attraction in its own right. Finally, Tioga Road provides a scenic alternative to Interstate 80 for those who must cross the Sierra Nevada mountain range on their journey to or from northern California. Rangers consider it a victory if they can entice such drive-by tourists to take a ten-minute walk into a meadow, but the chances of capturing such visitors in a survey are low. These and other factors may lend a certain particularity to the population that patronizes the visitor center in the valley.

To gain some idea of what visitors were experiencing outside of Yosemite Village and the visitor center, my options were limited. I had been instructed by the Park Service not to conduct any surveys outside of that one location, and I was told that "cold-calling" visitors out on the trails and recording interviews were also inappropriate. Nevertheless, I endeavored to talk to visitors as much as I could within these parameters. In the campgrounds, after interpretive programs, and as I walked the trails, I made efforts to engage visitors in conversation. When the subject turned to what had brought me there, I would tell them about my project, and often a de facto, informal interview (similar to the protocol used for the long-distance hikers, above) would follow. Afterwards I would record my observations in a running audio journal. Again, the idiosyncrasies of such exchanges preclude rigorous comparative analysis, rendering these interviews as conversations "on background."

My interviews with rangers displayed a similar indirect quality, although here the approach was formal. I used a written protocol (see below) and recorded the interviews as they were being conducted. As mentioned in the introduction, the prohibition against surveying rangers as a group led to my treatment of them as experts on the meaning of park experience rather than sources of raw data. In these interviews I did note their "private" religious orientations, and I inquired as to how these might have informed their professional duties. But I did not seek to amalgamate these private orientations into a collective picture. Instead I wanted to find out how much religion and/or spirituality rangers considered appropriate to the public sphere in which they worked. I focused on the process of communication, including the goals, techniques, and difficulties involved, and asked what role religion and/or spirituality might play in their collective mission. In this way I sought to draw a picture of public religion that could be distinguished from private religious convictions and behaviors.

Methods used to gather data at Muir Woods were similar to those used in Yosemite. After negotiation with the Park Service, I was given permission to conduct surveys outside the visitor center and entryway to the park. As in Yosemite, I was instructed to wear a nametag and bear a clipboard and to dress in a way that distinguished me from a Park Service employee. Here, however, the situation of visitors was much different from that of visitors surveyed in Yosemite. In Muir Woods, I caught visitors as they exited the park. Furthermore, this survey location caught the vast majority of visitors (given the location of the park and the steepness of the surrounding terrain, bypassing the entryway would require a significant amount of time and exertion). In addition to providing a more representative sample of park visitors, these factors also allowed me to speak with visitors after they had undergone significant exposure to the park environment and to Park Service programming. Under these conditions I surveyed 150 visitors during the summer of 2003.

As in Yosemite, permission for the survey came with the understanding that I would not approach visitors inside the park. And again, as in Yosemite, my contact with visitors inside the park consisted of informal conversations whose import I recorded in a running audio journal. Here one may note a particularity of the environment. The vast majority of visitors restricted themselves to the 1.5 mile loop along relatively flat terrain near the entryway to the park. This valley, traversed by a boardwalk and easy trails, contains the oldest and tallest trees as well as the interpretive installations, restrooms, gift shop, snack bar, and other amenities. Those who wish for a more solitary experience among the redwoods can take the steep trails leading out of the valley. While the trails are maintained and there are several benches where one can rest and enjoy the scenery, the steepness of the terrain discourages most visitor groups. In terms of experiential environments, there is therefore a basic distinction between, on the one hand, the well-trodden valley floor that can comfortably accommodate most visitor groups and, on the other, the slopes where one may find more athletic visitors.

Interviews with Muir Woods rangers occurred under conditions similar to those of the Yosemite ranger interviews.

Survey of Visitors to Yosemite National Park and Muir Woods National Monument

This survey investigates the relation between people's experience in national parks and their religious/spiritual views, if any, of nature. This research is being conducted through the Department of Religious Studies at the University of California, Santa Barbara. Participation in the survey is completely voluntary and all answers will remain confidential.

1. The National Park System consists of all the units managed by the National Park Service, including national parks, historic and cultural sites, and national monuments. How many times in the past two years have you visited a unit of the National Park System, including this one? _______
2. In which of the following activities have you participated during this visit (circle all that apply)?
   a. Sightseeing
   b. Hiking for more than two hours
   c. Taking a ranger-led interpretive nature tour
   d. Other: _______
3. How many people, including yourself, are in your group visiting the park? _______
4. How often do you spend time outdoors in a natural setting (daily, weekly, monthly, ______ times per year)?
5. What are your favorite natural areas to visit (please specify, with names if possible, whether these are local beaches, city parks, national forests, wilderness areas, national parks, etc.)?
6. How important are encounters with nature in your life (circle one: unimportant, not very important, somewhat important, very important, absolutely important)?
7. Please name any books, films, television programs, art works, etc., that have particularly influenced your view of nature.
8. Have you read any of John Muir's works? Which ones? _________
9. Do you consider yourself a (circle one if you prefer either term) religious/spiritual person? _______
10. Please name the religious tradition or denomination, if any, to which you feel you belong (please be as specific as possible).

11. How important is religion/spirituality in your life (circle one: unimportant, not very important, somewhat important, very important, absolutely important)?
12. How deeply is your religion/spirituality connected to your appreciation for nature (not connected, not very connected, somewhat connected, very connected, absolutely connected)?
13. Do you feel that there is anything religious/spiritual about your experience of national parks? Of this national park?

** Please explain your answers to questions 12 and 13 using the back of this form. If you prefer to communicate your responses verbally, feel free to approach me.

14. What is your zip code or the country of residence where you currently live? _____
15. What is the highest grade of school or year of college that you have completed? ______
16. Are you single, married, living with a life partner, or widowed?
17. In what race would you place yourself? Select one or more of the following groups.
    a. American Indian or Alaska Native
    b. Asian
    c. Black or African American
    d. Native Hawaiian or other Pacific Islander
    e. White
    f. Other: _____
18. What is your age? ______
19. Which one of the following best describes your employment situation?
    a. Working full-time for pay
    b. Working part-time for pay
    c. Self-employed/consultant
    d. Currently seeking work/unemployed
    e. Permanently disabled
    f. Homemaker/caregiver
    g. Student
    h. Other
20. How many children under the age of 18 are living in your household? ___

21. Which of the following income groups best describes your total household income in 2002 before taxes?
    a. Less than $20,000
    b. $20,000 to $49,999
    c. $50,000 to $99,999
    d. $100,000
22. What is your gender (circle one) M / F ?

If you would be willing to be contacted for a follow-up interview, please give your first name, telephone number, and times and days of the week when you are most easily reached.

If you would like learn the results of this survey, please provide an email address or other contact information:

This project is not sponsored by the National Park Service. If you have any questions or comments regarding this survey, feel free to contact Kerry Mitchell, Department of Religious Studies, University of California, Santa Barbara, California, 93106.

Answers to 12 and 13:

CHAPTER FIVE: FOLLOW-UP PHONE INTERVIEWS WITH VISITORS TO YOSEMITE AND MUIR WOODS

To investigate the theoretical claims advanced in this project more thoroughly, I interviewed twenty visitors to Yosemite and Muir Woods during the summer of 2007. On the written surveys that visitors filled out in the parks, they were given the option of providing their phone numbers for further contact. During June and July of 2007, I called all the numbers that were provided and conducted interviews with the first twenty who answered and had time for an interview.

Follow-Up Interview

Hi, this is Kerry Mitchell. Is _____ available?

We met several years ago in Yosemite/Muir Woods where I was conducting a survey of religious and/or spiritual attitudes towards nature in national parks. In responding to that survey you indicated that you would be willing to be contacted for a possible follow-up interview, and you gave me your phone number for that. This long-running project is still underway, but a few more moments of your time would help greatly in bringing it to completion. Do you have some time right now to answer a few questions? Do you mind if I record this interview? Your answers will remain confidential.

1. Could you describe your most memorable visit to a national park? What made that visit memorable?
   a. Were you alone?
   b. With family?
   c. In nature?
2. What stands out when you think of the management of the national parks that you have visited? All the programs, facilities, services—the civilized aspects of the park.
   a. What kind of contact have you had with rangers?
   b. Participate in park programs?
   c. How did you decide what to do? Where did you get info?
   d. What kind of lodging?
3. Have you ever been disappointed in your experience in national parks? Had something that bothered you?
4. You wrote that you considered your experience of national parks as religious and/or spiritual. Could you say a bit more about that?
5. The motto of the National Parks is "Experience your America." What does this mean to you?
   a. Explain it to a young relative, or perhaps a foreigner
   b. Why say "your"?
   c. Why "experience"? What does this mean?
6. How has your experience in the parks influenced the way you think about America? About being an American?
   a. Would you say your experience of the parks has made you more patriotic? How so?
7. How has your experience in the parks influenced the way you think about the government?
8. You wrote that you considered your experience of national parks as religious and/or spiritual. How do you think the management of the park may have influenced this dimension of your experience?
9. How might the religious/spiritual dimension of your experience influence the way you think about America? About the government?
10. In general, do you think it is important to have national parks? Why or why not?

NOTES

INTRODUCTION

1 See especially Asad, *Formations of the Secular*; Calhoun, Juergensmeyer, and VanAntwerpen, eds., *Rethinking Secularism*; Dressler and Mandir, eds., *Secularism and Religion-Making.*

2 *"Nones" on the Rise.*

3 See in particular Casanova, *Public Religions in the Modern World*, 61; Wuthnow, "Divided We Fall," 397.

4 Jacoby, *Crimes against Nature*, 2.

5 See Keller and Turek, *American Indians and National Parks*; Spence, *Dispossessing the Wilderness*; Burnham, *Indian Country, God's Country.*

6 This dynamic can be seen in the Authority of the Resource Technique (ART) that allows state agents to explain and enforce regulations in protected areas by appealing to the needs of the natural resource. A resource manual for managers of protected areas states that "[ART] transfers the authority (or that which asks a person to think or behave in a certain way) from the manager ranger or agency, to those things in nature (resources) that have their own requirements. . . . The AR technique . . . asks the ranger/manager to subtly de-emphasize the regulation and transfer part of the expectation back to the visitor by interpreting nature's requirements." The author gives an example of asking a visitor to put his dog on a leash for the sake of mule deer foals in the surrounding area. This is not just the state as nature. This is the state as Bambi. Wallace, "Law Enforcement and the 'Authority of the Resource.'"

7 For discussion of issues of secularism, intolerance, and violence, see Asad, *Formations of the Secular*, 56–62. See also Mahmood, "Secularism, Hermeneutics and Empire," 346–47. With respect to liberalism, see in particular Fessenden, "Religious Liberalism and the Liberal Geopolitics of Religion." I address these concerns more fully in the conclusion.

8 For scholarly discussion of the definition of this term see Roof, *A Generation of Seekers*, 67–68, 76–79, 119–48; Roof, *Spiritual Marketplace*, 33–35, 173–79; Zinnbauer et al., "Religion and Spirituality"; Albanese, Introduction; Taylor, "Earth and Nature-Based Spirituality"; Heelas and Woodhead, *The Spiritual Revolution*, 5–7, 12–32; Van der Veer, "Spirituality in Modern Society"; Taylor, *Dark Green Religion*, 3–4; Bender, *The New Metaphysicals*, 5–12; Gall, Malette, and Guirgis-Younger, "Spirituality and Religiousness"; Ammermann, "Spiritual But Not Religious?."

9 Anderson, *Imagined Communities*.
10 Corrigan and Sayer, *The Great Arch*, 3; emphasis in the original.
11 Luhmann, "Speaking and Silence," 26.
12 The scope of this project does exclude, however, the large number of "historical" parks within the National Park System. While the distinction between "natural" and "historical" parks is problematic, this project's focus on nature complements previous scholarship that has treated the religious and/or spiritual valuation of national parks that stand as historical monuments. See Linenthal, *Sacred Ground*; Glass, "'Alexanders All'"; Bremer, *Blessed with Tourists*.
13 Rich Weideman, Chief of Public Affairs and Special Events, Golden Gate National Recreation Area, telephone conversation, May 2003.
14 For a more detailed discussion of research methods, see the appendix.

CHAPTER 1. ESTABLISHING NATIONAL PARKS

1 Muir, *My First Summer in the Sierra*, 20–21.
2 Runte, *Yosemite*, 54–55.
3 Runte, *National Parks*.
4 See Kraus, *Recreation and Leisure in Modern Society*, 91ff. For a treatment of the broad intellectual context for the recreation movement, see Shivers, "Formation of an American Philosophy of Play and Recreation."
5 For Olmsted's larger legacy, see Spirn, "Constructing Nature."
6 Olmsted, Sr., "The Yosemite Valley and the Mariposa Big Tree Grove," 18.
7 Ibid.
8 Ibid., 22.
9 Ibid.
10 Ibid.
11 Ibid., 12.
12 Yellowstone Park Act of 1872, in Dilsaver, *America's National Park System*, 28.
13 These parks include Yellowstone, Yosemite, Sequoia, and Mt. Rainier. Sellars, *Preserving Nature in the National Parks*, 11–16.
14 Ibid., 28–46; Runte, *National Parks*, 65–81.
15 "Aboard the Underground Railroad," http://www.nps.gov/nr/travel/underground/.
16 See, for example, National Park Service, http://www.nps.gov/ever/index.htm.
17 For general treatments of heritage, see the work of historians David Lowenthal and David Glassberg. Highlighting the social function of heritage, Lowenthal asserted that "heritage passes on exclusive myths of origin and continuance, endowing a select group with prestige and common purpose," and that pride in heritage "inheres no less in precedence than in perpetuity—unbroken connections, permanent traits and institutions. Maintaining or restoring such links confirms that the groups we belong to are not ephemeral but enduring organisms" (*Possessed by the Past*, 128, 184). Echoing Lowenthal's conception of heritage, Glassberg analyzed what he called the "sense of history," or the "place of the past in the wider culture" beyond a university setting. Glassberg considered the sense of history as

akin to a "sense of place" that "locates us in space . . . in time . . . [and] in society, with a knowledge that helps us gain a sense of *with whom we belong*, connecting our personal experiences and memories with those of a larger community, region, or nation" (*Sense of History*, 7; emphasis in original).

18 One should note that within government documents, initial expressions of the symbolic function of national parks did not fall under any single term. Not until the 1960s did government officials begin to invoke the word "heritage" regularly to refer to the symbolic aspect of preservation. I use "heritage" as an interpretive category reflecting the enduring usage of the term within government literature up to the present day.

19 The National Park Service Organic Act of 1916, in Dilsaver, *America's National Park System*, 46.

20 Sellars, *Preserving Nature*, 40–41. Sellars's remarks referred to the manner in which Olmsted, Jr., suggested the revision—namely, at the end of a substantial letter and with minimal prefacing comments. One should note, however, that the elder Olmsted's report to the governor of California (which the younger Olmsted surely would have read) indicated thorough deliberation on the relation between nature preservation and a future public: "It should be remembered that in permitting the sacrifice of anything that would be of the slightest value to future visitors to the convenience, bad taste, playfulness, carelessness, or wanton destructiveness of present visitors, we probably yield in each case the interest of uncounted millions to the selfishness of a few individuals." Olmsted, Sr., elaborated on this point for several paragraphs. Dilsaver, *America's National Park System*, 23–24.

21 Yellowstone Park Act of 1872, in Dilsaver, *America's National Park System*, 28.

22 *Superintendents' Resolution on Overdevelopment*, 57. Despite this early intention to include education within the national park ideal, education played only a limited role in park programming during these early years. Not until the florescence of the ecological movement in the 1960s (discussed later in this chapter) did education become a primary vehicle for communicating the value of national parks. See Mackintosh, *Interpretation in the National Park Service*, 6ff.

23 Although Toll does not refer to the account in Genesis of the fall from grace, his understanding of industrial progress as a fall from a state of natural harmony echoes the themes of the biblical account most broadly. See Merchant, "Reinventing Eden."

24 *Superintendents' Resolution on Overdevelopment*, 59.

25 Ibid.

26 Work, "Statement of National Park Policy," 62.

27 Given the nationalist aspect of the first principle, the third principle of "national interest" may have functioned as a reassertion of federal, as opposed to state or local, sovereignty over the park lands.

28 Albright, "The National Park Service's Policy on Predatory Mammals," 87.

29 Even the slight change in the second principle suggests a reassertion of the symbolic value of the parks. Work wrote that parks are set apart for "use, education, health, and pleasure." Albright stated that parks are for "use, observation, health, pleasure, and inspiration." The addition of "inspiration," given the context of Roger Toll's explanatory letter discussed above, suggests an appreciation of the symbolic value of nature.

30 Albright, "The National Park Service's Policy on Predatory Mammals," 87.

31 Albright, "Office Order No. 228," 100.

32 As a matter of record, one should note that the Park Service maintains trails within wilderness areas. This may speak to the distinction between "general" protection of wilderness versus the protection against "all" development in smaller natural sites.

33 Edge, "Roads and More Roads"; White, "Atmosphere in the National Parks."

34 Drury, "The National Parks in Wartime," 168.

35 Ibid., 169.

36 Ibid., 168.

37 Ibid., 173.

38 Ibid., 171.

39 In addition to the notion of "balance . . . among all the elements" of a natural area, Drury illuminated his use of the term "ecological" by referring to the "harmonious relationship" of wildlife to an environment that was allowed to "evolve normally" ("The National Parks in Wartime," 173). This conception of "ecology" was broadly consistent with other uses of the term at this time. Donald Worster, in his study of the history of ecological ideas, noted that the U. S. government's land management policy at mid-century was dominated by a utilitarian approach that, while occasionally recognizing the complex interdependence among all elements of an environment, nevertheless subsumed all decisions under an anthropocentric view. Against this view, Worster highlighted the conservation ethic of Aldo Leopold, who postulated that humans stood in relationship to nature in terms of an ethical community. This idea of a personal, moral relationship to the nonhuman world offered an approach to policy decisions distinctive from that of utilitarianism. Interestingly, Drury's use of "ecology" did not fall strictly within either of these strains of ecological thought. According to Drury, the interdependent natural systems preserved in national parks were not to be exploited for human consumption, but the call to protect such systems was not a moral one, either. Rather, as I explain later in this chapter, the systems of relationship in nature were to be preserved as examples of "original design" ("The National Parks in Wartime," 173). From this perspective, nature provided connections among individuals and a common heritage that was now conceived not simply in nationalistic terms, but also in terms of ontological foundations. See Worster, *Nature's Economy*, 255–90.

40 See Merriam, *The Garment of God*. As a prominent paleontologist and conservationist during the early twentieth century, Merriam complemented his writings with political work oriented toward growing the system of state and national parks, particularly in California. See Mark, *Preserving the Living Past*.

41 Drury, "The National Parks in Wartime," in Dilsaver, *America's National Park System*, 173.

42 Ibid.

43 I use "ethical" here to connote a system of rules that may or may not involve an internal, moral feeling of community among those governed by the system (this contrasts with Aldo Leopold's understanding of an ethical community founded on a sense of moral bonds). Later sections of this chapter show that the systems paradigm, while in no way inimical to sensations of collective unity, appealed almost exclusively to order and necessity in presenting the value of ecological systems in the parks.

44 For the distinction between state and nation, see Gellner, *Nations and Nationalism*, 3–7. Gellner defined the state as "that institution or set of institutions specifically concerned with the enforcement of order" (3). Gellner defined the nation in both cultural and voluntaristic terms: "1) Two men are of the same nation if and only if they share the same culture, where culture in turn means a system of ideas and signs and associations and ways of behaving and communicating. 2) Two men are of the same nation if and only if they *recognize* each other as belonging to the same nation" (7). Under conditions specific to an industrial and nationalist age, Gellner continued, a nation arose as a combination of culture and will: "When general social conditions make for standardized, homogeneous, centrally sustained high cultures, pervading entire populations and not just elite minorities, a situation arises in which well-defined educationally sanctioned and unified cultures constitute very nearly the only kind of unit with which men willingly and often ardently identify. The cultures now seem to be the natural repositories of political legitimacy" (55). For an application of the nation/state distinction within the context of public religion in America, see Albanese, *America*, 434ff.

45 Wirth, "Mission 66," 194.

46 DeVoto, "Let's Close the National Parks."

47 Within the fields of economics and political science, this expanded conception of the value of public lands has found expression in the notion of "public goods." See Lowry, *Preserving Public Lands for the Future*. For a treatment of the intangible values of park lands, see Harmon and Putney, eds., *The Full Value of Parks*.

48 Wirth, "Mission 66," 193–94.

49 Ibid., 195–96.

50 Ibid., 194.

51 DeVoto, "Let's Close the National Parks," 183.

52 Ibid., 184.

53 Wirth, "Mission 66," 194–95.

54 Ibid., 194.

55 Tilden, *Interpreting Our Heritage*. Since it was first published, this work has appeared in three editions, has included forewords from two directors of the National Park Service, and serves to this day in Park Service training as the canonical statement of the principles of interpretation.

56 Ibid., 3, 8.

57 Ibid., 100.

58 Emerson, "History," quoted in Tilden, *Interpreting Our Heritage*, 11.
59 Merriam, *The Making of Citizens*, quoted in Tilden, *Interpreting Our Heritage*, 12.
60 Tilden, *Interpreting Our Heritage*, 110; emphasis in original.
61 Ibid., 93.
62 Cain, "Ecological Islands as Natural Laboratories," 202. Dilsaver noted that Cain's perspective was by no means entirely original and that for years critics had advocated that the Park Service integrate a more ecological approach into their management of the parks. For reasons that are not completely clear, however, Cain's speech received more attention than those earlier exhortations. Dilsaver noted that copies of Cain's speech, accompanied by a laudatory letter from an NPS scientist, were distributed widely within Park Service administration and served to reinvigorate previously sluggish research initiatives. Dilsaver, *America's National Park System*, 198.
63 Cain, "Ecological Islands," 208, 202.
64 Ibid., 208.
65 Ibid., 209.
66 National Park Service, "A Back Country Management Plan," 211–12.
67 Ibid., 212.
68 Ibid.
69 Ibid., 214.
70 Ibid., 214–15.
71 For a treatment of the ambiguities involved in applying the conception of carrying capacity to both humans and wildlife, see Shelby and Heberlein, *Carrying Capacity in Recreation Settings*, 3–5, 7ff.
72 National Park Service, "A Back Country Management Plan," 215. The quotation within this passage comes from Snyder, "How Wild the Wilderness."
73 Advisory Board on Wildlife Management, *Wildlife Management in the National Parks*. Board members included A. S. Leopold (son of *Sand County Almanac* author, Aldo Leopold), S. A. Cain, C. M. Cottam, I. N. Gabrielson, and T. L. Kimball.
74 Ibid., 240.
75 Ibid.
76 Ibid.
77 Ibid., 239.
78 *National Environmental Policy Act*.
79 *General Authorities Act*, 374.
80 National Park Service, *National Parks for the 21st Century*, 435.
81 Ibid.
82 Ibid., 436.
83 "Management Policies 2006," http://www.nps.gov/policy/mp/policies.html#_Toc157232597.
84 *National Parks for the 21st Century* (Chelsea Green ed.), 82; emphasis in original.
85 This focus on "diversity" included but went far beyond ethnic diversity or multiculturalism. One Park Service document embraced this broad understanding of diversity explicitly. Entitled "Coast to Coast Diversity in the National Park

System," this Park Service webpage divided its presentation into the categories of general, historic, cultural, professional, natural, and "experience" diversity. http://www.nps.gov/pwro/coast1.htm.

86 *National Parks for the 21st Century*, in Dilsaver, America's National Park System, 75. Despite its use of the term, this focus on diversity made no distinction between "culture" and nature. Immediately following this citation, the authors discussed the diversity of landscapes and historical events to illustrate their argument.

87 Ibid., 74.

CHAPTER 2. THE JOHN MUIR TRAIL

1 "The Wilderness Act," http://wilderness.nps.gov/document/WildernessAct%2Epdf.

2 Most JMT hikers travel north to south. At the northern end, Yosemite Valley stands at around 4,000-feet elevation and the nearby alternate starting point, Tuolumne Meadows, stands at 8,000. Starting here provides a gradual elevation gain towards the goal, the 14,495-foot Mt. Whitney, allowing easier adjustment to the altitude and less of a shock in terms of physical conditioning.

3 Work, "Statement of National Park Policy," 62.

4 Anderson, "Legacy of the American Frontier," 110–39.

5 "The Wilderness Act," http://wilderness.nps.gov/document/WildernessAct%2Epdf.

6 See previous chapter.

7 These dates reflect the beginning of the JMT hiking season, which, because of the dangers of snow on the passes, extends only from mid-June to late August/early September. Roughly six hundred permits are issued yearly for the John Muir Trail.

8 These frequencies arose from content analysis of interviews, and are therefore a result of deductive coding rather than responses to survey items on a questionnaire. I coded the interviews based strictly on their use of the terms "religion" and/or "religious," on the one hand, and "spiritual," on the other, when hikers described themselves and their experience.

9 Bratton, *The Spirit of the Appalachian Trail*, 44.

10 Ibid., 56.

11 See regional differences among the percentages of religiously unaffiliated. Pew Forum on Religion in Public Life, http://www.pewforum.org/files/2012/10/NonesOnTheRise-full.pdf, 38.

12 Bratton, *The Spirit of the Appalachian Trail*, 56–57.

13 Pew Forum on Religion in Public Life, http://www.pewforum.org/files/2012/10/NonesOnTheRise-full.pdf.

14 For a discussion of this tendency, as well as an important exception that will be discussed below, see Roof, *A Generation of Seekers*, 55–60.

15 Schmidt, *Restless Souls*, 1–23. Interestingly, Schmidt made pains to divorce this tradition of religious liberalism from any particularly Protestant lineage. However,

he presented evidence for making just such a connection, portraying certain liberal tendencies as "hyper-Protestant" to such an extent that they became "post-Christian" (111). See also Catherine L. Albanese's promotional blurb in ibid., n.p.

16 Roof, *Generation of Seekers*, 32–60.

17 http://www.pewforum.org/files/2012/10/NonesOnTheRise-full.pdf, 65–74.

18 Schmidt, *Restless Souls*, 12ff. While Schmidt here characterized nineteenth-century religious liberalism, he argued throughout the work that contemporary spirituality has shared these fundamental traits.

19 Roof, *Generation of Seekers*, 59–60. Roof applied these characteristics to the Baby Boom generation specifically. However, in subsequent work he argued that these same values has informed contemporary American culture much more broadly. See Roof, *Spiritual Marketplace*, 3ff.

20 Wuthnow, *After Heaven*, 7–8.

21 Ibid., 168–98.

22 One of these respondents, describing herself as spiritual and not religious, associated her spirituality with the act of writing and with solitude, both of which failed to manifest in her hike. I discuss her case in greater detail below. Heather McCarey, interview by author, digital recording, Whitney Portal, CA, July 23, 2002. The other respondent was a devout Catholic who associated religion and spirituality with church and other people, saying that his hike had more to do with personal concerns. Tom, interview by author, digital recording, Whitney Portal, CA., July 19, 2002. For reasons of privacy, some of my interviews with hikers were conducted on an exclusively first-name basis.

23 "I think everything around me is a god. We're all gods. I think every rock is god, every tree, every . . . everything. And I don't think every car, every building, every sidewalk—I don't get that same feeling. But when I come out here I'm just surrounded by the magic." Shake and Bake, interview by author, digital recording, Red's Meadow, CA, July 5, 2002. "Shake and Bake" is the "trail name" that this hiker acquired during an earlier long-distance hike. Shake and Bake explained that along the longer hikes such as the Pacific Crest Trail, running from Mexico to Canada, hikers tend to identify each other by names that arise out of particular experiences or reputations that develop along the trail. Her name arose out of her practice of putting foot powder in her boots.

24 Those who did not employ a wilderness/civilization distinction include a high school geology teacher who contrasted the "high country" of the majority of the trail with the lower elevations of the Sierra Nevada mountain range. Randy, interview by author, digital recording, Red's Meadow, CA, July 2, 2002. Another, an experienced long-distance hiker, distinguished between being on the trail as opposed to off it. Here one may note that long-distance trails move through both developed and undeveloped areas. Lone Chair, interview by author, digital recording, Whitney Portal, CA, August 3, 2002. "Lone Chair" is the interviewee's trail name.

25 Steve Grind, interview by author, digital recording, Whitney Portal, CA, July 12, 2002.

26 Billy Witort, interview by author, digital recording, Whitney Portal, CA, July 12, 2002.

27 Shake and Bake, Red's Meadow, July 5, 2002.

28 K. Hensiek, interview by author, digital recording, Whitney Portal, CA, July 15, 2002.

29 Kelly Paige, interview by author, digital recording, Whitney Portal, CA, July 24, 2002.

30 Brian, interview by author, digital recording, Red's Meadow, CA, July 8, 2002.

31 Matt, interview by author, digital recording, Red's Meadow, CA, July 8, 2002.

32 Slow Ride, interview by author, digital recording, Red's Meadow, CA, July 5, 2002.

33 While 84 percent of the interviewees (n=27) made reference to civilization through the terms described above, only six referred to America specifically.

34 There was an exception. One hiker said the experience of hiking the trail had renewed his commitment to start doing volunteer work. K. Hensiek, Whitney Portal, CA, July 15, 2002.

35 This and all following quotations in this section stem from the same interview: John, interview by author, digital recording, Whitney Portal, CA, June 28, 2002.

36 Steve Grind, Whitney Portal, CA, July 12, 2002.

37 Matt, Red's Meadow, CA, July 8, 2002.

38 Slow Ride, Red's Meadow, CA, July 5, 2002.

39 K. Hensiek, Whitney Portal, CA, July 15, 2002.

40 However, one, a devout Catholic, did not consider his experience religious or spiritual despite his evocation of the sublime: "The whole outdoors is so massive. As much as you think you're in control, you're out of control up there. . . . A big storm comes in and it could be over; you could fall off a cliff." Tom, Whitney Portal, CA, July 19, 2002.

41 Bill Thurman, interview by author, digital recording, Whitney Portal, CA, July 19, 2002.

42 Mark, interview by author, digital recording, Red's Meadow, CA, July 2, 2002.

43 Slow Ride, Red's Meadow, CA, July 5, 2002.

44 Steve Grind, Whitney Portal, CA, July 15, 2002.

45 Because of the particularities of this hiker's situation, I have used a pseudonym to identify him.

46 This and all following quotations in this section stem from the same interview: Matt, Red's Meadow, CA, July 8, 2002.

47 "PCTers" refers to those hiking the Pacific Crest Trail that runs for roughly 2,600 miles from Mexico to Canada.

48 Here I did not include reflections upon bonds that linked those who were already intimate: a deeper appreciation for friendships or siblings, for example. Rather, I coded responses under the category of community when hikers referred to "people in general" who were hiking the trail.

49 Randy, Red's Meadow, CA, July 2, 2002.
50 Shake and Bake, Red's Meadow, July 5, 2002.
51 K. Hensiek, Whitney Portal, CA, July 15, 2002.
52 Brian, Red's Meadow, CA, July 8, 2002.
53 This and all following quotations in this section stem from the same interview: Scott and Heather McCarey, interview by author, digital recording, Whitney Portal, CA, July 23, 2002.
54 For example, in high Sierra streams, the speed and volume of water flow varies depending on the season and the time of day, and the danger in fording such streams is often difficult to ascertain until after one has crossed. Hikers traveling in opposite directions can use hindsight to warn each other about where and when to make such crossings.
55 Bratton, *The Spirit of the Appalachian Trail*, 195–96.
56 Ibid., 195–202. Bratton contrasts this finding with Bron Taylor's assertion that many outdoor recreationalists "understand nature itself to be sacred" (Taylor, "Focus Introduction: Aquatic Nature Religion," *Journal of the American Academy of Religion* 75:4 [2007]: 863, quoted in Bratton, *The Spirit of the Appalachian Trail*, 211). The present study also interprets hiker spirituality in a way that points away from the sacredness of nature "in itself." However, this divergence would require much greater precision in definitions to yield a clear contradiction (that is, how would one separate an evaluation of nature "in itself" from [personal] modes of relation to it?).
57 Schmidt, *Restless Souls*, 12.
58 Schmidt, *Restless Souls*, 287. Exceptions would include those hikers (n=5) who invoked a biblical creator God in attributing religious and/or spiritual significance to their experience. The other sixteen hikers who found their experience spiritual, however, did not display such grounding in common texts, vocabulary, and theology. This discrepancy would prohibit one from claiming that, as a whole, hiker spirituality is an expression of biblical tradition.

CHAPTER 3. YOSEMITE NATIONAL PARK

1 For an in-depth treatment of the logic that informs this analysis, see Taussig, *Defacement*.
2 Marjorie Hope Nicolson has shown how the judgment of mountains as beautiful is a historically contingent phenomenon. She notes that before the influence of Romanticism took hold in the eighteenth century, Europeans tended to view mountains as frightful places. See Nicolson, *Mountain Gloom and Mountain Glory*.
3 In 1865 Samuel Bowles of the *Springfield Republican* (Massachusetts) wrote that the formations of Yosemite Valley matched "the great impressiveness, the beauty and the fantastic form of Gothic architecture. From their shape and color alike, it is easy to imagine, in looking upon them, that you are under the ruins of an old Gothic cathedral, to which those of Cologne and Milan are but baby-houses" (See

Samuel Bowles, *Across the Continent: A Summer's Journey to the Rocky Mountains, the Mormons, and the Pacific States, with Speaker Colfax* [Springfield, MA: Samuel Bowles Co., 1865], 226–27, quoted in Runte, *Yosemite*, 15). Runte discusses such claims under the rubric of "scenic nationalism," which he identifies as a central theme in arguments for creating national parks.

4 Muir, *John Muir*, 588.

5 Ibid., 589.

6 Runte, *Yosemite*, 54–55.

7 Here Muir's metaphor of a natural temple is still instructive. That is, one could argue that in terms of touristic development Yosemite Valley was run as if it were the preserve of a cathedral: monumental architecture surrounded by gift shops, tour guides, visitor accommodations, and so forth.

8 See Runte, *National Parks*; Sellars, *Preserving Nature in the National Parks*.

9 Notable exceptions to this scholarly neglect include McClelland, *Presenting Nature*, and Carr, *Wilderness by Design*.

10 Runte, *Yosemite*, 155.

11 Ibid., 88–90.

12 Ibid., 137–38.

13 This function would have been called "education" if not for the status of parks as vacation destinations. In the interest of attracting greater visitor participation, these educational programs were given a title that did not imply the work and/or sacrifice that many visitors (and their children) associated with the term "education." See Mackintosh, *Interpretation in the National Park Service*, 6ff..

14 Julia Parker, "Mewu Eh, Ahwahneechee Traditions," interpretive program presented in Yosemite, CA, August 9, 2003.

15 Julia Parker, conversation with author, Yosemite, CA, August 9, 2003.

16 Eric Westerlund, conversation with author, Yosemite, CA, September 9, 2002.

17 Ibid.

18 Ginger Burley, interview by author, digital recording, Tuolumne Meadows, CA, September 16, 2002.

19 Here one may note parallels with the themes of connection and perception in the spirituality of JMT hikers. See Chapter 2.

20 Ibid.

21 Ibid.

22 Margaret Eissler, interview by author, digital recording, Tuolumne Meadows, CA, September 7, 2002.

23 For this discussion of Eissler's program, and unless otherwise noted, all quotations refer to Margaret Eissler, "Ranger Walk—Music for Parks," interpretive program presented in Tuolumne Meadows, CA, September 7, 2002.

24 In her notes, which she made available to me after the program, Eissler attributes this quotation, drawn from the *Los Angeles Times* of November 27, 1978, to Hannah Morgan, "who moved with her husband and children from Appalachia to Dayton."

25 Anne Morrow Lindbergh, quoted by Eissler, "Ranger Walk—Music for Parks."
26 Kelley and Cousteau, eds., *The Home Planet.*
27 Data on the general public have been drawn from the National Park Service, Social Science Program, in Solop and Hagan, *The National Park Service Comprehensive Survey of the American Public.*
28 Bellah et al., *Habits of the Heart*, 148–50.
29 Ibid., 221, 246.
30 The phrase belongs to Alasdair MacIntyre, *After Virtue*, 33, quoted in Bellah et al., *Habits of the Heart*, 150.
31 Wuthnow, *The Restructuring of American Religion*, 153–64.
32 The concerns for social justice that rose to prominence in the 1960s, Wuthnow suggested, informed a national controversy with regard to American identity. He argued that the resulting split, seen in the difference between conservative and liberal versions of an American civil religion, continued up to the time of his writing. Wuthnow's discussion of legitimating myths concentrated on what is left as a basis for consensus underneath the controversies and therefore highlighted a concern for a type of freedom that, he suggested, remained as an assumed and unspoken foundation shared by Americans in general. Ibid., 257–64, 277–94.
33 Wuthnow, *After Heaven*, 7–8.
34 Roof, *Spiritual Marketplace.*
35 Roof, *A Generation of Seekers*, 42–48.
36 Inglehart, *Culture Shift in Advanced Industrial Society*, cited in Roof, *Generation of Seekers*, 43.
37 For reasons of privacy, survey respondents were not required to give their names. This and all following survey citations will therefore be identified by an alphabetic/numeric code. Y35, survey administered at Yosemite Village, CA, July 2003.
38 Y134, survey administered at Yosemite Village, CA, July 2003.
39 Y61, survey administered at Yosemite Village, CA, July 2003.
40 Y9, survey administered at Yosemite Village, CA, July 2003.
41 Y34, survey administered at Yosemite Village, CA, July 2003.
42 Ibid.
43 Y37, survey administered at Yosemite Village, CA, July 2003.
44 Y136, survey administered at Yosemite Village, CA, July 2003.
45 Y18, survey administered at Yosemite Village, CA, July 2003.
46 Y113, survey administered at Yosemite Village, CA, July 2003.
47 Y148, survey administered at Yosemite Village, CA, July 2003.
48 Ibid.
49 Y28, survey administered at Yosemite Village, CA, July 2003.
50 Y77, survey administered at Yosemite Village, CA, July 2003.
51 Y88, survey administered at Yosemite Village, CA, July 2003.
52 Y1, survey administered at Yosemite Village, CA, July 2003.
53 Y133, survey administered at Yosemite Village, CA, July 2003.
54 Y79, survey administered at Yosemite Village, CA, July 2003.

55 Y144, survey administered at Yosemite Village, CA, July 2003.
56 Y4, survey administered at Yosemite Village, CA, July 2003.
57 Y73, survey administered at Yosemite Village, CA, July 2003.
58 Y43, survey administered at Yosemite Village, CA, July 2003.
59 Y128, survey administered at Yosemite Village, CA, July 2003.
60 Y17, survey administered at Yosemite Village, CA, July 2003.

CHAPTER 4. MUIR WOODS

1 The plaque attributes these words to then secretary of the interior, Harold Ickes.
2 The following discussion draws historical data from Rothman, *The New Urban Park*, 4–6.
3 Muir, *John Muir*, 589.
4 *Muir Woods National Monument* (San Francisco: Golden Gate National Parks Conservancy, 2004).
5 Such limitation of God's power arises in discussions of theodicy, specifically with regard to the problem of evil. In addressing the question of how an all-good, all-knowing, and all-powerful God could allow evil to exist, certain philosophers and theologians have argued that the free will of human agents is a good that necessitates the existence of evil, if humans choose to do evil. A classic discussion of this problem can be found in Plantinga, God, Freedom, and Evil.
6 For the nation/state distinction that informs this analysis, see Gellner, *Nations and Nationalism*, 3–7; Albanese, *America*, 434ff.
7 See appendix for the full survey.
8 One significant difference between the two populations should be noted here. The Yosemite survey captured an equal number of men and women, with little difference between the two genders with regard to attitudes and sense of identity. The Muir Woods survey, however, captured more women than men (57 percent to 43 percent) and indicated a disparity between the two genders with regard to religious identity: 24 percent of men identified themselves as neither religious nor spiritual while only 11 percent of the women did. While this study is not equipped to explain this disparity, it may inform the content analysis of this section. Specifically, my analysis draws quotations from women more often than from men.
9 M144, survey administered at Muir Woods National Monument, CA, June 2003. Because of the need for confidentiality, respondents are here identified by an alphabetic/numeric code.
10 M39, survey administered at Muir Woods National Monument, CA, May 2003.
11 M1, survey administered at Muir Woods National Monument, CA, May 2003.
12 M128, survey administered at Muir Woods National Monument, CA, June 2003.
13 M3, survey administered at Muir Woods National Monument, CA, May 2003.
14 M5, survey administered at Muir Woods National Monument, CA, May 2003.
15 M7, survey administered at Muir Woods National Monument, CA, May 2003.
16 M37, survey administered at Muir Woods National Monument, CA, May 2003.
17 M30, survey administered at Muir Woods National Monument, CA, May 2003.

18 M29, survey administered at Muir Woods National Monument, CA, May 2003.
19 M17, survey administered at Muir Woods National Monument, CA, May 2003.
20 M138, survey administered at Muir Woods National Monument, CA, June 2003.
21 M27, survey administered at Muir Woods National Monument, CA, May 2003.
22 M96, survey administered at Muir Woods National Monument, CA, June 2003.
23 Respectively, M140, survey administered at Muir Woods National Monument, CA, June 2003; M34, survey administered at Muir Woods National Monument, CA, May 2003; M11, survey administered at Muir Woods National Monument, CA, May 2003.
24 M137, survey administered at Muir Woods National Monument, CA, June 2003.
25 M33, survey administered at Muir Woods National Monument, CA, June 2003.
26 M82, survey administered at Muir Woods National Monument, CA, June 2003.
27 M146, survey administered at Muir Woods National Monument, CA, June 2003.
28 M86, survey administered at Muir Woods National Monument, CA, June 2003.
29 M78, survey administered at Muir Woods National Monument, CA, June 2003.
30 M147, survey administered at Muir Woods National Monument, CA, June 2003.
31 In point of fact, the root system of redwoods is relatively shallow and broad.
32 M122, survey administered at Muir Woods National Monument, CA, June 2003.
33 See Welton, ed., *The Essential Husserl*, 135–60.
34 I draw the logic of this argument from Niklas Luhmann, and in particular from his assertion of the impossibility of intersubjectivity as a sociological concept. While Luhmann broke with Husserl, Luhmann's vision of society can be seen as an extension of the logic of subjectivity, replete with all the obscurities and impossibilities that Husserl built into it, to encompass social structure. See Luhmann, *Social Systems*, xxxvii–xliv; Habermas, *The Philosophical Discourse of Modernity*, 368–85.
35 Burley, interview, September 16, 2002.
36 The logic of the following analysis draws inspiration from Luhmann, "The Discovery of Incommunicability."
37 Marcus Combs, interview by author, digital recording, Muir Woods National Monument, CA, October 14, 2002.
38 Ibid.
39 Ibid.
40 Thickstun and Podesta, *Self-Guiding Nature Trail*, n.p.
41 Combs, interview, October 14, 2002.
42 Heather Boothe, interview by author, digital recording, Muir Woods National Monument, CA, October 14, 2002.
43 Ibid.

CHAPTER 5. THEORIZING RELIGIOUS INDIVIDUALISM

1 "Ken Burns's THE NATIONAL PARKS: AMERICA'S BEST IDEA Launched National Conversation about Country's Parks," http://www.pbs.org/aboutpbs/news/20100113_nationalparksimpactbaseball.html.

2 Duncan and Burns, *The National Parks*, xvi.
3 Ibid., 376–78.
4 Blatt, et al., "Roundtable."
5 Albanese, *Nature Religion in America*, 6–8.
6 Taylor, *Dark Green Religion*, 1–8.
7 Sponsel, *Spiritual Ecology*, xiii–xix.
8 Ross-Bryant, *Pilgrimage to the National Parks*.
9 "'Nones' on the Rise: One-in-Five Adults Have No Religious Affiliation," http://www.pewforum.org/files/2012/10/NonesOnTheRise-full.pdf, 45–47.
10 Modern, *Secularism in Antebellum America*; Fessenden, *Culture and Redemption*; Bender, *The New Metaphysicals*; Lofton, *Oprah*.
11 According to Niklas Luhmann, the ineffability of the subject, its impossibility as a sociological concept, lies at the center of these epistemological lacunae: "It is no accident that the modern concept of the subject . . . began its career at the historical moment when modern European society discovered it could no longer describe itself in the old categories of a stratified society, its essential forms and essential hierarchy, but could not yet say what the case was instead. . . . The hidden nonconstructability of 'intersubjectivity' is the theoretical counterpart of the indescribability of society" (*Social Systems*, xxxvii–xliv).
12 As Luhmann observes:

> What can the simultaneous autonomization and secularization of the leftover function system mean in relationship to religion? The first idea was: the divinization of society. From temples of virtue to the imitation of worship services the social was reformulated as religioid. . . . If a sociological theory wants to thematize religion in relation to society, certain consequences of the way the question is posed, along with a certain channeling of the theoretical analysis, become unavoidable. In response to the question, 'do we have religion today?' the theory must answer positively if it doesn't want to deny the existence of society. This has nothing to do with moral judgments regarding a corrupt world or the goodness of nature. It has to do with a verification of an expectation necessitated by certain theoretical dispositions. If there were no civil religion, the theory would have to invent it. ("Grundwerte als Zivilreligion," 184–86; translation by author)

13 Rousseau, *On the Social Contract*, 96–103.
14 Bellah, "Civil Religion in America," 168ff.
15 Richey and Jones, "The Civil Religion Debate."
16 Mathiesen, "Twenty Years After Bellah."
17 Bellah discusses this tension in his later modification of the civil religion thesis, but without offering a resolution. See Bellah, "Religion and Legitimation in the American Republic."
18 James Moseley concurred on the intractability of this problem, at least with respect to politics: "Given the characteristics of contemporary American life, I would conclude by suggesting that the quality of politics, on the one hand, and

of religion, on the other, may be better for being unamalgamated. At least, the picture will be clearer if politics and religion are not commingled in an ideal mixture. To wish it were otherwise, as advocates of civil religion tend to do, is to reach for a dream that is already irretrievably behind us. Perhaps it always was" ("Forum," 18). Michael Warner shared such despair in his piece entitled "Is Liberalism a Religion?": "I have no interest in answering the question of my title." He did, however, note how definitional vagueness had become such a feature of (particularly liberal) conceptions of religion that "any strong sense of the mysterious will be regarded as religious—and sometimes cultivated as such." Such ambiguity underlies the liberal characteristics of spirituality as discussed throughout this chapter. See Warner, "Is Liberalism a Religion?," 610, 616.

19 Wilson, *Public Religion in American Culture*, 143–68.

20 Casanova, *Public Religions in the Modern World*, 51–66. See also Weintraub, "The Theory and Politics of the Public/Private Distinction."

21 Here he distinguishes civil society from the state or political society. Casanova, *Public Religions*, 61.

22 Ibid., 52–55.

23 Ibid., 58–59.

24 Wilson, *Public Religion*, 88–89.

25 Anderson, *Imagined Communities*, 56.

26 Note the extremely broad scope of the liberal models of civil or public religion postulated by Robert Wuthnow and Jose Casanova. Wuthnow stated that liberal civil religion focused on "humanity in general" and concerned itself with issues of "nuclear disarmament, human rights, world hunger, peace and justice" ("Divided We Fall," 397). Casanova saw a more liberal form of public religion when churches put forth prophetic criticism in the name of "freedom, justice, and solidarity" (*Public Religions*, 61). While not devoid of particularity, these definitions are so broad that they could include more people than they exclude, thus giving these "religions" the character of general opinion rather than a particular way of life.

27 This is not to say that republican sentiment receives no reinforcement from spiritual experience. Rather, I concentrate on the liberal aspects because these have received less attention in the theoretical literature on public religion.

28 Olmsted, Sr., "The Yosemite Valley and the Mariposa Big Tree Grove," 12–27.

29 Ibid., 22.

30 Ibid. Here I note that the recreational movement, to which Olmsted's report contributed, has been recognized as progressive in its political orientation. See Kloppenberg, *The Virtues of Liberalism*, 126–27.

31 *Superintendents' Resolution on Overdevelopment*, 59.

32 This lack of recognition may contribute to the criticism of liberal, progressive politics as technocratic. As citizens would not need to know how the organization of the public sphere contributes to the public good, then the public good depends primarily on competent and efficient leadership.

33 Hiking the trail solo, an imminent father-to-be said, "I spent a lot of the time out there thinking that I couldn't wait to share this with my family when my kids are old enough to come out and be able to teach them—I mean I'm not going to be teaching them anything, they're going to teach themselves, just being out here out of respect for things that are greater than themselves." While his sense of passing down the public space of wilderness bespoke a notion of heritage, the idea that his children would generate a connection to wilderness out of "themselves" suggested a liberal perspective. K. Hensiek, Whitney Portal, CA, July 15, 2002.
34 See appendix for the full survey.
35 For reasons of confidentiality, respondents will here be identified by an alphanumeric code. Y19, phone interview by author, digital recording, June 12, 2007.
36 M55, phone interview by author, digital recording, June 19, 2007.
37 Runte, *Yosemite*.
38 Y56, phone interview by author, digital recording, June 8, 2007.
39 Y107, phone interview by author, digital recording, June 11, 2007.
40 Y137, phone interview by author, digital recording, June 29, 2007.
41 M123, phone interview by author, digital recording, June 18, 2007.
42 Y127, phone interview by author, digital recording, June 11, 2007.
43 Y95, phone interview by author, digital recording, June 11, 2007.
44 M102, phone interview by author, digital recording, June 29, 2007.
45 M69, phone interview by author, digital recording, June 18, 2007.
46 Wuthnow, "Divided We Fall," 397; Casanova, *Public Religions*, 61.
47 Y67, phone interview by author, digital recording, June 9, 2007.
48 One respondent failed to address the question.
49 Y126, phone interview by author, digital recording, June 29, 2007.
50 Ibid.
51 Kloppenberg, "Political Ideas in Twentieth-Century America," 126–27.
52 M69, phone interview by author, digital recording, June 18, 2007.
53 Ibid.
54 Y90, phone interview by author, digital recording, June 28, 2007.
55 Y19, phone interview by author, digital recording, June 12, 2007.
56 M68, phone interview by author, digital recording, June 26, 2007.
57 Y56, phone interview by author, digital recording, June 8, 2007.
58 Y95, phone interview by author, digital recording, June 21, 2007.
59 M55, phone interview by author, digital recording, June 19, 2007.
60 M102, phone interview by author, digital recording, June 29, 2007.
61 Y107, phone interview by author, digital recording, June 11, 2007.
62 Those who fell under the rubric of republican nationalism did not deny the natural appearance of the parks. Rather, in explaining the motto they put the principle of open access as primary.
63 Y19, phone interview by author, digital recording, June 12, 2007.
64 M55, phone interview by author, digital recording, June 19, 2007.

65 Two respondents expressed a distinctive religiosity that did not tie itself to creation. One, a self-described pagan, encountered "the Goddess" in nature with no reference to a point of origin. M69, phone interview by author, digital recording, June 18, 2007. The other, a Mormon, described his experiences in the parks with guardian angels whom he identified as family members. Y56, phone interview by author, digital recording, June 8, 2007.
66 Y127, phone interview by author, digital recording, June 25, 2007.
67 Y107, phone interview by author, digital recording, June 11, 2007.
68 M55, phone interview by author, digital recording, June 19, 2007.
69 M56, phone interview by author, digital recording, June 19, 2007.
70 Ibid.
71 Ibid.
72 M122, phone interview by author, digital recording, July 10, 2007.
73 Y137, phone interview by author, digital recording, June 29, 2007.
74 Y127, phone interview by author, digital recording, June 25, 2007.
75 Y31, phone interview by author, digital recording, June 6, 2007.
76 M68, phone interview by author, digital recording, June 26, 2007.

CONCLUSION

1 Tilden, *Interpreting Our Heritage*, 3.
2 Quoted in ibid., 11.
3 Ibid., 110.
4 See Keller and Turek, *American Indians and National Parks*; Spence, *Dispossessing the Wilderness*; Burnham, *Indian Country, God's Country*.
5 "In order that our nation may grow and prosper, forests must be cut, streams must be turned onto dry lands, cataracts must give up their power, meadows must be shorn to feed the flocks. These things are necessary. Scenery must often be destroyed by commerce, beauty must often be sacrificed to industry. But in order that we shall not squander all of our birthright, a few jewels of scenery are set aside for ourselves and for posterity to enjoy" (*Superintendents' Resolution on Overdevelopment*, 59).
6 Sellars, *Preserving Nature in the National Parks*.
7 Taylor, *Dark Green Religion*.
8 Sponsel, *Spiritual Ecology*.
9 Bratton, *The Spirit of the Appalachian Trail*.
10 Albanese, *Nature Religion in America*, 13.
11 Modern, *Secularism in Antebellum America*.
12 Fessenden, *Culture and Redemption*, passim.
13 Bender, *The New Metaphysicals*; Lofton, *Oprah*.
14 See Calhoun, Juergensmeyer, and Vanantwerpen, eds., *Rethinking Secularism*.
15 Asad, *Formations of the Secular*, 56–62. See also Mahmood, "Secularism, Hermeneutics and Empire," 346–347.
16 According to Taylor,

"Secular" refers to what pertains to a self-sufficient, immanent sphere and is contrasted with what relates to the transcendent realm (often identified as "religious"). This binary can then undergo a further mutation, via a denial of the transcendent level, into a dyad in which one term refers to the real ("secular"), and the other refers to what is merely invented ("religious"); or where "secular" refers to the institutions we really require to live in "this world," and "religious" or "ecclesial" refers to optional accessories, which often disturb the course of this-worldly life. (Charles Taylor, "Western Secularity," in Calhoun, Juergensmeyer, and Vanantwerpen, eds., *Rethinking Secularism*, 34).

17 "The liberal violence to which I refer (as opposed to the violence of illiberal regimes) is translucent. It is the violence of universalizing reason itself. For to make an enlightened space, the liberal must continually attack the darkness of the outside world that threatens to overwhelm that space" (Asad, *Formations of the Secular*, 59). See also Michael Taussig who argues "that this necessary institutional penetration of reason by violence not only diminishes the claims of reason by casting it into ideology, mask, and effect of power, but also that *it is precisely the coming together of reason-and-violence in the State that creates, in a secular and modern world, the bigness of the big S*" (*The Nervous System*, 116; emphasis in original.

APPENDIX

1 The term is more current among those hiking the Pacific Crest Trail (PCT), a 2,600-mile, five-month journey stretching from Mexico to Canada. During the months of my interviews, a large number of PCT hikers were hiking northbound along the JMT sections of the trail, leading to a certain degree of exchange with the largely southbound JMT hikers.

2 Yosemite Village does contain a Wilderness Center where backcountry hikers acquire their permits and bear-proof food canisters. Park rangers here are remarkably efficient. They run the backpackers through a brief review of the regulations, tell them where they can camp within the valley the night before their trek, answer any questions about routes and trail conditions, and send them on their way. I got the impression that both rangers and backpackers viewed Yosemite Village, and the valley in general, as little more than a way station in their visit.

BIBLIOGRAPHY

Advisory Board on Wildlife Management, Department of the Interior. *Wildlife Management in the National Parks*. Washington, DC: Department of the Interior, 1963.

Albanese, Catherine L. *Nature Religion in America: From the Algonkian Indians to the New Age*. Chicago: University of Chicago Press, 1990.

———. *America: Religion and Religions*, 3rd ed. New York: Wadsworth, 1999.

———. *Reconsidering Nature Religion*. Harrisburg, PA: Trinity, 2002.

———, ed. *American Spiritualities: A Reader*. Bloomington: Indiana University Press, 2001.

Albright, Horace, Director, National Park Service. "The National Park Service's Policy on Predatory Mammals." *Journal of Mammatology* 12, 2 (1931):185–86. Reprinted in *America's National Park System: The Critical Documents*. Edited by Lary M. Dilsaver. New York: Rowman and Littlefield, 1994: 87–88.

———. "Office Order No. 228: Park Planning," April 3, 1931. In *America's National Park System: The Critical Documents*. Edited by Lary M. Dilsaver. New York: Rowman and Littlefield, 1994: 99–103.

Alexander, Jeffrey, ed. *Durkheimian Sociology: Cultural Studies*. New York: Cambridge University Press, 1988.

Ammermann, Nancy. "Spiritual but Not Religious? Beyond Binary Choices in the Study of Religion." *Journal for the Scientific Study of Religion* 52, 2 (2013): 258–278.

Anderson, Benedict. *Imagined Communities*. New York: Verso, 1983.

Anderson, Donald Keith. "Legacy of the American Frontier: A History of the John Muir Trail." MA thesis. California State University, Fresno, 1997.

Asad, Talal. *Formations of the Secular: Christianity, Islam, Modernity*. Stanford, CA: Stanford University Press, 2003.

Bellah, Robert. "Civil Religion in America." In *Beyond Belief: Essays on Religion in a Post-Traditional World*. New York: Harper and Row, 1970: 168–89.

———. "Religion and Legitimation in the American Republic," *Society* (1978): 193–201.

———, Richard Madsen, William Sullivan, Ann Swidler, and Steven Tipton. *Habits of the Heart: Individualism and Commitment in American Life*. Berkeley: University of California Press, 1985.

Bender, Courtney. *The New Metaphysicals: Spirituality and the American Imagination*. Chicago: University of Chicago Press, 2010.

Blatt, Martin, Ed Linenthal, Karl Jacoby, Brenda Child, and Cindy Ott. "Roundtable: Ken Burns's 'The National Parks: America's Best Idea.'" *Public Historian* 33, 2 (2011): 9–36.

Bourdieu, Pierre. *Outline of a Theory of Practice*. Cambridge, UK: Cambridge University Press, 1977.

Bratton, Susan Power. *The Spirit of the Appalachian Trail: Community, Environment, and Belief on a Long-Distance Hiking Path*. Knoxville: University of Tennessee Press, 2012.

Bremer, Thomas S. *Blessed with Tourists: The Borderlands of Religion and Tourism in San Antonio*. Chapel Hill: University of North Carolina Press, 2004.

Burnham, Philip. *Indian Country, God's Country: Native Americans and the National Parks*. Washington, DC: Island Press, 2000.

Cain, Stanley. "Ecological Islands as Natural Laboratories." Sixth Biennial Wilderness Conference, San Francisco, March 20–21, 1959. Reprinted in *America's National Park System: The Critical Documents*. Edited by Lary M. Dilsaver. New York: Rowman and Littlefield, 1994: 200–10.

Calhoun, Craig, Mark Juergensmeyer, and Jonathan VanAntwerpen, eds. *Rethinking Secularism*. New York: Oxford University Press, 2011.

Carlson, Thomas A. *Indiscretion: Finitude and the Naming of God*. Chicago: University of Chicago Press, 1999.

Carr, Ethan. *Wilderness by Design: Landscape Architecture and the National Park Service*. Lincoln: University of Nebraska Press, 1998.

Casanova, Jose. *Public Religions in the Modern World*. Chicago: University of Chicago Press, 1994.

Chidester, David, and Edward T. Linenthal, eds. *American Sacred Space*. Bloomington: Indiana University Press, 1995.

Corrigan, Philip, and Derek Sayer. *The Great Arch: English State Formation as Cultural Revolution*. New York: Basil Blackwell, 1985.

Cronon, William, ed. *Uncommon Ground: Rethinking the Human Place in Nature*. New York: Norton, 1995.

De Vries, Hent. *Religion: Beyond a Concept*. New York: Fordham University Press, 2009.

DeVoto, Bernard. "Let's Close the National Parks." *Harper's Magazine*, October 1953, 49–52. Reprinted in *America's National Park System: The Critical Documents*. Edited by Lary M. Dilsaver. New York: Rowman and Littlefield, 1994: 183–89.

Dilsaver, Lary M., ed. *America's National Park System: The Critical Documents*. New York: Rowman and Littlefield, 1994.

Dressler, Markus, and Arvind-Pal S. Mandir, eds. *Secularism and Religion-Making*. New York: Oxford University Press, 2011.

Drury, Newton B. "The National Parks in Wartime." *American Forests*, August, 1943. Reprinted in *America's National Park System: The Critical Documents*. Edited by Lary M. Dilsaver. New York: Rowman and Littlefield, 1994: 167–73.

Duncan, Dayton, and Ken Burns. *The National Parks: America's Best Idea: An Illustrated History*. New York: Knopf, 2009.

Durkheim, Emile. *Sociology and Philosophy*. Translated by D. F. Pocock. New York: Free Press, 1974.

———. "Individualism and the Intellectuals." Translated by S. and J. Lukes. In *Durkheim on Religion*. Edited by W. S. F. Pickering. London: Routledge and Kegan Paul, 1975: 59–73.

———. *The Elementary Forms of Religious Life*. Translated by Karen Fields. New York: Free Press, 1995.

Edge, Rosalie. "Roads and More Roads in the National Parks and National Forests." Pamphlet No. 54, Emergency Conservation Committee, 1936, 1–6. Reprinted in *America's National Park System: The Critical Documents*. Edited by Lary M. Dilsaver. New York: Rowman and Littlefield, 1994: 137–141.

Fessenden, Tracy. *Culture and Redemption: Religion, the Secular, and American Literature*. Princeton University Press, 2006.

———. "Religious Liberalism and the Liberal Geopolitics of Religion." In *American Religious Liberalism*. Edited by Leigh Eric Schmidt and Sally M. Promey. Bloomington: Indiana University Press, 2012: 359–73.

Feuerbach, Ludwig. *Essence of Christianity*. Translated by George Eliot. Buffalo, NY: Prometheus Books, 1989.

Foucault, Michel. "Governmentality." In *The Foucault Effect: Studies in Governmentality*. Edited by Graham Burchell, Colin Gordon, and Peter Miller. Chicago: University of Chicago Press, 1991: 87–104.

Fox, Stephen. *John Muir and His Legacy: The American Conservation Movement*. Boston: Little, Brown, and Company, 1981.

Gall, Terry Lynn, Judith Malette, and Manal Guirgis-Younger. "Spirituality and Religiousness: A Diversity of Definitions." *Journal of Spirituality in Mental Health* 13 (2011): 158–181.

Gellner, Ernest. *Nations and Nationalism*. Oxford: Basil Blackwell, 1983.

General Authorities Act. U.S. Code. Vol. 16, secs. 1a et seq. (1970).

Georg-Moeller, Hans. *Luhmann Explained: From Souls to Systems*. New York: Open Court, 2006.

Glass, Matthew. "'Alexanders All': Symbols of Conquest and Resistance at Mount Rushmore." In *American Sacred Space*. Edited by David Chidester and Edward T. Linenthal. Bloomington: Indiana University Press, 1995: 152–86.

Glassberg, David. *Sense of History: The Place of the Past in American Life*. Amherst: University of Massachusetts Press, 2001.

Habermas, Jürgen. *The Philosophical Discourse of Modernity*. Cambridge: MIT Press, 1987: 368–385.

Harmon, David, and Allen D. Putney, eds. *The Full Value of Parks: From Economics to the Intangible*. New York: Rowman and Littlefield, 2003.

Heelas, Paul, and Linda Woodhead. *The Spiritual Revolution: Why Religion Is Giving Way to Spirituality*. Oxford: Blackwell Publishing, 2005.

Holmes, Stephen, and Charles Larmore. Translator's Introduction. In Niklas Luhmann, *The Differentiation of Society*. New York: Columbia University Press, 1982.

Hunt, Lynne. "The Sacred and the French Revolution." In *Durkheimian Sociology: Cultural Studies*. Edited by Jeffrey Alexander. New York: Cambridge University Press, 1988.

Inglehart, Ronald. *Culture Shift in Advanced Industrial Society*. Princeton: Princeton University Press, 1990.

Jacoby, Karl. *Crimes against Nature: Squatters, Poachers, Thieves, and the Hidden History of American Conservation*. Berkeley: University of California Press, 2001.

Keller, Robert H., and Michael F. Turek. *American Indians and National Parks*. Tucson: University of Arizona Press, 1998.

Kelley, Kevin W., and Jacques Yves Cousteau, eds. *The Home Planet*. Reading, MA: Pearson Addison Wesley, 1988.

Kieserling, André. Editorische Notiz. In Niklas Luhmann, *Die Religion der Gesellschaft*. Frankfurt: Suhrkamp, 2000: 357–58.

Kloppenberg, James T. *The Virtues of Liberalism*. New York: Oxford University Press, 1998.

Knodt, Eva. Foreword. In Niklas Luhmann, *Social Systems*. Translated by John Bednarz, Jr., and Dirk Baecker. Stanford, CA: Stanford University Press, 1995: ix–xxxvi.

Kraus, Richard. *Recreation and Leisure in Modern Society*, 3rd ed. Glenview, IL: Scott, Foresman and Company, 1984.

Laermans, Rudi, and Gert Verschraegen. "'The Late Niklas Luhmann' on Religion: An Overview." *Social Compass* 48, 1 (2001): 7–20.

Linenthal, Edward T. *Sacred Ground: Americans and Their Battlefields*. Urbana: University of Illinois Press, 1991.

Lofton, Kathryn. *Oprah: Gospel of an Icon*. Berkeley: University of California Press, 2011.

Lowenthal, David. *Possessed by the Past: The Heritage Crusade and the Spoils of History*. New York: Free Press, 1996.

Lowry, William. *Preserving Public Lands for the Future: The Politics of Intergenerational Goods*. Washington, DC: Georgetown University Press, 1998.

Luhmann, Niklas. *The Differentiation of Society*. New York: Columbia University Press, 1982.

———. "The Discovery of Incommunicability." In *Love as Passion: The Codification of Intimacy*. Stanford: University of California Press, 1986: 121–28.

———. "Grundwerte als Zivilreligion: Zur wissenschaftliche Karriere eines Themas." *Soziologische Aufklärung* 3 (1981). Reprinted in *Religion des Bürgers: Zivilreligion in Amerika und Europa*. Edited by Heinz Kleger and Alois Müller. Munich: Chr. Kaiser Verlag, 1986: 175–94.

———. "Speaking and Silence." Translated by Kristen Behnke. *New German Critique* 61 (Winter 1994): 25–37.

———. *Social Systems*. Translated by John Bednarz, Jr., and Dirk Baecker. Stanford, CA: Stanford University Press, 1995.

———. *Die neuzeitlichen Wissenschaften und die Phänomenologie*. Vienna: Picus Verlag, 1996.

———. *Die Religion der Gesellschaft*. Frankfurt: Suhrkamp, 2000.

MacIntyre, Alasdair. *After Virtue*. South Bend, IN: University of Notre Dame Press, 1981.

Mackintosh, Barry. *Interpretation in the National Park Service: A Historical Perspective*. Washington, DC: History Division, National Park Service, Department of the Interior, 1986.

Mahmood, Saba. "Secularism, Hermeneutics and Empire: The Politics of Islamic Reformation." *Public Culture* 18, 2 (2006): 346–47.

Mark, Stephen R. *Preserving the Living Past: John C. Merriam's Legacy in the State and National Parks*. Berkeley: University of California Press, 2005.

Marx, Karl. *Selected Writings*. Edited by Lawrence Simon. Indianapolis: Hackett, 1994.

Mathiesen, James. "Twenty Years after Bellah: Whatever Happened to American Civil Religion?" *Sociological Analysis* 50 (1989): 129–46.

McClelland, Linda Flint. *Presenting Nature: The Historic Landscape Design of the National Park Service: 1916–1942*. Washington, DC: United States Department of the Interior, National Park Service, 1993.

Merchant, Carolyn. "Reinventing Eden: Western Culture as a Recovery Narrative." In *Uncommon Ground: Rethinking the Human Place in Nature*. Edited by William Cronon. New York: Norton, 1995: 132–59.

Merriam, John C. *The Garment of God: Influence of Nature in Human Experience*. New York: Scribner's, 1943.

Modern, John Lardas. *Secularism in Antebellum America*. Chicago: University of Chicago Press, 2011.

Moseley, James. "Forum: American Civil Religion Revisited." *Religion and American Culture* 4 (1994): 1–23.

Muir, John. *The Mountains of California*. New York: Century, 1903.

———. *My First Summer in the Sierra*. New York: Houghton Mifflin, 1911.

———. *John Muir, His Life and Letters and Other Writings*. Edited by Terry Gifford. Seattle: Mountaineers, 1996.

National Environmental Policy Act. U.S. Code. Vol. 42, secs. 4321 et. seq. (1969).

National Park Service. "A Back Country Management Plan for Sequoia and King's Canyon National Parks." Washington, DC, 1960. Reprinted in *America's National Park System: The Critical Documents*. Edited by Lary M. Dilsaver. New York: Rowman and Littlefield, 1994: 211–16.

———. *National Parks for the 21st Century: The Vail Agenda*. Report and Recommendations to the Director of the National Park Service. National Park Service Document Number D-726, 1992. Excerpts reprinted in *America's National Park System: The Critical Documents*. Edited by Lary M. Dilsaver. New York: Rowman and Littlefield, 1994: 211–16.

National Parks for the 21st Century: The Vail Agenda. Post Mills, VT.: Chelsea Green, n.d.

Nicolson, Marjorie Hope. *Mountain Gloom and Mountain Glory: the Development of the Aesthetics of the Infinite* [1959]. New York: W. W. Norton Library, 1963.

"Nones" on the Rise: One in Five Adults Has No Religious Affiliation. Washington, DC: Pew Research Center, 2012. http://www.pewforum.org/2012/10/09/nones-on-the-rise/.

Olmsted, Frederick Law, Sr. "The Yosemite Valley and the Mariposa Big Tree Grove." *Landscape Architecture* 43 (1952): 12–25. Reprinted in *America's National Park System: The Critical Documents*. Edited by Lary M. Dilsaver. New York: Rowman and Littlefield, 1994: 12–27.

Parsons, Talcott. "The Life and Work of Emile Durkheim." In Emile Durkheim, *Sociology and Philosophy*. Translated by D. F. Pocock. New York: Free Press, 1974.

Peek, Ryan. "A Summer Spent Saving Frogs: Applying Research to the Real World." *Sierra Nature Notes* 1 (October 2001).

Peter-Müller, Hans. "Social Structure and Civil Religion: Legitimation Crisis in a Late Durkheimian Perspective." In *Durkheimian Sociology: Cultural Studies*. Edited by Jeffrey Alexander. New York: Cambridge University Press, 1988.

Pickering, W. S. F. *Durkheim on Religion*. London: Routledge and Kegan Paul, 1975.

Pike, Sarah. *Earthly Bodies, Magical Selves: Contemporary Pagans and the Search for Community*. Berkeley: University of California Press, 2001.

Platinga, Alvin. *God, Freedom, and Evil*. Grand Rapids, MI: Eerdmans, 1974.

Price, Jennifer "Looking for Nature at the Mall: A Field Guide to the Nature Company." In *Uncommon Ground: Rethinking the Human Place in Nature*. Edited by William Cronon. New York: Norton, 1995: 186–203.

Richey, Russell E., and Donald G. Jones, eds. *American Civil Religion*. New York: Harper and Row, 1974.

———. "The Civil Religion Debate." In *American Civil Religion*. Edited by Russell E. Richey and Donald G. Jones. New York: Harper and Row, 1974: 3–18.

Roof, Wade Clark. *A Generation of Seekers*. San Francisco: Harper, 1993.

———. *Spiritual Marketplace*. Princeton, NJ: Princeton University Press, 1999.

Ross-Bryant, Lynn. "Sacred Sites: Nature and Nation in the U.S. National Parks." *Religion and American Culture* 15 (2005): 31–62.

———. *Pilgrimage to the National Parks: Religion and Nature in the United States*. New York: Routledge, 2013.

Rothman, Hal K. *The New Urban Park: Golden Gate National Recreation Area and Civic Environmentalism*. Lawrence: University Press of Kansas, 2004.

Rousseau, Jean-Jacques. *On the Social Contract*. Indianapolis: Hackett, 1983.

Runte, Alfred. *National Parks: The American Experience*. Lincoln: University of Nebraska Press, 1979.

———. *Yosemite: The Embattled Wilderness*. Lincoln: University of Nebraska Press, 1990.

Rushdie, Salman. "Is Nothing Sacred?" The Herbert Read Memorial Lecture, read by Harold Pinter at the Institute of Contemporary Arts, London, February 1990. Reproduced at http://www.imaginary.com.au/2004/02/is-nothing-sacred.

Schmidt, Leigh Eric. *Restless Souls: The Making of American Spirituality*. San Francisco: Harper San Francisco, 2005.

Schmidt, Leigh Eric, and Sally M. Promey, eds. *American Religious Liberalism*. Bloomington: Indiana University Press, 2012.

Sears, John F. *Sacred Places: American Tourist Attractions in the Nineteenth Century.* New York: Oxford University Press, 1989.

Sellars, Richard West. *Preserving Nature in the National Parks: A History.* New Haven, CT: Yale University Press, 1997.

Shelby, Bo, and Thomas A. Heberlein. *Carrying Capacity in Recreation Settings.* Corvallis: Oregon State University Press, 1986.

Shivers, Jay S. *Leisure and Recreation Concepts: A Critical Analysis.* Boston: Allyn and Bacon, 1981.

Smart, Ninian. *The Religious Experience*, 5th ed. Upper Saddle River, NJ: Prentice Hall, 1996.

Snyder, Arnold P. "How Wild the Wilderness." *American Forests*, May 1961, 34–35, 62–63.

Solop, Frederic I., and Kristi K. Hagan. *The National Park Service Comprehensive Survey of the American Public, Technical Report.* Washington, DC: Department of the Interior, 2001.

Spence, Mark David. *Dispossessing the Wilderness: Indian Removal and the Making of the National Parks.* New York: Oxford University Press, 1999.

Spirn, Anne Whiston. "Constructing Nature: The Legacy of Frederick Law Olmsted." In *Uncommon Ground: Rethinking the Human Place in Nature.* Edited by William Cronon. New York: Norton, 1996: 91–113.

Sponsel, Leslie E. *Spiritual Ecology: A Quiet Revolution.* Santa Barbara, CA: Praeger, 2012.

Superintendents' Resolution on Overdevelopment. With explanatory letter by Roger Toll. Prepared at the National Park Service Conference, November 13–17, 1922, Yosemite National Park, California. Reprinted in *America's National Park System: The Critical Documents.* Edited by Lary M. Dilsaver. New York: Rowman and Littlefield, 1994: 57–65.

Taussig, Michael. *The Devil and Commodity Fetishism in South America.* Chapel Hill: University of North Carolina Press, 1980.

———. *The Nervous System.* New York: Routledge, 1992.

———. *Defacement: Public Secrecy and the Labor of the Negative.* Stanford: University of California Press, 1999.

Taylor, Bron. "Earth and Nature-Based Spirituality: Part I." *Religion* 31 (2001): 175–93.

———. *Dark Green Religion: Nature Spirituality and the Planetary Future.* Berkeley: University of California Press, 2010.

Taylor, Charles. "Western Secularity." In Calhoun, Craig, Mark Juergensmeyer, and Jonathan VanAntwerpen, eds. *Rethinking Secularism.* New York: Oxford University Press, 2011: 31-53.

Thickstun, Carole, and Victoria Podesta. *Self-Guiding Nature Trail Tour: Muir Woods, Golden Gate National Recreation Area.* Tempe, AZ: Golden Gate National Parks Association, 2001.

Tilden, Freeman. *Interpreting Our Heritage*, 3rd ed. Chapel Hill: University of North Carolina Press, 1977.

Tiryakian, Edward A. "From Durkheim to Managua: Revolutions as Religious Revivals." In *Durkheimian Sociology: Cultural Studies*. Edited by Jeffrey Alexander. New York: Cambridge University Press, 1988.

Van der Veer, Peter. "Spirituality in Modern Society." *Social Research* 76, 4 (2009): 1097–1120.

Wallace, George N. "Law Enforcement and the 'Authority of the Resource.'" Missoula, MT: Arthur Carhart National Wilderness Training Center, n.d. http://carhart.wilderness.net/docs/manuals/waappg.pdf.

Warner, Michael. "Is Liberalism a Religion?" In *Religion: Beyond a Concept*. Edited by Hent de Vries. New York: Fordham University Press, 2009: 610–625.

Weber, Max. *The Protestant Ethic and the Spirit of Capitalism*. Translated by Talcott Parsons. New York: Charles Scribner's Sons, 1958.

Weintraub, Jeffrey. "The Theory and Politics of the Public/Private Distinction." In *Public and Private in Thought and Practice*. Edited by Jeffrey Weintraub and Krishan Kumar. Chicago: University of Chicago Press, 1997: 1–42.

———, and Krishan Kumar, eds. *Public and Private in Thought and Practice*. Chicago: University of Chicago Press, 1997.

Welton, Donn, ed. *The Essential Husserl*. Bloomington: Indiana University Press, 1999.

West Is Best: How Public Lands in the West Create a Competitive Economic Advantage. Bozeman, MT: Headwaters Economics, 2012. http://headwaterseconomics.org/land/west-is-best-value-of-public-lands.

Wolfe, L. M., ed. *John of the Mountains: The Unpublished Journals of John Muir*. Boston: Houghton, Mifflin, 1938.

White, John R. "Atmosphere in the National Parks." Address to Special Superintendents' Meeting, Washington, DC, February 10, 1936. In *America's National Park System: The Critical Documents*. Edited by Lary M. Dilsaver. New York: Rowman and Littlefield, 1994: 142–48.

Wilkins, Terence. *John Muir: Apostle of Nature*. Norman: University of Oklahoma Press, 1995.

Wilson, John. *Public Religion in American Culture*. Philadelphia: Temple University Press, 1979.

Wirth, Conrad, Director, National Park Service. "Mission 66." Special Presentation to President Eisenhower and the Cabinet, January 27, 1956. In *America's National Park System: The Critical Documents*. Edited by Lary M. Dilsaver. New York: Rowman and Littlefield, 1994: 193–96.

Work, Hubert, Secretary of the Interior. "Statement of National Park Policy." Memorandum for the Director, National Park Service, March 11, 1925. In *America's National Park System: The Critical Documents*. Edited by Lary M. Dilsaver. New York: Rowman and Littlefield, 1994: 62–65.

Worster, Donald. *Nature's Economy: A History of Ecological Ideas*, 2nd ed. New York: Cambridge University Press, 1994.

Wuthnow, Robert. *The Restructuring of American Religion: Society and Faith Since World War Two*. Princeton: Princeton University Press, 1988.

———. "Divided We Fall: America's Two Civil Religions." *Christian Century* 105 (1988): 395–99.

———. *After Heaven: Spirituality in America since the 1950s*. Berkeley: University of California Press, 1998.

Zinnbauer, Brian, et al. "Religion and Spirituality: Unfuzzying the Fuzzy." *Journal for the Scientific Study of Religion* 36 (1997): 549–64.

INDEX

ABOUT THE AUTHOR

Kerry Mitchell directs the Comparative Religion and Culture Program at Long Island University Global. He earned his BA in Religious Studies and French at Indiana University, followed by an MA and PhD in Religious Studies from the University of California, Santa Barbara. He currently lives and works in Brooklyn, New York.